A STREET DIVIDED

STORIES FROM JERUSALEM'S ALLEY OF GOD

DION NISSENBAUM

St. Martin's Press
New York

www.stmartins.com

Lines from the poem "Jerusalem, 1967" by Yehuda Amichai, from the book *Poems of Jerusalem and Love Poems*, are printed with the permission of Sheep Meadow Press.

Library of Congress Cataloging-in-Publication Data

Nissenbaum, Dion.
    A street divided : stories from Jerusalem's Alley of God / Dion Nissenbaum.
        pages   cm
    ISBN 978-1-250-07294-8 (hardback)
    1. Jerusalem—Boundaries. 2. Jerusalem—Ethnic relations. 3. Jerusalem—Politics and government—20th century. 4. Jerusalem—Description and travel. 5. Israel-Arab War, 1948–1949—Influence. 6. Partition, Territorial. I. Title.
    DS109.93.N57 2015
    956.94'42—dc23

                                                                            2015010735

ISBN 978-1-250-07294-8 (hardcover)
ISBN 978-1-4668-8489-2 (e-book)

Our books may be purchased for educational, business, or promotional use. For information on bulk purchases, please contact the Macmillan Corporate and Premium Sales Department at 1-800-221-7945, extension 5442, or write to specialmarkets@macmillan.com.

First Edition: September 2015

10   9   8   7   6   5   4   3   2   1

For Seema, the Love of My Life, my Jan,
yesterday, today, and for all our tomorrows

In vain you will look for the fences of barbed wire.
You know that such things
don't disappear. A different city perhaps
is now being cut in two; two lovers
separated; a different flesh is tormenting itself now
with these thorns, refusing to be stone.

—Yehuda Amichai, "Jerusalem, 1967"

CONTENTS

ACKNOWLEDGMENTS

First and foremost, thanks go to the families on Assael Street. This story is theirs, and the book would have been impossible without their willingness to share their captivating tales.

Nawal and Zakaria Bazlamit, along with the entire Bazlamit family, always welcomed me into their homes over many years. Hijazi and Abdullah Bazlamit were particularly generous with their time. Rachel Machsomi and her many adult children, especially Rivka, were just as gracious when I came to visit them in Ma'ale Adumim. David, Alisa and Avital Maeir-Epstein repeatedly opened their doors to talk about their lives and were always willing to answer the smallest of questions. Khaled, Rita, Jamal, Amjad and Wafa Rishek were especially thoughtful hosts. Malka Joudan and her grown kids, Itzik, Maya, and Yaacov; Shimshon Jacoby; Rafi Goeli; Maha Salhab and her parents, Moussa and Khulood; Ziad and Randa Yaghmour all took time out of their busy lives to sit and talk. Elon and Linda Bezalely, Sara Arnold, the Gazawi family, the Mujaheds and Brent all helped make this story possible.

This tale owes a special debt to the people on the street who told their stories even though they had reservations about talking, especially "Imm Fadi," her kids, and "Carol," all of whom had their names changed in this book. (A few other names, such as Leyla's, also have been changed.)

I am grateful for the help of many people from Abu Tor, especially Hedva Harekhavi, Judith and Jeffrey Green, Saliba Sarsar, Sarah Sallon, Ricki Rosen and Jordan Herzberg.

This book wouldn't have been possible without three particular friends who helped as translators and served as important sounding boards: Nuha Musleh, Orly Halpern and Cliff Churgin. Nuha, a Palestinian journalist, well known as a whirlwind who always juggles work, family and friends with grace, has an unparalleled empathy that opened every door we knocked on, year after year. Orly, a veteran Israeli-American reporter in Jerusalem, carved out time in her crazily busy days to provide advice, translation and perspective. And Cliff, an Israeli-American colleague I worked with for years, tracked down vital information and always saw the same thing I saw on Assael Street: a unique Jerusalem tale.

Here at home, I owe immense thanks to my family for offering constant support and encouragement. Most importantly, I am grateful for the unconditional love of my wife, Seema, whose compassion and beauty make me always thankful to be her partner. From the UN archives in New York to Assael Street in Jerusalem, Seema helped shape this story from start to finish. This book is infused with her insights, which helped me see the story from a different perspective.

Thanks to my mother, Barbara Vincent, for raising a son who I hope reflects her values and intellectual curiosity. My older brother, Kent Grayson, sparked my imagination as a kid and has always been one of my biggest champions. Thanks to Kent and my sister-in-law, Leslie, for being inspirations for me and for raising two independent daughters, Eliza and Helena. To Susan and Roy Henshaw, thanks for showing us all courage, faith and resilience.

I am thankful to my father, Gerald Nissenbaum, and his wife, Madeline Celletti-Nissenbaum, for the boundless love, guidance and support that they offered over the years. And to my younger siblings Ben, Nick and Marleah for their help answering esoteric late-night questions or providing their artistic perspectives on this book.

I am grateful to be part of the Jilani family, which embodies the best qualities of our faith: compassion, humility and kindness. I am particularly thankful to Afshan and Airaj, my mother- and father-in-law, for raising their fearless daughters and for being role models for Seema and me by creating rewarding, enriching and adventurous lives for themselves. Thanks to my sisters-in-law, Saira and Sana, and my brothers-in-law, Junaid and Mosaddiq, for their suggestions and jokes that kept me laughing along the way. To my niece Zaynab and my nephews, Zayd and Yusef: Thanks for reminding us all that life doesn't have to be so serious all the time! And a special thanks to Mohammad Shafiuddin, whose intellectual fire at age 92 is something to behold, and to his 81-year-old wife, Munir, who embodies humble generosity—with a sharp wit.

I owe a debt of gratitude to many others who made this story possible: photojournalist David Rubinger; architects Yehuda Greenfield-Gilat, Karen Lee Bar-Sinai, Chen Farkas and Senan Abdelqader; the YMCA's Forsan Hussein; Khader Musleh, Nuha's husband and a longtime friend; Israeli researcher Doron Oren, who probably knows more about Abu Tor's Jewish history than anyone; Professor Rhona D. Seidelman, an expert on Israel's early immigration challenges; Amanda Leinberger at the UN Archives in New York; Meron Benvenisti and Daniel Seidemann, who offered important perspectives; Steve Linde, Elaine Moshe and Tovah Lazaroff at the *Jerusalem Post* for taking on a last-minute research mission; Arlene Balkansky at the Library of Congress; Judith Feierstein, for her candor; and Adam Brill, Yossi Katz and the Jewish National Fund for helping dig up insightful details about the 1957 fight over their tree-planting project.

I am particularly thankful to my friends who read early drafts and offered candid feedback: Mike Phillips, Stephanie Koven, Eric Westervelt and Anna Blackshaw. I'm also grateful for friends who provided encouragement and timely advice: Sharline Chiang, Tim McKee, Dave Read, Lisa Woo, Quil Lawrence, Shahed Amanullah, Thanassis Cambanis, Tammer Ramini, and Conor and Atia Powell. I am grateful to the *Wall Street Journal* and my editors, Bob Ourlian and Jerry Seib, who gave me the time and space to write this book. Thanks to Katherine Kiviat for her photos of Assael. Thanks to Busboys and Poets, the 14th Street DC café inspired by Langston Hughes, where I spent countless hours writing. And I couldn't be more appreciative of my agent, Robert Guinsler, who believed in this story enough to make sure that it found a good home at St. Martin's Press, where Laura Apperson guided the book through the process and Karen Wolny took it under her wing.

A STREET
DIVIDED

INTRODUCTION

Above all, this is a story.

It is set on one 300-yard, dead-end street in one little city.

The people who live there always asked me: Why are you writing about this street? Nothing happens here. There's nothing special about this place.

On one hand, they're right. There *is* nothing special about this street. The people here go to work. They have big holiday parties that last long into the night. There are birthdays and funerals. They get angry about little things that sometimes blow up into big ones. They sing. They pray. They laugh. Occasionally, a punch or two is thrown.

On the other hand, there is no other street in the world like this one.

This is where West first met East, where Jew meets Muslim, where Palestine could someday meet Israel. This is where *Shabbat* meets *Jummah*. If there is going to be any common ground, this street is where it may one day be found. Literally.

The border of future states is being defined, every day, on this street. Every inch here does matter. It matters whether a Jewish family lives on one side or the other. Buying or selling a home on this tranquil, cobblestone cul-de-sac is a risky political act that could reshape the future borders of Israel and Palestine. The narrow width of the road could one day determine whether you carry an Israeli passport or a Palestinian one.

This street has been home to priests and prostitutes, poets and spies. It has been the stage for an improbable flirtation between an Israeli girl and a Palestinian boy living on opposite sides of the barbed wire along the front lines. It has even been the scene of an unsolved murder.

This is a true Jerusalem story, one filled with love, war, exodus, deception and betrayal.

On this street, nothing is too small to fight about. A deteriorating outhouse on this hillside once sparked a UN investigation. So did a homemade tin manhole cover. And a rooftop pigeon coop. There have been rock-throwing street brawls over parking spots and bloody clashes over missing holiday lights. Guns have been pulled. Men have been hauled off to jail. The stone and concrete walls outside people's homes carry an ever-changing series of spray-painted Arabic prayers, political slogans and veiled threats. Some of the doorways have small, tubular Jewish mezuzahs attached to them to keep a biblical commandment to honor G-d. Other gates feature spray-painted images of the Ka'aba, the widely recognized towering black cube at the center of Islam in Mecca, where Muslims believe the Prophet Abraham and his son Ishmael laid the foundation for their religion.

Black-masked Israeli police in full riot gear have broken through Abu Tor bedroom windows to arrest Palestinians accused of one crime or another. Palestinian blue-jeaned teens with layers of checkered kaffiyehs covering their faces have hurled stones through bedroom windows and Molotov cocktails onto tiled roofs. Palestinian families have raised mourning tents for young men brought down by Israeli bullets.

It doesn't take much to see where the lines are drawn on Assael Street. Everyone knows where they stand. Some people who live on this serene cul-de-sac think there is no hope, that Jews and Muslims will never really be able to live, side by side, in peace. Others believe realigning spiritual energy—and a little yoga—could produce miracles for Jerusalem.

Before this street ever had a name, it was just a small shepherd's path carved into the side of a Jerusalem valley said to contain the Gateway to Hell.

When warring generals sat down in 1948 to split Jerusalem, their hand-drawn lines curved along this hillside. Israel took control of the top, said to be the Hill of Evil Counsel, the biblical site where Jerusalem's Jewish high priests plotted with Judas to bring down Jesus Christ.

Jordan took the part that ran down through Hinnom Valley, the accursed Valley of Slaughter, the biblical scene of ritualistic child sacrifices and other unspeakable crimes. It was a cursed gash in the earth where well-worn horse trails ran past a mysterious cliffside tomb shaped like an ancient Egyptian pharaoh's hat. On the other side, in Jordanian hands, stood the part of Jerusalem that mattered most: the Old City.

As they drew their lines through Jerusalem, the military commanders created a narrow band of land on the Jerusalem hillside that was controlled by neither side. Israelis called it *shetach hekfer;* Palestinians called it *al Mantiqa Haram.* In both languages it meant the same thing: the Forbidden Area. Jerusalemites sometimes called it "Barbed Wire Alley." Whatever name they used, they all saw it the same way: It was a dangerous No Man's Land that separated enemy nations.

For more than 15 years, poor Jewish immigrants from the Middle East and North Africa lived on this border, across the barbed wire from poor Palestinian families. The two sides got to know each other from afar. The occasional waves of hello grew into people quietly tossing food and gifts over the border fence. Kids traded cigarettes thrown over the barbed wire for the dads on the other side to try. One boy lobbed a cheap ring that the girls on the other side thought might be cast with a secret love spell. Mothers tossed warm pita bread for a pregnant neighbor on the other side. One long-robed grandfather handed fresh-picked poppies over the fence to the younger woman who'd been secretly watching him from above.

All the while, Israeli and Jordanian soldiers looked on from their border posts, keeping an eye out for any suspicious activity. Anything could be reason for concern. Even a bouquet of flowers.

When the barbed wire came down in 1967, after Israel pushed Jordan out of Jerusalem during the Six-Day War, neighbors that once had to worry about being thrown in jail for talking to each other suddenly became friends. Muslim families brought lavish trays of food to Jewish families at the end of Passover. Mothers would gather in each other's kitchens to cook and knit while they taught each other Arabic and Hebrew. The kids, Jewish and Muslim, played together as well: The older kids shot pool in a tiny club down the hillside while the younger ones played soccer in the field at the top.

After the fence was pulled aside, Barbed Wire Alley got a new Israeli name: Assael. Literally: Made by God.

"This is where God connected Jerusalem," said Moussa Salhab, a grizzled, chain-smoking Palestinian father whose family home in this No Man's Land was used by Jordanian border guards until 1967.

It seemed as if it really was possible to bridge seemingly unbridgeable divides. The differences seemed negligible. They were neighbors. They became friends. Some got along better than others.

It didn't take long for their lives to diverge.

As it became clear that their fortunes were heading in different directions, the physical and psychological barriers started going back up. Gates were barricaded. The walls grew taller, and doors were sealed shut. Neighbors who once considered each other family stopped talking. The friendly waves became increasingly rare. People installed security cameras to keep watch on who was doing what on the street. Onetime friends quietly called Israeli police to report their neighbors for one problem or another. Some people started stringing barbed wire across the tops of their walls to keep others out. Sometimes it seemed like the only thing connecting the two sides of the street was a small beam of invisible, New Age healing energy.

Redrawing Middle East nations is not a theoretical question to the families on Assael Street. If some people have their way, this old dividing line could become the new one separating Israel and Palestine. A few centimeters on a map matter to the people here whose entire lives have been shaped by poorly defined lines. Creating borders on a map is hard. Doing it on the ground, on this street, is even harder. The closer you get to the line, the more blurred it seems to get. But if Israel is ever going to live next to Palestine, the lines have to be drawn somewhere. And that could be here, down the center of Assael Street.

This is a story about how people see themselves, how they want to be seen, and how they are seen by others. Unsurprisingly, the stories don't always line up. People remember things the way they want to. People forget things. Memories fade. We fill empty spaces with details that make stories a little more interesting. And the stories change a little bit each time they are told. In some cases, there are ways to figure the truth of a story by checking out newspaper articles, UN reports and other shreds of information that have survived the years. In others, all that's left of moments in time are people's imperfect memories. People remember the same thing differently, especially the neighborhood feuds. Families have secrets they prefer to keep private. Like all of us, they have stories they'd rather not have told. Some stories have been repeated so many times that they have become family legends. There are the ones they like to tell about themselves and the ones other people like to tell about them. In many ways, the stories people tell here are more important than what actually happened. The tales are passed, imperfectly, from one generation to the next. People define their lives by the memories they choose to remember and the ones they decide to forget.

This is not the whole story of Assael Street. This is not the definitive story of Assael Street. This book barely scratches the surface of the lives of a few families on one narrow road. There is no shortage of tales to be told about the people living along this 300-yard dividing line. These are just a few.

*　*　*

There is no escaping a suspicion of bias when writing about Jerusalem.

"Do you think that people will assume biases because of your name?" one friend asked me.

Probably so.

My last name, I was taught, is a Jewish-German one meaning "Nut Tree." My name was an easy target for school-hall wisecracks. I knew what matzoh was, but Judaism played a small role in my life. My mother was the oldest daughter of devout Catholic parents from a Massachusetts mill town. I was baptized in a church, not bar mitzvahed in a synagogue. Growing up, Judaism meant little more than going to my paternal grandmother's place to eat horseradish at Passover and haul in some comic-book money at Hanukah. Christianity meant going to my maternal grandmother's place for Christmas to fill up on her warm Spritz sugar cookies and search for hard-boiled, pastel-colored Easter eggs one Sunday morning each spring. While living in Afghanistan in 2010, I met an enchanting Pakistani-Texan doctor who was volunteering at a Kabul hospital. I soon embraced Islam in Indonesia and eventually married that doctor—the love of my life.

I've offered silent prayers in front of the Western Wall, at the Church of the Holy Sepulcher and in al Aqsa mosque. I am also a vegetarian; one who wears leather boots. I like to think that I am able to set aside my imperfect vegetarian beliefs when I write about nonvegetarians. I hope I am able to set aside my preconceptions in telling this story and that people will be forgiving of inherent biases that may seep into the tale. I hope readers won't get tripped up if a person is described in one place being Arab and in another as being Palestinian. I hope people won't dwell on whether a particular piece of land should be characterized as "occupied" or "disputed." Though the little things are the ones that matter on Assael Street, this story is about much more than the details.

This book doesn't provide a political road map with new ideas on how to solve what seems like an unsolvable problem. It's a snapshot of a small street that was, is, and may always be the front line for one of the world's most intractable conflicts.

*   *   *

To me, Assael isn't just any street. For many years, it was the one right outside my living room window. Like a lot of Western journalists at the time—from the start of 2006 to the end of 2009—I lived in Jerusalem's Abu Tor neighborhood.

Choosing a home in Jerusalem is about more than finding a place with lots of light that's close to a market. Where you live is often seen as an unspoken declaration about your political leanings. For many Americans, living in West Jerusalem is the default, and any decision to live somewhere else might very well be seen as a slight against Israel. To Israelis, Westerners living in East Jerusalem are likely to be viewed warily because of their presumed pro-Palestinian leanings. Westerners living in Ramallah, in the West Bank, are likely to be branded anti-Israel. To Palestinians, any Westerner who chooses to live in an Israeli settlement is presumed to be unsympathetic to their dreams. Living in Abu Tor, living on the old dividing line, was often meant to signal a willingness to treat both sides fairly, to look at the situation from both perspectives. Politically, culturally, psychologically, this is the street where it mattered which side you chose to make your home. Just living in Abu Tor, choosing a "mixed" neighborhood, was seen by some Israelis as a subtle sign that you harbored anti-Israeli views.

The invisible border in Abu Tor was easy to see. It was obvious where West Jerusalem came to an end and East Jerusalem began. West Jerusalem ended at the edge of the garden below my living room window, and East Jerusalem started in the forest of satellite dishes rising from the crowded compounds on the other side of Assael Street. It looked as if development had swept over the top of the neighborhood, crept down to the western edge of Assael Street, and stopped.

The higher side of the street was dominated by modern, multistory decorative stone apartment buildings covered with fragrant tangles of jasmine and thick canopies of purple bougainvillea. The balconies were covered with pots of flowering cacti and spiky aloe plants, snapping clothes lines and stacks of three-legged plastic chairs, Buddhist wind chimes and rainbow flag banners flying alongside Israel's blue Star of David. The big buildings sprawled out alongside a smaller number of refurbished stone homes, places once owned by Palestinian families, with elegant arched doorways, high ceilings and mosaic-tiled floors that were often rented out—at lucrative prices—to Westerners like me. In four decades, the crown of Abu Tor had been transformed from one of the worst places to live in Jerusalem to one of the city's most desirable neighborhoods.

The eastern side of Assael, and the lower part of Abu Tor, well, that was a different story. It was the edge of what some Jewish Abu Tor residents called "the ghetto." The well-maintained homes at the top of Abu Tor that were owned by influential Israeli politicians, former spies, retired university professors and well-known Jerusalem artists gave way to large warrens of homes that all seemed to be filled with three or four generations of Palestinian families. The stone walls and metal storefront shutters were spray-painted with Arabic and English slogans: FREE PALESTINE. FREE GAZA. HAMAS. Cabbies and pizza delivery guys on their scooters sometimes refused to drive through the narrow streets where groups of Palestinian men always seemed to be sitting outside their homes and shops, keeping an eye on who drove past. Few cars came down Assael. It's a dead-end street used mostly by the people living there. Palestinian kids sped up and down the blue-gray herringbone stone street on their bikes, scooters and skateboards. They set up street-side dumpsters and piles of clothes as soccer goals in the middle of the road. And they grudgingly stepped aside whenever some driver rudely interrupted their games by driving through their "field."

Every spring, to commemorate the reunification of Jerusalem, thousands of demonstrators, some carrying rifles, others carrying Israeli flags, march down Assael Street singing nationalist songs in a provocative reminder of their political dominance over the Palestinians living on the eastern side of the road.

Israeli tour guides and young Israeli soldiers regularly lead groups on walks past the tall, salmon-colored, decorative stone retaining walls where they point to battle scars from 1948 and to homes that served as frontline bunkers until 1967.

My apartment rooftop looked out on Assael and the East Jerusalem valleys. To the north, through stands of tall, pointed fir trees, came the illuminated glow of the Dome of the Rock in the Old City. The Old City wall ran along the horizon until it gave way to the Mount of Olives and its thousands of white graves holding Jewish souls waiting for the Messiah to return. Sloping white carpets of graves eventually gave way to pillars of gray concrete walls snaking across the horizon where Israel's controversial separation barrier has cut off the Palestinian neighborhood of Abu Dis from the rest of Jerusalem. The horizon curves back south where herky-jerky stacks of houses and paint-chipped apartment buildings cede the hillsides to sharply rising valleys filled with pine, fir, cypress, eucalyptus, lemon and olive trees. On a ridge at the top of the tree line sits the historic stone compound with sunken gardens and its own private pet cemetery that once served as the Jerusalem headquarters for the British High Commissioner in charge of post–World War I Palestine. Soldiers fought for this ridgeline when Israel was created in 1948. And it's where the first shots were fired in the 1967 battle for Jerusalem.

On Friday afternoons, the pulse of Jerusalem slows. Muslim families gather after weekly prayers for big meals, long naps and late nights of drinking cardamom-flavored coffee. The pale, tangly bearded, black-hat Orthodox Jewish men drag bike racks into the middle of all the streets leading into their neighborhoods to keep anyone from driving through the area on Shabbat. It kept a lot of wayward tourists in rental cars, delivery scooters, lost foreigners and mischievous teenagers from being stoned. Most shops in West Jerusalem, save for a few cafés, bars and markets, close their doors until sundown on Saturday.

On a spring evening, as a warm desert breeze swept over the low, cinnamon-hued hills and through scrub-filled valleys, it was easy to sit on my rooftop and envision a unified city. At dusk on Friday nights, the air would fill with the sounds of Jewish families marking the start of their Shabbat with loud dinnertime readings from the Torah, Muslim muezzin calling the Jerusalemites to prayer on Jummah from a half-dozen mosque minaret megaphones spread out across the valley below, and Christian church bells clanging from stone towers in the Old City on the far horizon.

On the best of nights, an oversized, orange full moon would rise over the Jordan Valley as fireworks from Palestinian wedding celebrations shot across the sky. On the worst of nights, blue flashing lights bounced off the walls as clouds of tear gas drifted through the streets.

When the acrid jolt of burning trash mixed with pungent tear gas and the singe of gasoline-soaked burning tires, it wasn't hard to imagine that the valley might actually lead to the Gates of Hell.

It's a neighborhood where skinny teenage street peddlers walk through the cobblestone streets shouting *"kaak kaak kaak,"* with wooden trays balanced on their heads and stacked with freshly baked sesame seed bread, sold with small paper packets of fresh *za'atar* that smelled of toasted sesame seeds and warm oregano. Every morning during the holy month of Ramadan, a lone Palestinian drummer will march through the neighborhood before dawn keeping a pounding beat to wake everyone within earshot who wants to eat before a long day of fasting.

There were also plenty of neighborhood feuds. I saw my share of late-night arguments that spilled out into the streets. I got caught up in a few Abu Tor disputes myself. Israeli police officers knocked on my front door more than once to complain about the late-night bass beats coming from my rooftop and waking annoyed neighbors. I was even the unsuspecting target of an ill-considered, and ill-conceived, attack on my home. One night, a pair of mischievous, hazily inebriated Western journalists for well-known American media companies decided it would be a hilarious joke if they fired massive bottle rockets and heavy-duty fireworks at my rooftop, 100 yards away. They fired—and missed. Badly. Instead of hitting my long, rectangular rooftop deck, the fireworks slammed into the modern stone apartment building right below me, on the western side of Assael Street. At the time, the place happened to be home of the US consulate's top security officer—the kind of guy who was trained to jump when things go bang. It wasn't long before black Suburbans with flashing blue lights came screeching to a halt on Assael Street, and muscular men with sidearms stepped into the street to take control of the situation.

Abu Tor is a gritty neighborhood in more ways than one. The physical grit settles on cups and dishes. It dusts rugs, tables and chairs. Storms coming from the Dead Sea gather force in the narrow valleys and tear through wood-framed canvas Bedouin tent encampments in the Judean Mountains before slamming into Jerusalem's Abu Tor hillside homes with a fury that can knock heavy iron window shutters from their hinges. When the rolling thunder stops echoing through the valleys and the skies clear, you can turn east to see the shimmering waters of the Dead Sea and the dull glow of Amman's city lights 50 miles away in Jordan's rolling desert hills.

* * *

It was easy to settle into the city's rhythms. I moved into my new home in 2006 and sat for hours drinking coffee on the rooftop, soaking in the sounds and scents of Jerusalem. There was a small dog yapping in the garden right below my living room window, but what neighborhood doesn't have barking dogs? I didn't think too much of it at first. But because I often worked from home, the yappy Chihuahua soon became the bane of my existence. The dog barked day and night. There never seemed to be an hour when he wasn't yapping at something.

I didn't want to be the new foreigner who started complaining about things the minute I arrived. But as the days of relentless barking dragged into weeks, I walked down the concrete stairs next to my building and knocked on a rusting metal gate leading to the garden home right below mine. A small, elderly woman with tangles of dark hair and a thin, flowered dress came out and stood on the porch, giving me the eye. She spoke in a loud, gravelly voice, as if she could hardly hear herself. She didn't know much English. I didn't understand much Hebrew. Her suspicious daughter-in-law finally came out to translate. I had a feeling it wasn't going to end well.

"Can you please keep your dog inside when you're gone?" I asked the two women in my best friendly-new-neighbor voice. "He barks all the time."

"Yes, yes," the daughter-in-law said in a way that made it clear they weren't going to think much about it after they closed the door.

The yappy dog, Timmy the Sixth, became my Telltale Heart, the incessant soundtrack to my life, driving me a little battier every day. I left my neighbors printouts of brochures for gizmos they could buy to train Timmy the Sixth not to bark. One afternoon, when the yapping seemed unbearable, I stormed back down to the house and asked the old woman to do something about her dog—this time with a bit more Jerusalem anger in my voice.

"It's the Arabs," her irritated Filipina daughter-in-law told me as she translated for a mother-in-law she seemed to dislike. "She says it's the

Arab kids that make her dog bark. She says the Arab kids run up and down the street all day and bang on our fence to make the dog bark and upset her."

It felt like an argument I wasn't going to win, so I turned to the long arm of the law. The long, legal process of having the woman fined for violating city noise ordinances became a torturous, time-consuming affair that led nowhere. When all hope appeared lost, one longtime Abu Tor resident offered a grim solution: She offered to kill Timmy the Sixth for me.

"I'll just put poison in some meat and throw it over the fence," she told me matter-of-factly one night after listening, again, to my complaints about the barking. "It's no problem. We've had problems with them for *years.*"

I didn't think she was serious until she mentioned it again. Like it was a done deal.

"It's OK," I told her. "It's not so bad that you have to do that."

"Oh, don't worry," she said. "I'll take care of it."

I wasn't giving her a wink-and-a-nod to go ahead with it. I really didn't want her to poison the dog. But she seemed to think I was giving her an implicit green light.

"Really though," I said before we hung up. "Please don't poison the dog."

"Don't worry about it," she reassured me in a way that wasn't reassuring at all. "I understand."

Sure enough, she tried to kill Timmy the Sixth by throwing poisoned meat into the dog's yard. But it didn't work. Timmy the Sixth lived to bark another day. I gave up. The yapping dog appeared unbeatable. The day I moved out of the apartment at the end of 2009, the irritable little Chihuahua was still barking at shrieks and shadows.

When I returned to Abu Tor in 2014 to talk with the family, the woman's son, Yaacov, a guy known in the neighborhood as Yanki, recognized me almost immediately. Like his mom, Yanki had put down his roots in Abu Tor. He'd brought his wife there, proudly took their twins on afternoon walks, and watched the three of them move away when the feuding couple decided some distance was best. Like the kid he must have been, Yanki still roamed around his mom's house in flip-flops, baggy shorts and sleeveless T-shirts that showed off his dark, hairy arms. The house smelled of wet dog and chicken soup. Timmy the Sixth was still alive—and still barking at anyone who knocked on the gate.

Yanki's mother, Malka Joudan, the one who'd blamed the Arab kids for making her dog bark, still lived on Assael in the abandoned Palestinian home she'd moved into in 1951. Malka's mind had been hobbled by a stroke that made it difficult to talk to her. It was hard to follow all the tangents in her meandering stories and harder to know which tales were true. Yanki's wife and their twins were long gone. Yanki and his mother had stopped talking to each other. They moved around the cold, damp house in their own orbits. Malka's brown curls popped out of the edges of the scarf tied around her head as she asked her guests, again and again, why they were there, whether they had seen her daughter, what her son was doing in the kitchen . . .

Malka sat near a small electric space heater under several puffy comforters while she shouted at the television news. Yanki paced around the darkened rooms as he talked on the phone. His flip-flops slapped against the cold tile floors while he rummaged about in the shadows for something. When he was nearly done with the call, he came into the living room where his mom was watching TV with the volume blasting.

"I remember you," he said to me as he sat down near his mother and hung up the phone. "You wanted to be in control."

I waved my hand and laughed it off. The sound of Timmy the Sixth's barking felt like nails on the chalkboard in my brain. I wanted to chase the memories from my mind as soon as I could.

"It's in the past," I told him.

Yanki chuckled and looked me over.

"It's OK," he said before getting up again to get tea and water for his guests. "Forget it."

Yanki, who was born and raised on the street, took a long view of the fight. He'd seen plenty of foreigners pass through the neighborhood. He could tell who was going to be around for the long haul.

"I knew you were a visitor here," he told me as he slipped away into the darkness once again. "I knew you were going to go."

* * *

Living in Jerusalem sometimes felt like being in Dr. Seuss's illustrated children's story "The Zax," about a North-Going Zax who runs straight into a South-Going Zax in the middle of the wide-open Prairie of Prax. Whether

North-Going or South-Going, the Zaxes are loud, hairy, stubborn, argumentative creatures. Although the open prairie stretches out on either side of them, neither the North-Going Zax nor the South-Going Zax is willing to step aside so the other can pass.

The North-Going Zax threatens to stand firm for 59 days. The South-Going Zax vows to stay put for 59 *years*. If there is to be a showdown, the South-Going Zax says, he will come out on top. As a boy, the South-Going Zax tells his North-Going rival, all young Zaxes learned a simple rule: "Never budge in the least! Not an inch to the west! Not an inch to the east!" The patronizing lecture only seems to make the North-Going Zax dig in, so his South-Going adversary makes it clear that he's not going to back down.

"I'll stand here, not budging!" the South-Going Zax warns, "I can and I will, if it makes you and me and the whole world stand still!"

The North-Going Zax and the South-Going Zax do stand still. For years and years and years and years and years. But the world doesn't. It moves on. People eventually build a freeway right over the un-budgeable Zaxes, still defiantly glaring at each other in the middle of the desert.[1]

Jerusalem brings out the Zax in a lot of people. It came out in me one particular day as I was pulling out of a space in a narrow, gated downtown parking lot. As I was leaving, a guy who regularly used the spot drove up to the parking lot entrance while the metal gate rolled open. I couldn't get out of the cramped, triangular lot until he backed out of the entrance, but the driver signaled for me to pull deeper into the tiny lot so he could take the parking space before I drove away. I refused to budge. So did he. We wildly waved our hands at each other and shouted curses from afar. We sat there for minutes. Finally, I threw open my car door, marched over to his window and let all my pent up frustration blow.

"If you'd just move your *fucking* car we could both be on our way!" I shouted at the man.

The driver looked at me, said something in Hebrew under his breath, turned off his engine, got out, and locked the car.

"You don't know who you're dealing with," he said as he walked away, leaving his car blocking the entrance. No one could get in or out of the small parking lot. Not me. Not him. Not anyone. It didn't matter to him how many people would be inconvenienced by his actions. He made his point. He would not budge.

We were at a stalemate. Everyone else just had to figure out for themselves how to deal with our standoff. These kinds of fights happen over and over in Jerusalem. When people can, they move on. They wash their hands of the problems, or they find ways around them. But stalemate takes its own kind of toll. Stagnation leaves a mark. Over time, the small slights and daily frustrations build up like a pressure cooker until they explode, one way or another. You can feel it, every day, on Assael Street.

* * *

This story is built around the memories of the people who lived in this neighborhood, including my own. Some people were more willing to talk than others. Several residents asked that their real names not be used, so a few have been changed. Some of these stories are bolstered by UN documents, memoirs of key players, government records and newspaper reports from the time.

I'm sure you could find another 300-yard street somewhere in the world that has as many stories as this one. But there is no doubt that Assael has a tale like no other.

* * *

There is a story they tell on Assael Street that goes something like this . . .

ONE

NO MAN'S LAND

Many men dream of redrawing Middle East borders.

Eliyahu Goeli is one who actually has.

Singlehandedly, the young Iranian immigrant became one of the first people to stretch Israel's borders and grab a little more land for his new country. And not just any land. Eliyahu claimed more ground for Israel in Jerusalem, the city where the Jewish high priests could speak directly to God. There could be nothing more rewarding.

Expanding Israel's poorly defined boundary wasn't Eliyahu's first priority when he arrived in Israel in 1950. The Jewish father of four was just looking for someplace to live. He'd done well in Iran, where he made Arak, the region's popular licorice-flavored alcohol. With the growing surge of immigrants pouring into a new country struggling to find places for everyone, Eliyahu had to go to the edge of Israel to find a home.

There was a reason no one had taken over the concrete block house set above Israel's new border with Jordan. It seemed like a horrible place to live. There was no electricity or running water. Dusty winds whipped through open windows and coated the floors with a thin, grainy carpet of red sand blown up from the Judean Desert. There was no indoor bathroom, an inconvenience that would eventually trigger a major international quarrel requiring United Nations intervention. The house also stood in the crosshairs of two enemy nations. On one side, just past the pine trees to the west, Israeli soldiers kept 24-hour watch. On the other side, down the slope to the east, Jordanian Legionnaires, said by Israelis to have itchy trigger fingers, set up new border posts. Somehow, to Eliyahu, these things seemed like obstacles that could be overcome.

There was just one little wrinkle in Eliyahu's plan: The house he wanted to move into wasn't in Israel. It was part of the dangerous No Man's Land separating Israel and Jordan. Eliyahu was undeterred. He enlisted help from some Israeli soldiers to drag the barbed wire away from the house so he could move his family to the rim of his new country. It may have seemed like a small thing to Eliyahu at the time, but his actions helped set the stage for generations of international quarrels over the smallest of things.

In Eliyahu's case, it would be a volatile international dispute over an outdoor toilet. For others living along this short ridgeline, it would be a makeshift manhole cover, pigeons and freshly picked flowers. On this street, nothing was too small to fight over. Because Israel and Jordan were still arguing over exactly where the border between their two countries ran, the people living along the blurred lines knew every little thing did matter. The border lines were fluid. They were poorly defined. As Eliyahu proved, they were malleable. Where people lived, where they planted their trees, where they built their walls, all of it could change the border separating warring nations.

By design, Israel and Jordan had created long stretches of No Man's Land between the two countries to serve as a temporary buffer zone, separating enemy armies until seasoned diplomats could agree on permanent boundaries. That created open geographic wounds all along Israel's new borders. The most sensitive ones were in Jerusalem, where the lines severed streets, homes and neighborhoods. The zone cutting below Eliyahu's home would come to be known as Barbed Wire Alley.

The imperfect division of Jerusalem set the stage for late-night rescue missions to find runaway horses and special UN search parties sent to hunt for false teeth lost in No Man's Land. Israeli and Jordanian officers held special court hearings in No Man's Land to decide the fate of wayward cows that wandered from one country into the other. There were arguments over missing sheep. Lots of arguments over missing sheep. One Israeli tree-planting project in No Man's Land led to one of most surreal arguments ever to be fought at the UN Security Council before the world's most powerful nations.

Young couples divided by war started their marriages in Jerusalem's No Man's Land. At least one husband with a volcanic temper ignored the very real possibility that he might be killed by a sniper's bullet when he angrily stormed into No Man's Land after a violent argument with his estranged wife.

The problems were the creation of a pair of battlefield generals who had no intention of cementing the borders of Israel and Jordan when they drew the lines in 1948.

In the waning months of the war, Israeli and Arab League officers crowded into a small Jerusalem home, just outside the Old City walls, where they lay out a large map and began to argue over the lines. For the Israelis, the mapmaker was Moshe Dayan, the easily recognizable military commander with the iconic black eye patch, who was then leading the country's forces in and around Jerusalem. For the Arab Legion, it was Abdullah El-Tell, a tall commander wearing a red-and-white diamond-checked scarf carefully accenting his crisp uniform; he would become a vital emissary for leaders of the two nations.

CARVING UP JERUSALEM

It was November 30, 1948. Israel was seizing the advantage across the Middle East battlefields. Tens of thousands of Palestinians were on the run, heading for Lebanon, Jordan, Syria and Egypt. Israel had taken control of most of Jerusalem but didn't have the most important part: Arab forces had routed Israeli fighters from the Jewish Quarter and taken full control of the Old City. Israel and Jordan were ready to stop shooting at each other. And they were asking Dayan and Tell to create new maps to ensure that the guns would stay silent.

Sitting in the abandoned house that day in 1948, the two military commanders faced the difficult job of splitting Jerusalem. They laid the map out on an uneven surface as dozens of officers from both sides looked on. Dayan used a red grease pencil. Tell used a green one. Their lines rarely met. For the men, the lines were drawn only to reflect the general position of their forces on the front lines. They were supposed to be temporary cease-fire lines that would give diplomats some breathing room. The two men didn't expect their rough work to mark the final, firm border.

So, without much concern, the men created chunks of No Man's Land between their red and green lines. It amounted to nearly 750 acres of land in Jerusalem to keep fighting over.[1] In some places, No Man's Land was wider than a football field. In others, it was thinner than a tight city alley.

One reason the line failed to completely end the fighting was that the map the military officers used wasn't detailed enough. When the map was magnified to settle land disputes, it became clear that the grease pencil lines weren't thin enough—about four millimeters thick in some places—to accurately fix the borders. Israel and Jordan would continue to argue over every millimeter. When the generals finished their work in 1948, the United Nations set up a special committee—the Mixed Armistice Commission, or MAC—to broker border disputes between Israel and Jordan. The UN team set up shop in the new No Man's Land near the heavily guarded border crossing between East and West Jerusalem. The office would be the scene of endless disputes over the serious and the surreal. The absurdity of the arguments seemed to grow each year. A rotating series of UN commissioners tried in vain to stop the bickering. But how could the commission settle disputes if Israel and Jordan couldn't agree on where one country ended and the other one began?

"It's not enough to have a line," said Raphael Israeli, a Hebrew University scholar who served for five years as an Israeli representative to the MAC. "The question is: What do you understand about the line?"

In the densest parts of Jerusalem, the "thick of the line" cut through the streets, cleaving buildings in half or enveloping them entirely. The border drawn by Tell around the Old City posed a particular conundrum for Jordan. Tell's line covered the Old City walls where Jordanian soldiers kept constant watch. That made it impossible for Jordan to agree to any interpretation of the border that accepted the inner edge of the line as the outer edge of Jordan's border. It would have created an absurd situation in which the walls of the Old City were in No Man's Land and the walled city itself was part of Jordan.

Meron Benvenisti, an Israeli politician who served as deputy mayor of Jerusalem soon after Israel captured the city in 1967, later described the map as a "cartographer's nightmare and a geographer's catastrophe."[2]

The inability to resolve the issue led to years of fatal confrontations in No Man's Land. Israeli soldiers patrolling along the disputed lines were shot and killed by Jordanians hiding behind the archers' arrow slits in the

Old City's stone ramparts. Jordanian soldiers were killed by Israeli snipers. Civilians on both sides who got too close to the borders were gunned down. Residents had to rush through Sniper's Alleys in Jerusalem and hope that the hidden soldiers watching them through rifle scopes wouldn't take aim as they ran for safety.

Israel and Jordan argued incessantly over No Man's Land. Israel suggested cutting the land in half and eliminating it entirely. Jordan refused.

"JERUSALEM IS A POWDER KEG"

Problems along the border only got worse as the years dragged on with no agreement on what to do about the problem. Snipers from both sides kept shooting. Civilians kept dying. The United Nations kept holding emergency meetings to try to contain the violence. At one special emergency UN meeting, called on April 23, 1953, Lt. Gen. William Riley, a decorated American Marine running the Jordan-Israel MAC, warned both countries that the situation was getting out of hand. The night before, someone had opened fire along the Jerusalem border. It wasn't clear who fired first, but the shooting quickly spread up and down the dividing line. Though there was now a cease-fire in place, Riley said an Israeli sniper had opened fire that morning. Riley was alarmed—and his frustration was evident as the meeting began.

People on both sides "are living in a state of terror," he told the Israeli and Jordanian officers.[3]

"We have had casualties before, but in this case casualties of civilians living on both sides of the line were the worst I have ever seen in my time in this area," he said.[4]

Riley chastised both sides for using the poorly drawn lines as an excuse for their deadly tit-for-tat arguments.

"You have the right to defend yourselves with fire, but the question of resorting to retaliatory fire if one side or the other opens fire is contrary to the letter and the spirit of the General Armistice Agreement," he told them. "I have urged the parties on numerous occasions to eliminate the No Man's Land. However, as this has not been done, the parties themselves must mutually agree on the steps that must be taken to eliminate some of the difficulties that face each side of this No Man's Land."[5]

The head of Israel's delegation at the meeting, Lt. Col. Haim Gaon, rejected the American's perspective as out of touch with reality. Israelis, he told Riley, were living in an "impossible situation." Jordanian forces were killing civilians, and gangs were crossing the border into Israel to carry out unspeakable acts. He characterized the UN MAC as useless.[6]

Riley knew it was futile to argue over who started what. No matter what one side complained about, the other side would respond with a complaint of its own. There seemed to be no end to the kinds of things the Israelis and Jordanians could fight over. At that point, all the general was trying to do was to prevent the spiral of violence from getting worse.

"I have always maintained that it was not a question of building a box score on votes or on decisions that affected one side or the other, but that the MAC was here for the purpose of finding ways and means of avoiding similar types of complaints in the future," Riley told the two delegations. "Now, if your MAC is not doing that, then of course you defeat the purpose of the MAC itself and the parties must be held responsible for failure to raise the question of avoiding future types of complaints by getting together and finding a way to stop them."[7]

The commission might not be ideal, he said, but it was the only hope Israel and Jordan had of settling their disputes.

"It is the only official contact between the parties whereby each party can talk to the other in attempting to maintain a status quo until somebody finds a solution to the overall problem," he said.[8]

The Jordanian delegation urged Riley to settle the issue at hand. They saw things one way. Israel saw them another. Why else was the United Nations here if not to break the deadlock?

"The Israelis believe they are innocent, we believe we are innocent," Lt. Col. Sadek Bey Shar said. "We shall not know until somebody tells us who is right. We are here to discuss matters, explain difficulties and find solutions. We are not here to waste our time, talk and go away with no results. We agree that Jerusalem is a very sensitive point. People live too close to each other. However, both our people should have the right to live in peace."[9]

The Israelis were especially antagonistic toward Riley and refused to accept his suggestions. Riley pushed the two delegations to come up with a new plan to protect civilians living in No Man's Land. He thought it was time to stop killing people there. The problem was especially serious because neither side would agree on where, exactly, the No Man's Land borders started.

"There is a tacit agreement between the parties whereby a civilian can be fired upon when he enters No Man's Land, but even this action is not to be condoned and should be reduced to a minimum as firing of any kind is not justified under the terms of the General Armistice Agreement," Riley said. "I believe both sides could agree that if somebody enters No Man's Land, he should be picked up instead of being fired at."[10]

The argument dragged on without driving toward any agreement. After three hours, the meeting broke up with no action taken to reduce tensions. It was a pattern that would repeat itself for weeks, months and years. Israel and Jordan would spend hours arguing over procedure and then run out of time to discuss the substantive incidents at hand. Figuring out who fired first always proved to be difficult. And there seemed to be no agreement on how to prevent more clashes.

"The question as to who opened fire first is almost impossible to ascertain," Riley said before the April 23, 1953, meeting broke up. "I am not interested in the question of who is right or who is wrong. I am interested in the parties reaching conclusions whereby they can avoid similar incidents in the future."[11]

His appeals swayed no one. Six months later, Maj. Gen. Vagn Bennike, a famed member of the Danish resistance to Nazi rule in World War II who was then serving as chief of staff for the UN Truce Supervision Organization that oversaw the commission's work, warned the UN Security Council that the problems in the divided city were about to explode.

"Jerusalem, when tension increases between Israel and Jordan, is a dangerous powder keg," he wrote in a report to the UN Security Council in New York.[12]

After years of circuitous arguments over the "width of the line," Israel and Jordan finally made one breakthrough in 1955: They agreed that their borders would stretch to the outer edge of the lines drawn by Dayan and Tell. That helped resolve one problem with the map. But it failed to address the bigger one created by the existence of No Man's Land in the first place.

KILLING WILD DOGS IN ABU TOR

In May 1956, *Life* magazine photojournalist David Rubinger got a call from an Israeli member of the MAC who had a tip: The United Nations was preparing for an unusual rescue mission in Jerusalem. They were co-ordinating a cease-fire so they could search for dentures lost in No Man's Land.

The dentures belonged to Miriam Zahade, a 42-year-old cancer patient at a French hospital that sat right on the edge of Jerusalem's No Man's Land.[13] Zahade was living out her last days on the border line, under the care of Catholic nuns. The West Jerusalem hospital sat on one of the narrowest strips of No Man's Land between Israel and Jordan. The arched windows of the three-story stone building looked directly across at the Old City walls and the gateway to the Christian Quarter. Israeli soldiers used the hospital rooftop to keep watch on Jordanian Legionnaires on the Old City wall ramparts 100 feet away. This section of No Man's Land was one of the most volatile. Coils upon coils of barbed wire stretched along the street. More than one person at the hospital was hit by errant bullets over the years. In the hospital's church, the stained-glass image of St. Francis of Assisi took a bullet hole right through his heart. Nuns, doctors and patients all entered the hospital from the back. The entrance facing the Old City, with stairs leading right onto No Man's Land, was closed off. Going out that door could be deadly.

So when Miriam's dentures tumbled out a window and into No Man's Land that day in May, it seemed like a lost cause. It was spring, and Miriam was sitting by a window overlooking the border. She accidentally coughed her dentures into a piece of paper and threw them out the window. The paper fell into the weeds and trash below. By the time Miriam realized she'd tossed her dentures into No Man's Land, there was nothing she could do. Miriam was distraught. She refused to speak for days.[14]

The nuns came up with an improbable solution: Why not ask Israel and Jordan to declare a cease-fire so the UN could send a search party into No Man's Land to recover the dentures? In a rare moment of unity, both armies agreed to hold their fire so the UN could rescue the dentures.

With Jordanian Legionnaires watching from the Old City walls on the other side of No Man's Land, a French officer carrying a white flag led five nuns and an Israeli soldier into the rubble to hunt for the false teeth. It wasn't an easy mission. The street between the hospital and the Old City was cluttered with boulders, trash, overgrown bushes, shrapnel and, quite possibly, unexploded mines from the 1948 war. Miriam kept watch on the search from the hospital windows above.

"It was like looking for a needle in a haystack," said Rubinger, who took photos of the unusual rescue party.

Dressed in their white habits with their distinctive *Flying Nun*-esque hooded cowls, the women picked through the detritus without any luck. As the minutes dragged on, the search seemed futile. Then one of the nuns spotted something in the grass, rummaged through the garbage and hoisted the dentures into the air. Smiling, Sister Augustine triumphantly showed the dentures to Miriam looking down from the window above as Rubinger snapped photos. When the pictures appeared in *Life* magazine, the French commander who led the search party complained that it made him look like a fool.

"It is not fitting for a French commandant to be seen looking for false teeth," the French officer told Rubinger.*

The incident came to define the hospital and the small ways Israel and Jordan were able to find common ground, at least for some false teeth.

"For humanitarian reasons, you can do a lot, even in a time of war," said Sister Monika Duellmann, who took over as director of the French hospital in 2004. "It's difficult to get a cease-fire that will hold, and they got one for the teeth—because it's not political and it's not religious."

Rubinger, arguably Israel's most famous photojournalist, often sought out surreal stories along the jagged dividing line. The photographer went everywhere he could go. One place he always worried about entering was No Man's Land.

"It wasn't very good for your health to go to No Man's Land," Rubinger said. "It was easier to get to the moon than it was to get across the border."

Seven months after the search for the dentures, Rubinger got a chance to get another look at No Man's Land. In December 1956, faced with a growing wild dog problem in the city, Israel and Jordan agreed to join forces to lay out poisoned meat in No Man's Land as part of a joint anti-rabies campaign. The dog problem was particularly bad in Jerusalem's Abu Tor neighborhood. Abu Tor had been cut in two by the 1948 war. The top of the hillside neighborhood was inside Israel, but most of Abu Tor was part of Jordan. The two countries were separated by a skinny band that cut across a steep hillside of stone homes and small orchards.

---

*Italicized quotes in the book are based on memories of one or more people who were part of the conversation.

Led by a Scottish major with the UN and with an Israeli paratrooper keeping watch, Rubinger clicked away as Israeli and Jordanian veterinary workers tossed the deadly meat into the fields. Rubinger followed the team along the coils of barbed wire running between the homes and neglected terraced gardens. No Man's Land seemed deserted, and bitter winter winds swept up the valley. The team walked along Barbed Wire Alley, a rocky path that would one day become Assael Street.

"It felt like you were going somewhere nobody ever goes," Rubinger said. "Like virgin territory."

While they were throwing out the meat, they heard something moving in the abandoned homes below. They watched warily as a Jordanian soldier came their way. He wore a long wool coat and a scarf that covered all but his eyes and nose. The soldier waved and made his way toward Rubinger and the anti-rabies team. In the chilly afternoon breeze, the Jordanian soldier walked up to a low stone wall in No Man's Land and handed the Israeli paratrooper a glass of hot tea so he could warm himself up. Rubinger was amazed to see this small act of kindness between two soldiers from enemy nations.

"That was unique," he said. "Not just rare. Unique. The border between Israel and Jordan was such that nobody crossed alive."

A few months later, Rubinger drove to Qalqilya, a small village up north that was right on the Israel-Jordan border. The dividing line put the village in Jordan and its fields to the west in Israel. That created endless problems. The villagers had a hard time accepting that they lived in one country while their old farmlands were now in another. It was even harder to explain to their sheep, cows and donkeys, which gave little thought about new nations and wondered more about where they were going to get their next meal. It was a problem that dogged UN officials who complained that the borders made no sense.

"Had the line been drawn to respect village boundaries, little trouble would have resulted," said E. H. Hutchison, a commander in the US Navy who took over as chairman of the Jordan-Israel MAC in 1953. "The inhabitants of the villages so affected are not prepared to respect the invisible line or political decrees that are supposed to keep them from the lands they and their forbearers have owned and cultivated for hundreds of years."[15]

That day in 1957, Rubinger had been tipped off that a big international trial was going to be held in Qalqilya. When he arrived, Israeli and Jordanian officers were gathering on the border to decide the fate of a cow.

"They had a court sitting on the road, in the middle of the road, that had to decide whom the cow belonged to," said Rubinger, who was so captivated by the unfolding legal battle that he shot three rolls of film.

The uniformed Jordanian and Israeli officials set up three folding metal tables on the road in No Man's Land between large metal anti-tank barricades shaped like big toy jacks. The aggrieved Arab farmers, wearing long formless *thobes* and white flowing kaffiyehs held on the head by a double knot of black cord, met on the road to plead their case. Jordanian and Israeli soldiers milled around as the men argued over whose cows were whose. The cows in question were led before the judges for examination. The court issued its decree. Decades later, Rubinger couldn't remember just how it played out. And nothing was left in his photo archives to jog his memory.

COOLING OFF IN NO MAN'S LAND

Livestock disputes weren't all that unusual at the time. UN records from that era are filled with files upon files about stolen mules, missing cows and "imposter" sheep. Diplomats assigned to Jerusalem routinely found themselves mediating feuds over livestock. Journalists in Jerusalem could only take them so seriously. "Jordan Yields Wrong Sheep," read one headline on a short story in the February 11, 1958, edition of the *Jerusalem Post*.

"Mandelbaum Gate in Jerusalem became a sheepfold yesterday morning when the Jordanian authorities herded 30 sheep into no-man's-land for return to Israel," the reporter wrote. The sheep were finding their way back through Mandelbaum Gate, the central link between Jordanian-controlled East Jerusalem and Israeli-controlled West Jerusalem.[16]

The handover seemed to be going along well, until the Israelis inspecting the returnees discovered that most of the sheep weren't theirs. They were, the article reported, "imposters." The sheep were turned back by Israel to Jordanian officials who vowed to track down the real sheep.[17]

Crossing the border was impossible for most people. Mandelbaum Gate was used mostly by UN officials, diplomats, merchants and few others. Little about it was inviting. The 50-yard crossing was dominated by the remnants of a two-story stone home owned by a Jewish immigrant named Simcha Mandelbaum. The only piece of the house to survive the 1948 war was part of a wall with an elegant stone arch that rose above a No Man's Land cluttered with rusting armored personnel carriers, coils of barbed wire and lines of conical, concrete anti-tank barriers known as Dragon's Teeth.

At Christmas, busloads of Christians on the Israeli side were allowed through the gate into Jordan so they could visit the biblical birthplace of Jesus in Bethlehem, just down the road from Jerusalem. Occasionally, Israel and Jordan used the gate to hand over mischievous boys caught exploring No Man's Land.

The No Man's Land at Mandelbaum Gate served as an unusual backdrop for engagements and weddings between brides living on one side of the border and grooms living on the other. Israel and Jordan agreed to hold their fire so some couples, separated by the border, could get engaged amid the tangles of barbed wire and Dragon's Teeth.[18] They looked on as the families raised toasts to newlyweds married in No Man's Land.[19]

In 1958, Raphael Israeli, then a 24-year-old Israeli army captain, was chosen to be a delegate on the Jordan-Israel MAC. His youth and inexperience meant that Israeli came to the job with distinct disadvantages, so the ambitious Israeli officer did all he could to even the scales. Israeli, who was born in Morocco and left when he was 14, used his knowledge of Arabic to establish a decent rapport with the Jordanian delegation led by Col. Mohammad Daoud Al-Abbasi, a deft debater who would go on to become his country's prime minister. The two officers got so close that Abbasi, nearly 20 years older than Israeli, quietly gave his Israeli counterpart a present at the UN commission office in No Man's Land when one of Israeli's kids was born.

"Don't tell anybody," Abbasi told Israeli as he handed him the gift, *"because if anybody knows I brought a present to a Jew, to a Zionist, they will hang me."*

One of the biggest tests for the two came in 1962 when Israeli got an urgent call in the middle of the night telling him to get dressed and come to the UN office in No Man's Land right away to meet Abbasi.

"What's happened?" Israeli asked, fearing the worst.

"Just come," the UN official told Israeli.

When Israeli got there, Abbasi was in a panic.

"*Rafi,*" the Jordanian officer said, "*you have to help me. We have a problem.*"

The crisis wasn't over a deadly shooting or a child missing in No Man's Land. It was over a runaway horse. And not just any horse. This one belonged to the head of Silwan, the crowded Arab village outside the Old City that rose on the hillside across the valley from Abu Tor. The man's horse had run across the valley, up the Abu Tor hillside, past the barbed wire and into Israel, where it was set to be placed under quarantine for 40 days.

In this case, with this horse, that wasn't going to work. The horse's owner called Abbasi and told him in no uncertain terms to bring his horse back without delay.

"*You have to help me,*" Abbasi told Israeli. "*The entire village expects me to bring it back. All my honor and respect hangs on this. Please help me get it back quickly.*"

Israeli was happy to help—so long as he could use the crisis to Israel's advantage. Israeli wanted to use the handover to take a swipe at the United Nations. He suggested that Israel give Abbasi the horse the next day at the UN headquarters on a ridge next to Abu Tor, not at Mandelbaum Gate. Abbasi blanched at the idea, but Israeli persuaded him to go along with the plan. Israeli called the general in command at the UN Government House and told him about the agreement. The general, Israeli said, rejected the idea out of concern it would damage the UN gardens. "OK," Israeli told the United Nations, "I'll call some reporters and tell them that the UN is blocking a deal between Israel and Jordan."

The handoff took place the next day at the UN headquarters.

Horses, sheep, cattle and dogs weren't the only ones to venture into No Man's Land. Adventurous kids would sometimes sneak through the fence to rescue playground balls. Soldiers from one side or the other would risk being shot to gather eggs, vegetables or fruit in No Man's Land. And young men on the hunt for a daring adventure also tested border security. One night sometime in the early 1950s, while Rubinger was drinking with friends at a neighborhood bar—Fink's—in West Jerusalem, two guys came in waving a pair of movie tickets from a cinema in the Old City, across the No Man's Land, in Jordan. How they got into East Jerusalem, they didn't say.

"It was a suicidal thing to do," Rubinger said.

The failure of Israel and Jordan to eliminate No Man's Land paved the way for it to become the setting for surreal moments that trumped cow courts and sheep counts. One man claimed he was the Messiah and wandered babbling into No Man's Land near the Old City. Another guy made local news when he stormed out of his house during an argument with his wife and marched straight into No Man's Land before he did something he might regret.

"Husband Cools Off in No Man's Land," read the headline of a tiny August 16, 1959, *Jerusalem Post* article about the domestic fight that became an international dispute.[20]

> A 27-year-old resident of Jerusalem's Musrara quarter, Avraham Abu-Gzar, got into a quarrel with his wife yesterday afternoon and, after beating her, announced his intention of crossing the border into Jordan. He actually went into No Man's Land and disappeared among the empty houses.
>
> Police were called and asked to contact the U.N., and Jordanian authorities . . . but, wise in the ways of quarreling husbands, [they] advised everybody to sit tight for awhile. Sure enough, at 4:15 p.m.—three quarters of an hour after Abu-Gzar had disappeared—he reappeared, having decided not to cross into Jordan after all. Police detained him and released him on . . . bond.

The beating appeared to be part of a turbulent train wreck of a marriage. The short story only hinted at its troubles: a violent husband; a wife who was living with another man in another city; and three children looking for a stable home.

"They will decide today if and how to charge the contrite husband," the reporter wrote. "Two years ago, Mrs. Abu-Gzar left her husband to live in Haifa with another man. She came to Jerusalem on Friday to see her husband before a Rabbinate Court this week which is to decide on the custody of their three children."

JORDAN TO ISRAEL: STOP THE TOILET

Perhaps the most absurd fight over No Man's Land took place at Eliyahu Goeli's hillside home in Abu Tor.

Living in the cross fire, the Goelis settled into an unusual routine. They would creep through the barbed wire and into No Man's Land to

recover eggs laid by their chickens. Sometimes they had to scramble after the chickens themselves. They waved to friendly Jordanian soldiers,
who kept constant watch from a rooftop below. They rushed across
open ground on the hilltop to avoid being targeted by malicious border
guards. The family learned to tell the difference between the snap of
rifle rounds over their heads and the echoes of machine gun fire across
the valley.

The Goelis' home was part of a small compound owned by Jerusalem's
Greek Orthodox Church. There was a small monastery on the other side of
the property from the Goelis and a few other homes tucked under the trees.
After Eliyahu staked his claim, others moved in.

In February 1966, the Goelis and their neighbors decided they needed
to repair their outhouse. The bathroom was in serious disrepair. So they
brought in some concrete blocks and started rebuilding, oblivious to the
outrage boiling on the Jordanian side.

On February 10, Jordanian officials fired off an urgent demand that
the United Nations immediately step in and bring the construction in No
Man's Land to a halt. The next day, when Jordanian officials learned the Israelis were still building, Abbasi, then head of the Jordanian military team
in Jerusalem, sent a charged warning to the United Nations: *"If you don't
stop the construction, we will."*

"Col. Daoud said that if we didn't take measures to get the work
stopped, he would find the way of stopping it himself," a UN official told
his superiors.[21]

But it didn't stop. The workers kept coming. On the third day, the
Jordanians fired off a more threatening complaint.

"To keep the peace in Jerusalem, we request immediate stoppage of
the work being done until the case is discussed by the MAC," the Jordanian
delegation demanded.[22]

UN investigators converged on Abu Tor to investigate the latest border
dispute. They secretly snapped photographs that captured blurred images
of young men working on the outhouse. They interviewed people building the toilet. They measured the size of the outhouse and the thickness of
its concrete blocks. The dispute dragged on for weeks. Jordanian officials
accused Israel of using the toilet as a pretext for covertly building a new
military post in No Man's Land. Israelis mocked the Jordanians for being
so worked up over a tiny five-foot by eight-foot toilet.

On March 8, the Israeli and Jordanian delegations met at the MAC offices for a second time to argue over the home improvement project. The two sides agreed that the house was in No Man's Land. They didn't see eye-to-eye on the toilet itself. In 1951, Israel and Jordan had reached an agreement under which a few people already living in No Man's Land—people like the Goelis—would be allowed to stay. Israel and Jordan selected a few dozen homes in No Man's Land they wanted to protect and agreed to provide power and services to a few on each side. The deal tacitly ceded parts of No Man's Land to one nation or the other. Israel and Jordan agreed that people living in the homes should be allowed to live a "normal life." In this case, the two countries couldn't agree on what that meant. Exasperated UN officials tried to mediate. Israelis thought it was absurd to think that repairing the bathroom would be forbidden.

"What does it mean?" asked Lt. Col. Yair Biberman, the Israeli military representative called upon to fight for the outhouse. "Does it mean that this building will remain without a toilet?"[23]

No, the Israeli colonel could not accept this.

"Once it was agreed that normal life will proceed there, that means that such an elementary thing as a toilet is entirely within the authority of the people living in that building to repair and to change."[24]

The Jordanians disagreed. Abbasi said no deal between the two countries allowed people in No Man's Land to build extra rooms on their houses, no matter the size. If Jordan allowed Israel to repair the toilet, it would set a precedent for Israelis to build dozens of buildings that would be perfect new sniper positions for their soldiers.

"If this kind of work is allowed to continue for a few months more, we will have 25,000 annexes to one house," he said at a March emergency meeting at the UN office. "This is the intention of those who built up this agreement, and I am sure that you know it."[25]

On March 14, the diplomats met to decide the outhouse's fate. By a vote of two to one, the MAC condemned Israel for building the outhouse and called for its removal from No Man's Land.

"Let my concluding words be an earnest appeal to the parties to find a satisfactory solution which will prevent future similar situations with a view to preventing tension in this sensitive area," said Lt. Col. M. C. Stanaway, an army officer from New Zealand who was then serving as chairman of the UN commission, at the close of the fourth hearing and 18 hours of arguing.[26]

For the Israelis this was a victory. The United Nations condemned the construction, but the outhouse remained standing.

"We used to draw up a balance-sheet of condemnations, and even evolved a kind of tactical strategy during these protest wars," Israeli Gen. Uzi Narkiss wrote in his memoir. "I, of course, was fully aware that the real decision would be made not at the debating table of the MAC, but on the line itself, where the number of hands raised for or against would not decide the issue, but the number of Israeli civilians living permanently on the line, earning their living and raising their children."[27]

Narkiss understood that having civilians like the Goelis, who were willing to put down roots on disputed land—what modern politicians would call "facts on the ground"—mattered more than placing soldiers on the border.

"I will always remember a talk I had with a young officer early in my command," he wrote. "I pointed out to him that his patrol passed a part of the line in one of the mixed quarters. 'But we don't need to demonstrate our presence there,' he said innocently. 'The Jewish children playing near the fence demonstrate the presence.'"[28]

It was a constant battle over inches. The inability to agree on what to do with the No Man's Land meant that there was always new ground to fight over. It wasn't just about toilets or sheep. One of the biggest fights of the time was over trees.

"BULLDOZERS AREN'T MACHINE GUNS"

Few people probably paid much attention to the small story on page three of the *Jerusalem Post* on August 15, 1957: "100,000 Trees for Jerusalem Border."

The story seemed to be a yawner, a little newspaper filler, about Israel's latest tree-planting project.

It was actually an early public salvo in another Arab-Israeli fight that would have to be settled by the UN Security Council.

"Over 100,000 trees are to be planted this coming season near the ceasefire lines in Jerusalem," the three-paragraph story began. "The trees will be planted by the Jewish National Fund [JNF], right up to the border from Talpiot to Abu Tor. Preparatory work for the planting is already being carried out at the site. The Forest Division of the Ministry of Agriculture has announced that over 20,000 dunhams [5,000 acres] of marginal lands unfit for cultivation are to be planted with Eucalyptus trees, starting this winter."[29]

As Israel put it, this was environmental activism at its best. Israeli officials described the tree planting as a citywide beautification effort meant to eventually encircle then-divided Jerusalem in a green belt. To Jordan, it was a blatant act of aggression. These weren't just trees; Jordan viewed the saplings as another way for Israelis to steal contested property from Arab owners who were powerless to stop the land grab.

The fight had quietly begun earlier that summer when Israeli workers, protected by soldiers, entered No Man's Land to begin planting. Tractors and bulldozers uprooted dozens of olive trees to make way for the Israeli reforestation effort.[30] Jordanian soldiers watched from afar as the project grew. Day after day more workers came. So did the soldiers. They began plowing fields, carving out new roads, building barbed wire fences and installing what appeared to be new mortar positions.[31] On July 24, Lt. Col. M. M. Izhaq, the senior member of the Jordanian team at the MAC, fired off a detailed demand to the United Nations for an emergency meeting.

"Statement of Facts," his complaint began. "On 21 July 1957 Israeli labourers escorted by Israeli security forces entered the No Man's Land between the lines at approximately MR 1724 1288 and MR 17240 12893 and started digging." This, Col. Izhaq wrote, was a "flagrant violation of the status quo." An emergency meeting had to be called to force Israel to stop the work. Immediately.[32]

The head of the MAC unsuccessfully sought to defuse the situation by asking the Israelis to halt the tree-planting project. Israeli officials said no. They refused to take part in an emergency meeting to discuss it. They were going to keep digging.

The fight over the trees brought No Man's Land back to center stage. In this case, the battle took on special importance because the two sides were fighting over land near the UN headquarters in Jerusalem. Built in the early 1930s, the UN Government House served as home and headquarters for the British High Commissioner while England ruled Palestine. The locals called it the Government Palace. It was where the British elite hosted parties in elegant halls with high ceilings and chandeliers.

When Dayan and Tell sat down to draw their map in November 1948, they drew wide lines around the Government House, creating a fat No Man's Bulge over the sparsely populated valley. As in Abu Tor, Israel and Jordan agreed that a fixed number of civilians already living in the area "between the lines" would be allowed to stay. Around the UN compound, Israel and Jordan both agreed to limit that number to 200 apiece. The area became a wide demilitarized zone.

Dayan repeatedly tried to convince Jordan to divide No Man's Land. In Jerusalem, Dayan persuaded one of his Jordanian counterparts to accept division of the area by creating an informal "civilian line" through the middle, but the idea was rejected in Amman, where Arab leaders weren't prepared to willingly cede any part of Jerusalem to Israel. Although the two sides never officially agreed to divide the No Man's Land, they sometimes acted as if they had, creating a de facto split that was tacitly accepted—as long as neither side complained.

While Israel portrayed the program run by the Jewish National Fund as a beautification project, Jordanian officials knew that tree planting was a political act in Jerusalem, one that could be used to establish the digger's rights to the land. Israel knew it too, and the government approved the move into No Man's Land to demonstrate its claims to the area.

With Israel refusing to stop, Jordan took its case to New York. UN secretary-general Dag Hammarskjold, the Swedish diplomat who'd just helped avert a 1956 war in the Middle East by creating a new UN peacekeeping force, privately urged Israel to stop planting the trees. So did London and Washington. Everyone was leaning on Israel to bring the digging to a halt.[33]

On August 28, 1957, as pressure built on Israel, its top leaders gathered to discuss their predicament. Golda Meir, then Israel's foreign minister, painted the whole debate as an absurd overreaction by jittery Jordanians.

"In Jordan during the first days there was great panic, when near the border, very near the border, we went in with heavy equipment, tractors and bulldozers," Meir told Israeli prime minister David Ben-Gurion and other Israeli leaders. "Possibly, they were really panicked and turned to all their friends: 'For God's sake, Israel is preparing to attack!'"[34]

Israel wasn't preparing to attack Jordan. But the tree planting had triggered a war of its own. In New York, Meir said, Hammarskjold kept warning Israel to cool things down before they got out of control.

"When someone approached Hammarskjold he said: 'You don't really want a discussion in the Security Council. There is a feeling that America also does not want this discussion any too much,'" Meir told the group. Just that morning, a UN official gave Israel another warning: Stop the tree-planting work or we will bring this before the UN Security Council. Meir urged Ben-Gurion not to bow to the pressure.[35]

"There is no reason to make a commotion," Meir said during the meeting. "There is no logical reason that we be forbidden to prepare the area and plant trees."[36]

"They do not want our rights to be established," Ben-Gurion told her.[37]

"I want to suggest that we continue the work," Meir replied. They had to stand up to the pressure. "We will go to the Security Council. We will go there. Common sense does not tolerate that we have to stop the work."[38]

Meir warned that Israel would lose the upper hand if it agreed to stop digging up the hillsides.

"We know that if we stop this one time, it is harder to start again later," she said. "I think that the best thing we can do is to finish quickly, at the very least, the work with heavy equipment, indeed, bulldozers are not machine guns."[39]

The Israeli leaders emerged from the meeting ready to fight. The United Nations, America, England and other world powers kept privately prodding Israel to stop the work before they were forced to bring it before the Security Council. No one wanted to see the world superpowers fighting over trees in the Middle East.

"The Americans are afraid that Syria and Russia will be given the opportunity to appear as though protecting Arab interests," Meir said in another meeting on September 1. Meir urged the Americans to get Jordan's King Hussein to back off. She saw no reason to back down.[40]

"I do not care if Hussein says this is a victory because we took our heavy equipment out of the area," Meir said. "But to stop crucial work—that we cannot do. Hussein has to supply sensations to public opinion, we also have public opinion to whom we will not be able to explain why we must stop work that doesn't cause damage to anyone and that there is no objection to our doing this work."[41]

Neither side would bend. Five days later, Israel was hauled before the UN Security Council to defend its decision.

The 11-member Security Council included Henry Cabot Lodge Jr., the American diplomat who would go on to become Richard Nixon's vice presidential running mate when he lost to John F. Kennedy in 1960. Ambassadors from the Soviet Union, England, the Philippines and Iraq all gathered in the Security Council chambers to hear Jordan's ambassador to the United Nations lay out the ominous implications for peace in the Middle East. This wasn't about trees, he told them. This was about the ground they were planted in. This land wasn't "no man's land." It belonged to Palestinian farmers forced from their homes by war. Now, the Jordanian ambassador told the Security Council, Israel was using tree planting as an excuse to seize more ground in Jerusalem.[42]

"We are now faced with a particular form of Israeli violation of the Armistice Agreement, the aim of which is the same as that of other aggressions on the part of Israel, namely, to get access to, to exploit and occupy privately owned Arab lands," Ambassador Yusuf Haikal told the Security Council.[43]

Haikal left no doubt that Jordan was prepared to go to war over the trees if the United Nations didn't do something.

"In the event of the persistence by Israel in the work described earlier," he warned the council, "my government would have no alternative but to take the necessary steps and measures to ensure the safety of the area and the preservation of the status quo."[44]

When his turn came to speak, Israel's deputy UN ambassador, Mordecai Kidron, immediately mocked Jordan for bringing the issue to the Security Council. He characterized the Jordanians as petty rivals who were willing to pick a fight over the most absurd things. Like trees.

"It might appear that the appropriate place for a discussion of this nature is the Food and Agriculture Organization of the United Nations rather than the Security Council," Kidron said, "because, despite the assertions of the Jordan foreign minister, there are no aggressive or other military aspects to the planting of trees in this area."[45]

Kidron cast Jordan as hopelessly trapped in a pitiful paradigm that made the country's leaders reflexively anti–anything Israel did, even planting trees. He deftly framed Jordanians as reactionary rejectionists who saw dark deeds and hidden agendas on Jerusalem's innocent hillsides.

"We have in Israel a particular feeling about trees," Kidron told the ambassadors from the world's leading powers. "Among the things of which we are most proud in the history of modern Jewish settlement in the Holy Land is the conversion of large stretches of barren hills and rock strewn mountains into verdant forest."[46]

Kidron went on at some length about the importance of trees to Israelis. They planted them when people were born. They planted them when people died.

"Trees are for us symbols of life and of growth," he told the Security Council. "It was thus with a particular feeling of amazement and lack of comprehension that we heard that Jordan wished to put a stop to the planting of trees in the former Government House area."[47]

There was nothing nefarious about the tree planting, Kidron said. It was little more than Israel doing on its side of No Man's Land what Jordanians were doing on their side. When Kidron was done, Arkady Sobolev, the Soviet Union's ambassador to the United Nations, leaned in on Jordan's side. Like the Jordanians, Sobolev saw Machiavellian hands pulling hidden strings. He blasted Kidron for trying "to belittle the significance of these works" that the Israeli leader "seemed to regard . . . as a joke."[48] This was no laughing matter to the Soviet ambassador. Sobolev agreed with Jordan: This wasn't about trees. It was about Israel doing America's bidding by stirring up conflict to keep the Middle East in a constant state of chaos.

"Aggressive circles in certain governments are interested in the maintenance of such tension and are using Israel as a tool for the implementation of their own plans," Sobolev said.

When he decided to speak, America's ambassador ignored the Soviet implications entirely and backed calls for continued UN examination of the situation.

"We do hope," Lodge said in time-tested, mealymouthed diplomatic speak, "that . . . both parties would refrain from taking any action between the armistice lines that would tend to increase tensions."[49]

With the United Nations punting, Israel was able to keep planting. For the rest of the year, UN officials kept tabs on every tractor, bulldozer, young tree and soldier that entered the area between the lines. UN observers drew detailed maps documenting the tree-planting efforts that showed the Israeli work stretching across hundreds of acres in No Man's Land, from the edge of Abu Tor to the south. When the issue came back to New York in January

1958, the UN Security Council unanimously backed a US-crafted resolution that called on Israel to suspend the tree-planting project until the United Nations could carry out a new survey of No Man's Land that would examine whether Israel was planting trees on land owned by Palestinian Jerusalemites.

"Israel should not be allowed to use Arab-owned properties and Arabs should not be allowed to use Israeli-owned properties," the resolution read.

The UN action was meant to defuse tensions. In reality, it did almost nothing to curtail Israel's work in No Man's Land. By the time the UN Security Council voted on the dispute, Israel had been working on the tree-planting project for six months. New "facts on the ground" were taking root. When Israel seized control of East Jerusalem in 1967, the JNF declared part of No Man's Land next to Abu Tor, where the 1957 tree-planting project had taken place, to be a new "Peace Forest."

"The Peace Forest was intended to connect the eastern and western parts of Jerusalem, representing the reunification of Israel's capital city in 1967," one Israeli tour guide wrote on a tourism website. "Its name reflects a wish that all of Jerusalem's residents will be able to live together in harmony, and its location serves as an ideal gathering place for people of all walks of life."[50]

The Peace Forest's origins have long been forgotten. When I asked the JNF in 2014 about the history of the forest, the group hired an Israeli geology professor, Yossi Katz, to investigate. Katz looked over JNF records and checked Israeli government archives before reporting back to the JNF. Katz said he could find no evidence that the JNF planted trees in the disputed No Man's Lands that later became the Peace Forest. The geologist couldn't explain why detailed UN maps in 1957 showed the Israeli tree-planting project expanding across the area now known as the Peace Forest. He couldn't say who did the work, but it wasn't the JNF.

In the end, it didn't really matter who planted the forest along the Jerusalem ridgeline. The dispute became one more reminder that feuds over small things along the unsettled border, from toilets to trees, could become the spark for a major confrontation, if not a new Middle East war.

TWO

FATHER OF THE BULL

I n the beginning, there was a hillside. It rose steeply above the Old Testament's accursed Valley of Slaughter, high enough to give people living there an enviable view of the Middle East city where G-d created Adam from the dust, Jesus Christ was crucified for our sins and the Prophet Muhammad ascended to Heaven.

This hillside may have been the place where Judas cut a deal with Jerusalem's high priest to betray Jesus Christ for 30 pieces of silver. It may be named after a Muslim warrior—but it's not entirely clear which one. Some Israelis say it is named for a revered Jewish high priest who lived and died here.

If you ask the head of the Greek Orthodox Church in Jerusalem, he might tell you this neighborhood on the hill, Abu Tor, isn't named after a famed Muslim fighter general at all. It's named after a Greek Orthodox saint known for healing the city's animals. Some researchers say the hilltop actually draws its name from pagan worshippers who carved out stone caves where they paid homage to their gods 3,000 years ago.

In Abu Tor, people tell different stories about the neighborhood's name. So it's not surprising that people can't agree on what has actually happened here. Some researchers will stake their reputations on saying that Abu Tor is the place where Judas conspired with the Jewish high priest Caiaphas to bring down Jesus—a place known as the Hill of Evil Counsel.

Abu Tor would have been a perfect place for plotting and scheming. From the open vista, it feels like you can almost jump over the valley and land inside the Old City's walls. On quiet mornings, the sun rising over the Judean Desert casts the Old City in silhouettes of domes, minarets and steeples washed in a hazy indigo-apricot hue. The city's crowded neighborhoods roll out below Abu Tor as the echoes of howling dogs and crunching tires ricochet through the streets. Winds the color of iodine sometimes slam into Abu Tor, battering the hillside with endless waves of desert sand. It feels like the kind of place where you might conspire to bring down a heretic who claimed to be the Son of God.

Some tour guides and historians say the *real* Hill of Evil Counsel lies farther south, on the ridgeline used first by the British to rule post–World War I Palestine and then by the United Nations as it tried to keep the peace in the Middle East. Even if the UN Government House doesn't actually sit on the Hill of Evil Counsel, it's a good story for tour guides.

THE TOMB OF ABU TOR

In English, the Arabic name *Abu Tor* is usually translated as "Father of the Bull" or "Father of the Ox." In this case, it is believed to have referred to a fierce Muslim general who fought alongside Saladin as his fearsome army rousted Christian Crusaders from Jerusalem in 1187.

Depending on who you ask, the general's full name might have been Ahmad Bin Jamal ad-Din or Sheikh Shehab ad-Din el Cudsi. In either case, he was given the name Abu Tor for riding a bull into battle with Islam's most celebrated warrior. As a thank-you for his bravery, Saladin gave Abu Tor a small village on a hillside outside the Old City's Jaffa Gate. Even after the war, the bull remained loyal to the general. When Abu Tor needed things from the market, he would tie a note around his faithful bull's neck and send it lumbering toward town. Without fail, the bull returned to the hillside every time with all the things that Abu Tor needed.[1]

Some longtime residents of Abu Tor say that both those stories are wrong, that the real Abu Tor is Abu al-'Abas Ahmad ibn Jamal al-Din 'Abdallah ibn Muhammad ibn 'Abd al-Jabar al-Kudsi, who helped Islam's second caliph, Umar ibn al-Khattab, conquer Jerusalem the *first* time, in 637.

Little known to most people, even many of those living in the neighborhood, is that, whoever he is, Abu Tor is buried at the top of the hillside in a small stone crypt that has been transformed into a backyard storage shed.

(Even this is sometimes disputed by the Greek Orthodox Church. The man buried there isn't Muslim, the church leaders might argue. He's a sixth-century Christian martyr.)

Abu Tor's final resting place is in the shadows of a broad fig tree, under a cement-and-stone block shed that's used to store bikes and gardening tools, right next to a plastic garbage can.

The tomb's location can be found in the UN archives on copies of the cease-fire map used by Dayan and Tell in 1948, where it is marked as that of "Sh. Ahmad et Turi," Sheikh Ahmad of the Bull. Sometimes old Muslim men from the neighborhood down the hill will come to the narrow stone alley outside Abu Tor's tomb and raise their hands in quiet prayer.

Some locals say there is good reason to stay on Abu Tor's good side: He will haunt the people who don't look after his tomb. Bad things happen to those who don't take good care of his final resting place. And so Abu Tor's tomb remains. He has been buried alongside one of the neighborhood's most captivating homes: a one-story stone house with a central domed roof and high ceilings that may have served as a mosque, a Greek Orthodox patriarch's home, and a brothel.

Others say the origins of the neighborhood's name can be traced back much further than the seventh century. Some people say the name Abu Tor dates back thousands of years, to the time of Canaan, when pagans worshipped gods like Baal, a deity often depicted as a bull. As in the Valley of Slaughter below, some locals say, small cults used the Abu Tor hillside to honor their gods with fiery offerings and bloody sacrifices.

One of the suspected sacrificial spots is near Eliyahu Goeli's home, inside the walled compound that has been owned by the Greek Orthodox Church for centuries. For the Greeks, for all Christians, this spot holds special significance beyond its reputation as the Hill of Evil Counsel. Hidden beneath the sloping hilltop is a claustrophobic catacomb that once held the bones of some of Jerusalem's important Christian pioneers, one of whom was beheaded in the fourth century when he refused to betray his faith.

The small stone monastery is built above a beautiful, long mosaic floor that some people say is a clear sign that the hillside was an important spiritual center in days gone by. The monastery seems to be jammed into the hillside at an angle, like it's been yanked around a few times. The building, with its short, narrow, arched stone entrance and its rusting crucifix hanging from the heavy iron front door, dates back to the seventh century when Saint Modestus restored Jerusalem's decimated holy sites, including the Church of the Holy Sepulcher. Modestus wasn't just a Christian hero: Church leaders say he protected and healed animals. For that, the Greek Orthodox Patriarch has said, Modestus was the one from this hillside known as the real, the original, Abu Tor.

Of course, there are some modern-day residents of this neighborhood who say that the original name is actually Givat Hananya, the hill of Hananya, a Jewish priest from the city's Second Temple era who had a summer home there. But most people, Arab and Jewish, simply know this place as Abu Tor: home of the stubborn-headed.

THE GATES OF HELL

Until the late nineteenth century, many people thought this hillside was too far from the Old City to be safe from marauders. Though only a half mile from the safety of the Old City walls, Abu Tor is on the far side of an ignominious valley with steep drops that make it difficult to quickly move through by foot, horse or car.

The Old Testament refers to it as the Valley of Slaughter. On this the city's Jews, Christians and Muslims can agree: This rough-stoned valley leads to the Gates of Hell. This is where the wicked will be held to account for their deeds.

It is among the spotty grass and olive trees that Jewish kings are said to have once sacrificed their sons. The choking smoke that once rose from the darkened valley floor came from innocent children thrown by pagans into funeral pyres to honor their gods.

It may be the valley where an inconsolable Judas hanged himself from a tree after realizing the result of his betrayal of Christ. It may be where Judas bought a potter's field and had a mysterious—and fatal—fall. It's a place known in the New Testament as the Field of Blood.

To the southeast of Abu Tor is the city's Peace Forest, a plunging ridgeline filled with hundreds of acres of pine, eucalyptus and olive trees. The modern-day forest promenade has been the setting, depending on the level of tension, for everything from Jewish-Muslim musical performances to small-time criminal dognapping rings, from Palestinian kids' malicious stone throwing to fatal Palestinian stabbing attacks on Israelis out for a walk in the park.

In 1887 a German banker and two Jewish partners decided to build a block of affordable housing on a ridgeline in Abu Tor. They got halfway through the construction of Beit Yosef before they gave up. In the 1920s, about ten Jewish families were living in Beit Yosef when the city was hit by a wave of tension focused on restricted Jewish access to the Western Wall. Though local residents tried to protect the Jewish families in Beit Yosef, a bloody 1929 revolt sparked by the tensions made it clear that Jewish families were imperiled.[2]

The Jewish families moved away from Abu Tor and a new Palestinian business class moved in. The neighborhood became a magnet for merchants from Hebron, who settled in Abu Tor and built many of the stone homes with arched windows, mosaic floors and high ceilings that still define its historic character.

FINDING MARTIN BUBER IN A WAR ZONE

In the run-up to the 1948 war, Abu Tor had little strategic value. It had served mostly as a staging ground for a few militant attacks along Hebron Road, the busy route on the edge of Abu Tor that connected the Old City with Bethlehem and Hebron to the south. It also connected the British Mandate headquarters, on the ridge some called the Hill of Evil Counsel, with central Jerusalem. Militants planted roadside bombs, hit the government printing press building on Hebron Road and launched small attacks on the railroad station right next door.[3]

When Israel's new army made its push to control Jerusalem's Old City in 1948, it swept through Abu Tor with relative ease. The soldiers faced little resistance on the hillside as Jordanian fighters fell. Most of the families had fled. And it wasn't a place where Arab forces could easily hold ground. Israeli soldiers held just enough of Abu Tor to protect the train station and government buildings on the western edge of the neighborhood along Hebron Road.

As Israelis moved from house to house in Abu Tor looking for enemy soldiers trying to hide among the civilians, they ran into an unexpected resident: Martin Buber, the famed existentialist philosopher known for his wild, white beard, which sometimes made him look like a deranged, home-less prophet.[4]

"He had a weird look," said one Israeli soldier in a military report un-earthed by Doron Oren, an Israeli researcher who wrote a dissertation on Abu Tor. When the Israelis asked Buber why he hadn't sought safety some-where else, he apparently told them he wasn't worried.[5]

"He was sure no one would hurt him," the soldier said.[6]

Buber moved away from the new border drawn by Dayan and Tell. The crown of Abu Tor became the eastern edge of Israel. The houses abandoned by the Palestinian merchants were given to dozens of low-level Israeli government clerks who had been forced to move from Tel Aviv to Jerusalem if they wanted to keep their jobs.

Many of them weren't happy to be moving from their more temperate coastal lives in Tel Aviv to abandoned homes on Israel's new border with Jordan. The clerks filed complaint after complaint asking the new Israeli government to fix up their houses. When the government dragged its feet, the clerks banded together in protest.[7]

They complained about being placed on the border; they said they couldn't help noticing that other government workers, those with connec-tions and more responsibility, had been given nicer homes away from the border in Katamon. The complaints and protests usually went nowhere.[8]

As more and more people began moving to Israel, a country the Jewish people could finally call their own, its leaders struggled to find homes for them all. Abu Tor became the new neighborhood for scores of immigrants from the Middle East and North Africa. The new families came from Iran, Morocco and Tunisia. They began to take over homes right on the barbed wire border separating Israel from No Man's Land and the Jordanian sol-diers beyond.

WAITING FOR SANTA CLAUS

Down the hillside, below the narrow stretch of Abu Tor No Man's Land separating Israeli-controlled West Jerusalem and Jordanian-controlled East Jerusalem, Arab residents retained their connection to work and life in the Old City across the valley.

Many took buses and walked to their jobs as cobblers, shopkeepers and sandwich makers. They all knew there was a new country at the top of the hill. It wasn't clear how long it was going to stay. Arab leaders across the Middle East assured their citizens that Israel wasn't going to last. Jordanian soldiers moved into the neighborhood and took over Palestinian homes to use as forward posts along the new border with Israel. They rolled out barbed wire to mark the western edge of the Hashemite Kingdom of Jordan, a newly independent country that freed itself from British rule in 1946.

Right beyond the barbed wire, as the hillside pitched up sharply, was No Man's Land. Most of the homes there were empty. Loose metal shutters slammed against stone walls when storms swept across Abu Tor. For the kids living below the barbed wire, No Man's Land was a No-Go Zone. It was dangerous. It could be deadly. They knew Israeli soldiers were keeping watch from positions hidden in the tree line above them, but they could rarely see them. They knew, as some say in Islam, that Allah was as close to them as their jugular vein.

Saliba Sarsar was born in East Jerusalem seven years after the city was split by Dayan and Tell. Saliba grew up on the lower slope of Abu Tor, where he would sometimes sneak into the deep, wide fields and forests in the more lightly guarded No Man's Land to the south of Abu Tor, out where the United Nations had its headquarters. But Saliba and his friends steered clear of the dangerous gash of No Man's Land that ran above their neighborhood.

"We heard all kinds of horror stories about people being shot in No Man's Land and we never ventured in there," Saliba said.

Jordanian Legionnaires kept close watch on Abu Tor and got to know the families living in the neighborhood. They were suspicious of everything, even candy innocently tossed over the barbed wire.

One day in Abu Tor, Saliba said, a pack of gum came sailing over the barbed wire along No Man's Land and landed in the dirt. A man living nearby walked over to pick it up. The gum caught the attention of a Jordanian soldier, who came over to interrogate the man and make sure that the packet of gum didn't contain any secret messages.

The Sarsars were one of the families split by the 1948 war. When the shooting started, Saliba's grandfather, Jani Korfiatis, was living with his wife in Jerusalem's largely Arab neighborhood of Katamon. When the gunfire stopped, Jani was on one side of the border and the rest of his family was on the other. The son of Greek pilgrims didn't see the need to leave his

Katamon home when Israel was established. But his decision cut him off from the rest of his family living in Abu Tor. Like others living in Jerusalem in 1948, Jani had no clear idea what dividing the city was really going to mean.

"It was their home," Saliba said, "so they just stayed where they were."

When the barbed wire went up, Jani went down to see the Jordanian Legionnaires in charge of the neighborhood: *"Take good care of my daughter,"* he told them. *"Take good care of my family."*

Every year at Christmas, Israel and Jordan allowed a few thousand Christian pilgrims to cross from West to East Jerusalem, through Mandelbaum Gate, so they could see family and visit Christ's biblical birthplace in Bethlehem. Saliba's grandfather was one of the few living on the west side of the city who got the yearly pass to visit. Each year, Saliba and his siblings counted the days until they could see their grandfather. Jani always brought them sweets from Israel and other gifts that they couldn't get in East Jerusalem.

"We waited each year for Santa Claus, and Santa Claus was none other than my grandfather," Saliba said.

The visiting permits were always short—usually a few days. Then Saliba's grandfather would cross back through Mandelbaum Gate and disappear again for another year.

BEATNIK ABU TOR

There was something about living on the edge of a new country that attracted eclectic characters to Jerusalem. On the Israeli side, as the country dug in, artists established a small bohemian outpost in Abu Tor. Abandoned Palestinian houses in Abu Tor filled with young, adventurous Israeli poets, writers, television directors and sculptors who wanted to live—spiritually, psychologically and physically—on the edge. Director Tom Shoval, who produced a short documentary about the artistic life of Abu Tor, described the neighborhood in the 1950s and 1960s as "an international center of Beatnik life."[9]

"People, artists made pilgrimage to the area," he said. "There was a unique spirit here."[10]

The London-born poet Dennis Silk, known for filling his place with hand puppets and wind-up toys, moved into a house next to the Goeli family. He practiced his marionette plays at his house. Yehuda Amichai, one of Israel's most celebrated poets, came to Abu Tor to live, as he put it in one poem, "inside the silence." So did poet Arieh Sachs and Micah Shagrir, a pioneer of Israeli film and television.

The neighborhood represented the frontier of the young country, the place where artists felt like they could stew in Israeli angst. Living in Abu Tor meant simmering in the idea of what it meant to be Israeli. The artists gathered at each other's homes for parties and poetry readings. American writers and British poets came to drink wine along the border and scribble down anguished ideas about life on a precipice.

The artists who lived in Abu Tor ruminated on what it meant to live in homes abandoned by Palestinians and what they would say to the old owners if they ever came back. On one visit to see Arieh, British poet Elaine Feinstein marveled at the Israeli poet's elegant, curved Arab ceilings, a compliment that appeared to sober him up during a long night of drinking. Arieh smiled bitterly and told Elaine that he had recently seen Palestinians burning tires in the road nearby. *"I got the message,"* he said.

"CAKES, NOT WAR"

One of those attracted to life on the edge in the 1960s was Hedva Harekhavi, a 25-year-old, dark, curly haired design student who was questioning her place in the divided city. When a real estate agent asked her what she wanted in a house, Hedva told the realtor that she wanted two things: "silence and sun."

"I have something for you," the agent replied: *"Abu Tor."*

The house Hedva's realtor had in mind looked down on one of two Jordanian guard posts in the neighborhood. The back wall of the home was pockmarked with shell fragments. One blast had blown a car-wheel-sized hole in the back wall of an unfinished section of the house. A wide garden with fruit trees and grapevines bumped into the fence marking No Man's Land, right above a dirt path that would one day mark the beginning of Assael Street. You couldn't get any closer to the end of the country.

Hedva was sold.

"It was a place nobody wanted to live," she said. "Nobody except me."

"I bought it," she said, "for the cost of a blender."

Hedva was intrigued by life on the border. She would climb onto the roof of her new home and wave to the Jordanian soldiers no more than 50 yards away. The Israeli soldiers always told her not to get too friendly with the enemy.

"Girl, girl, don't say hi to them," the soldiers told Hedva. *"Not so much peace."*

From Hedva's vantage point near the Israeli and Jordanian guard posts, No Man's Land and the valley below seemed to be devoid of human life.

"We didn't hear or see any people—just birds and chickens," she said. "I lived here for a year and a half before the war and I didn't hear a single voice."

Hedva kept to herself along the border, unaware that, just a few houses away, Jewish and Muslim teens were flirting over a part of the barbed wire where cigarettes and bread flew through the air.

When the 1967 war began, Hedva launched a one-woman protest: She went to a nearby grocery store to buy a bunch of cakes and handed them out to drivers.

"Cakes, not war," Hedva told them. "Cakes! Not war!"

Within a few days, as it became clear that the fighting in Abu Tor was over and Israeli soldiers were in control, people like Hedva set out to visit the valley for the first time.

Hedva was stunned to see children, women, men, animals, all living a few hundred yards below her home. She wasn't the only Israeli taking advantage of the power vacuum to explore the newly conquered parts of Jerusalem. Hedva watched as scores of Israelis—artists, thugs, soldiers—crossed through the barbed wire so they could loot Palestinian homes abandoned during the fighting. Some people simply moved in, intent on claiming the homes as their own.

Among those who led the takeover, she said, was Shlomo Baum. Baum was a physically intimidating Israeli military commando who had helped Ariel Sharon set up a special unit in the 1950s to cross Israel's border with Jordan and carry out reprisal attacks. Commando Unit 101 launched one of the biggest such assaults in 1953, when Sharon and members of the unit led an attack on the village of Qibya in the northern West Bank. Nearly 70 civilians were killed.

When the 1967 war broke out, Baum and his allies were accused of beating, threatening and intimidating Arab residents in Abu Tor. Israeli police were so concerned about Baum's actions that they forced him and his friends to sign legal orders barring them from taking over Arab homes in the neighborhood.[11] Baum and his friends, including the owner of a Jerusalem nightclub called Bacchus, said they were doing nothing wrong. They said they had permission from the Israeli army to take over the empty homes. Police confiscated a small, Swedish submachine gun from an empty home they linked to Baum and kept an eye out for his return to Abu Tor.[12]

"It was brutal," Hedva said. "But it passed."

Baum and his fellow opportunists weren't the only ones taking advantage of the security vacuum in Abu Tor. Hedva knew several young artists who also tried to move into abandoned homes. If everyone else was doing it, Hedva figured she would scout around to see if she could find a better place to live too.

"I always dreamed of living in an isolated place, along with sun and nature," she said.

Hedva's search led her into No Man's Land, through unkempt trails south of Abu Tor used by wild dogs, where she found a large stone building she decided to take as her new home. It was empty. She had no idea whose it was, but now it was going to be hers. Hedva didn't have much with her to stake her claim. It seemed unlikely that anyone was going to find her. She was deep in the secluded ravine. For Hedva, it was the fulfillment of a fantasy. The war she'd opposed had ended up leading her to her dream home.

"I am a dreamer," she said. "And it was like a fairy tale."

Although it was isolated from most other houses, Hedva slept on the floor of the building for several days. She listened to the creaks of the windows and the rustling of hungry animals outside. She could hear distant voices now and again, but they never got very close.

"It was very dangerous, but I so wanted to live there," she said.

The fantasy didn't last. It wasn't long before Israeli soldiers came across Hedva in the home.

"You can't stay here," the told Hedva. *"Go home."*

Hedva returned to her house along the border, where Israeli officials were in the process of transforming the barbed wire dirt path into a new Jerusalem street that would eventually be named Assael.

"MADE BY GOD"

Literally, *Assael* means "made by God."

Some residents say the Israelis chose the street name to symbolize the place where the jagged wound cutting across Jerusalem was healed.

But the street name isn't meant to be translated literally. Jerusalem officials actually named it after one of King David's nephews, Asa'el, who grew up to become one of his uncle's battlefield commanders, a fighter "fleet-footed as a wild gazelle" whose death in battle was one in a series of tit-for-tat biblical killings. People here will argue over how the name should even be spelled in English: Assaell. Assael. Asa'el. They all refer to the same place, but different people will tell you that one way is the right way to refer to this narrow Alley of God.

Some Palestinian kids from Abu Tor simply refer to it as the "Street of the Martyr Jawad," a young man from Assael Street who was killed by Israeli forces at al Aqsa mosque one Friday afternoon in 1996, becoming the second man in his family to be shot dead by an Israeli gunman. His grandfather, Hijazi Bazlamit, was the first.

THREE

THE MARTYRS

The shot came from a hidden rifle on the hillside above, and Hijazi Bazlamit fell by his son's side.

Another bullet crack echoed across the valley—and down went Hijazi's brother.

Abdullah Bazlamit, then a toddler still unsteady on his feet, froze.

While his wounded uncle crawled to safety, Abdullah watched his father slowly bleed to death as the sun cast afternoon shadows across the Abu Tor No Man's Land.

Along Jerusalem's border, the death of Hijazi Bazlamit in February 1951 was one of many. Sniper shots killed women, children and farmers on both sides. Jerusalem's border was far from settled. Especially here in Abu Tor. Most of the Palestinian families living in Abu Tor fled in 1948 when the Jordanian Legionnaires fought to a stalemate on the hillside.

When Dayan and Tell sat down with their pens to carve up Jerusalem in November 1948, the Israeli general drew a red line on the map that passed to the west of Hijazi Bazlamit's house and the Jordanian officer drew a green line that passed to the east.

The Bazlamits' home, like countless others along the newest Middle East borders, was now trapped, as UN officials would dub it, "between the lines."[1]

In this section of Jerusalem, the No Man's Land was a narrow belt about 50 yards wide and 300 yards long. A short strip of homes in Abu Tor was caught in No Man's Land—maybe a dozen compounds in all.

Many of the Bazlamits' neighbors, along with those who lost houses on the other side of the barbed wire to the new state of Israel, sought safety with relatives somewhere else. Others wound up in refugee camps between Jerusalem and Jordan. Not the Bazlamits. Wajeeh Bazlamit, Hijazi's wife and the matriarch of the family, refused to let war drive her from the family's Abu Tor home.

The family had shuttered their house when the war swept through Jerusalem and quickly returned once the shooting stopped. They found they weren't welcome in their own home. They were in limbo. Their house sat on land that belonged to neither Israel nor Jordan. It posed a problem for everyone. There was good reason to kick the families out of No Man's Land. By definition, it was unsettled territory. Something for Israel and Jordan to keep fighting over. Although the Bazlamits' simple stone block house lacked the grandeur of the nicer homes in Abu Tor, the family wasn't going to leave.

Israel and Jordan were never able to agree on a plan to officially divide No Man's Land. So there remained, as Dayan put it, "two front lines" across Jerusalem.[2]

In some places, the No Man's Land cut a wedge several hundred yards wide, creating vast, open, neglected fields that became a home for howling dog packs, wayward sheep herds, and—at least once—a foreigner suffering from messianic delusions.

In 1951, after two years of continual disputes over the border, relations with Israel and Jordan were fraying. Both countries were flooding the UN Mixed Armistice Commission (MAC) with demands for emergency meetings and immediate investigations. Some were trivial matters meant to gum up the system. Others involved serious allegations of rape, cross-border attacks and retaliatory massacres. Israel accused Jordanian soldiers of breaking the peace by firing on Israel's West Jerusalemites as they raced for safety across open ground. Jordan accused Israeli forces of sneaking across the border and attacking innocent villagers.

On that fatal day in February 1951, there had been some shooting along the border, but it had not reached Abu Tor. Hijazi Bazlamit left his Old City shoe shop in the hands of Zakaria, his 13-year-old son, and caught an early afternoon bus back to Abu Tor. The Bazlamits' house sat on the lower slope of No Man's Land, below the barbed wire marking the border of Israel. The family's backyard bumped right into the new country up above. The only things separating their little courtyard from the border were a couple of tilting stone retaining walls and some thin, young fruit trees.

The family's house was effectively surrounded by soldiers. Four border posts kept watch along this small stretch of Abu Tor. One Jordanian unit kept watch from an abandoned Palestinian home on the border about 100 yards to the south of the Bazlamits' home, and another looked over things from a house about 100 yards to the north. On the hillside above, Israeli positions essentially mirrored the Jordanian ones.

Hijazi, a slender man with a thin Charlie Chaplin mustache, knew going in the backyard could always be risky, especially when there had been shooting along the border. That didn't stop him that afternoon. He headed up the rocky hillside with his youngest son, Abdullah, wobbling after him.

Though he was not even three years old at the time, Abdullah has vivid memories of that day. He remembers the smell of the grapevines and the fruit trees. He remembers the sound of the shot that killed his father. He remembers seeing his dad fall.

"He lay bleeding for three or four hours," he said.

Abdullah sat in the garden, holding his dying dad's hand, as his relatives tried to coax the little boy off the hillside. No one was willing to risk being shot to rescue Hijazi and his son. Abdullah didn't know what to do. Abdullah's mother, brothers, uncles and aunts were all trying to coax the young boy out of the sniper's view.

"*Come, Abdullah,*" his aunts and uncles said. "*Come down from the garden.*"

Abdullah was too scared to move. And there was no way for his relatives to get to Hijazi without exposing themselves to the hidden sniper.

As Hijazi lay dying, 13-year-old Zakaria Bazlamit returned from the Old City and saw a crowd gathered at a home down the road, outside the No Man's Land. It was near dusk, and Zakaria stopped to see what was going on.

"*What are you doing here?*" one of his friends asked Zakaria. "*Run home, your father's been killed.*"[3]

"The neighborhood is built on a slope," Zakaria said in a 2007 interview with Israeli journalists. "I was downhill and our house at the time was the highest up in the neighborhood. It was difficult to climb, but I ran like a deer. I jumped over the rocks. And, even when I fell, I got up and ran as fast as I could."[4]

When Zakaria got home, his family was gathered in the back of the house, helplessly trying to rescue Hijazi and Abdullah.

"When I got there, my uncles were already there. I asked where my father was and they told me that he was lying wounded, outside, in the courtyard, but they couldn't pull him in (because) as soon as someone would stick his head out, the Jews would begin firing," he said.[5]

Like Abdullah, Zakaria's memories of that day were vivid and detailed. "I saw him from the window, lying in the courtyard, right here, 10 meters from the Jewish houses, moving his arm, his foot," he said. "He was suffering—and I couldn't do anything."[6]

The family had to wait until dusk to get Hijazi and Abdullah off the hillside.

"I was pale and my mother was hysterical," Zakaria said. "They laid him out on a ladder, which they made into a stretcher, and took him down to the village. There they put him on a vehicle that quickly took him to a hospice in the Old City."[7]

By then it was too late. Hijazi was dead. He was 35.

If Hijazi had been able to say any final words to his son, they didn't stick in Abdullah's mind.

The next day, the family buried Hijazi outside the Old City walls, in a cemetery close to al Aqsa mosque. Because their house was in No Man's Land, the Bazlamits had to set up a mourning tent at a family home in the Old City.

At 13, Zakaria dropped out of school and started taking care of his father's shop.

"My uncles told me, 'You are now the man of the family, you have to support them,'" Zakaria said.[8]

For a while, his friends came to visit him at the shop. Then they trickled off. Before long, they just stopped. Zakaria would see his buddies playing in the Old City streets and thought about the life he'd lost that afternoon in February.

"I hated the Jews for this," said Zakaria.[9]

For the Bazlamits, Hijazi was the first, but not the last, family martyr in the struggle for control of Jerusalem. His wife and kids framed a hand-colored photograph of Hijazi and kept it in their home. Hijazi looked out from the gilded frame with a bewildered gaze. He is smartly dressed in a dark jacket covering a gray pullover. But the black cord wrapped around his white cotton head scarf looks slightly askew. His bushy black eyebrows seem raised in surprise, like he can't figure out what's gone wrong. For years, the Bazlamits have looked at Hijazi's portrait when things go wrong.

"Our father's blood is in this earth," Hijazi's kids all say in one way or another. *"We are not going to leave willingly."*

No one ever saw the shooter hidden in the tree line on Israel's side of the border. It could have been an Israeli soldier. Maybe it was an Israeli civilian. Whatever the case, the family said, Hijazi was gunned down in gangland-style retaliation.

"At the time, whenever a Jew was shot at, an Arab was shot at," said Abdel Halim, another of Hijazi's sons. "My father was the victim of a revenge attack."

SPARKS OF WAR IN NO MAN'S LAND

After the Bazlamits buried Hijazi and came to terms with the void he left, things got worse along the border.

On February 5, Jordan accused Israeli soldiers of fatally shooting two civilians. The following day, Israel accused Arab attackers of raping a woman and killing her husband in West Jerusalem. The day after that, Jordan accused Israeli forces of attacking a village in East Jerusalem, killing ten women and children.

By the time the two sides agreed to meet to discuss the rising death toll, Israel and Jordan had turned in a dozen complaints requesting emergency meetings.

The delegations finally met on Monday, February 12 in the UN commission office in No Man's Land, near Mandelbaum Gate.

From the start, the UN-brokered meetings were thinly veiled political skirmishes between Israel and Jordan. The two countries found plenty to fight over. Often they argued over deadly shootings and serious attacks along the border. But the meetings would frequently devolve into hours of meaningless bickering.

On that Monday afternoon, Col. Bennett L. de Ridder, the Belgian officer then leading the MAC, started the meeting with an appeal to both sides not to get bogged down in minor disputes.

"Many of these incidents are of small importance, such as cattle straying across the demarcation line," he said. "If we can avoid these long talks on small things which happen, we will save a lot of time."[10]

The Israelis and Jordanians wholeheartedly agreed. Then they started arguing.

Israel and Jordan launched into a debate about whether to discuss the complaints in order of importance, or chronologically.

Jordan wanted to start with the February 6 attack that killed ten women and children.

This wasn't just *one* incident to the Jordanians. It was a potential spark for a new war with Israel.

"I would not be exaggerating at all if I say that it might very well lead to the breach of the peace, and the resumption of hostilities, and perhaps in a major war," warned Azmi Bey Nashashibi, head of the Jordanian delegation.[11]

Israel was not intimidated. The Israeli delegation wanted one of its still-unresolved complaints from nine months earlier to go first.

The Jordanian officials happily agreed to stay and consider *all* 11 pending complaints—but wanted to start with the killing of women and children the previous week.

"What does it matter if we consider their first complaint at one, three or five o'clock?" Sadek Bey Shar, at the time a major in the Jordanian army, asked sardonically.[12]

"I can ask you the same question," replied Lt. Col. Shaoul Ramati, who likely knew the Jordanians could easily dominate an entire meeting talking about their complaints without getting to the Israeli ones.[13]

And so the two sides argued, argued and argued over this point.

"It does not change the nature of our meeting if we discuss the most serious case first," Shar said.

Ramati grew increasingly frustrated as the endless bickering dragged on into afternoon.

"During the time we have now wasted discussing the matter of priority, we could have dealt with at least two or three complaints, and still we are talking and doing nothing," he said.

Shar refused to budge. He suggested that they discuss the issues in order of importance, an agreement that would have immediately been followed by an argument over which complaint *was* the most important.

"You can argue about the order of importance for days," Ramati argued. And he was right.

After three hours of irresolvable bickering, the two sides walked away from the meeting without discussing anything of substance.

Nashashibi and Ramati expressed equal disgust with the stalemate, one the Jordanian officer once again warned might lead to a new Middle East war.

"It is useless to go on this way," Nashashibi said as it became clear they were not going to overcome the impasse. "I would hate to imagine what my government and public opinion would say when we meet here to discuss a tragic incident which the whole world is talking about, and which might endanger the peace of the whole world, if we went back to vote on a matter which took place nine months ago, and was discussed four months ago. If we cannot do any better, we had better adjourn."[14]

Ridder could do nothing. The only thing the two sides could agree upon was stalemate.

"If you cannot come to any agreement, we had better adjourn," he said. "But I think it is a great pity."

"So do I," Nashashibi replied.

"So do I," echoed Ramati.[15]

The dysfunctional meeting was reflective of a dysfunctional system that struggled to bring some quiet to the border.

Raphael Israeli, the young Israeli officer working with the MAC in the 1960s, suggested that the attacks that winter, like the shot that killed Hijazi Bazlamit, could have been averted—if the United Nations had done more to bring the two sides together before things got out of hand.

"It is difficult to dismiss the thought that, had the MAC acted immediately after the Israeli complaint of 16 December 1950 [about the killing of an Israeli civilian by a shot from the Old City walls inside Jordanian-controlled East Jerusalem], the ensuing unfortunate chain of events might have been avoided," Israeli wrote.[16]

But the problems were so serious that the two countries couldn't keep bickering over points of procedure. The killings along the border kept happening with regularity. And the No Man's Land seemed especially problematic.

By that summer, Israel and Jordan came up with a new plan meant to make sure people like Hijazi Bazlamit weren't shot dead along the border.

In July 1951, Israel and Jordan sat down with a detailed map of Jerusalem that showed which houses fell within the No Man's Land borders.

Israel and Jordan went house by house and marked about 70 homes in the city's No Man's Land in which Israeli or Jordanian families would be allowed to live. Israel marked the houses it wanted to protect in red; Jordan marked its homes in blue. For the people living there, it cleared the way for "normal civilian life" in No Man's Land. Israel agreed to provide city services to those on the Israeli side. Jordan agreed to do the same for those to be connected to the Jordanian side. The agreement cemented the stubbornness of the families living along the borders who refused to budge.

Now a widow, Wajeeh Bazlamit was even more determined to stay in her home. She made a vow she would ultimately keep: to die living on her land, just as her husband did. Abdullah remembers something his mom said again and again: *"I will leave this land the same way my husband did."*

The UN agreement had another significant provision: Any other families were barred from moving into No Man's Land. People already living there could come and go for things like work and family visits. But both sides had to retain the "status quo" in No Man's Land: Neither side could build or repair any homes there—suspicious acts both sides often viewed as aggressive attempts to gain new advantages.

Jordan created a small entrance through the barbed wire right below the Bazlamits' house so the family could get in and out of No Man's Land.

Life between the lines was supposed to be a little bit safer, even though everyone in the family knew that going out to their courtyard could be fatal. But it seemed like the trips to get water from the well or to pick lemons, olives and figs might be a little less dangerous.

On searing summer nights, when it was quiet along the border, Abdullah, Zakaria and their other brothers would sit in the courtyard where their father had been shot dead and look out at the darkened horizon. They could hear the clank of rifles and coffee pots coming from the Jordanian soldiers in their nearby outpost. And they could hear the occasional shouts and laughter of the Israelis up above. When the moon was full, they could see the silhouettes of the Old City walls and the Dome of the Rock through the haze of campfire smoke drifting across the valley. When the winter storms pelted the city with hail, and rolling thunder spilled over Abu Tor with flashes of lightning, it did sometimes feel like they were looking down on the Gates of Hell.

CROSS-BORDER BREAD SMUGGLING

As things settled into more of a routine, the Bazlamits went up into their gardens more and more. The more time they spent out back, the more often they caught sight of the Israelis on the other side, living in the homes of the Bazlamits' former Palestinian neighbors. Every now and again a kid's ball would come sailing over the fence and roll down the hillside. The balls were rarely returned. Dawlat, Abdullah's wife, was one of the women who thought of the Israeli families on the other side of the street as neighbors, even if they lived in different countries. Whenever one of the Israeli chickens wandered into No Man's Land, Dawlat would shoo it back across the border.

"That would please our neighbors a lot, because it showed that we were honest," she said one night, decades later, as her husband, kids and grandchildren squeezed together on their living room couches to hear old family stories. "Especially because people were afraid to talk to each other on both sides of the barbed wire."

In 1959, Zakaria married a young girl from the Old City, a 14-year-old named Nawal. She had a broad smile and dark, fiery eyes that let you know that she wasn't one to be too deferential to her husband when she thought he was wrong. Nawal grew up in a home not far from al Aqsa. She spent her childhood learning the twists and turns of the Old City's cobblestone alleys. She liked living off Chain Street, so close to *al buraq*—the wall where the Prophet Muhammad tied his buraq before riding the winged horse to Heaven. (It was the same 60-foot-tall wall that Jewish worshippers called the Wailing Wall.) And living so close to al Aqsa mosque was a blessing.

Moving to No Man's Land took time to get used to. The Bazlamit family was big. Her new mother-in-law was strong-willed. And Nawal had to come to terms with living between coils of barbed wire separating warring nations.

The most dangerous part of any day was the trip out back to the neighborhood well, which rested up on a vulnerable part of the hill, close to the fence, well within rifle range of the Israeli guard posts obscured by the tree line above.

The women would go to the well in the early morning or at dusk. Never when the sun was highest and tempers along the border seemed to be hottest. When they brought their buckets and pots for water, the women would catch glimpses of Israeli life on the other side of the barbed wire:

children playing hide-and-seek in their gardens; women hanging laundry from clothes lines between the twisting tree branches outside their homes. It was a mirror image of life on their side of the border.

One afternoon, while Nawal was at the well, she saw a lean Jewish man on the other side of the barbed wire trying to get her attention. She'd seen him before. He had big glasses and wore one of the little caps the Jewish men all seemed to wear. His shirt and jacket hung off his thin frame as he stood on the balcony of his home on the hillside above the well. He made a bulge over his belly and kept repeating a word in a language she didn't understand. He kept putting his hand to his mouth.

She didn't know what to make of it all. Nawal didn't know if this guy was crazy or hungry. He tried to reassure her and the other women at the well that he meant no harm.

"Get some bread," one of the women said to Nawal, who went back down to her house, wrapped up some freshly baked pita bread in a towel and brought it back up to the well. They unwrapped it and looked around to see if any soldiers might be watching. Nawal tossed it over the fence. The man rushed toward his side of the border, grabbed the bread with a wave of thanks and retreated to his stone home on the other side.

Nawal laughed at her surreal life as she walked back down to her home with the other women.

NEW NEIGHBORS IN NO MAN'S LAND

Zakaria, one of the shorter, rounder, quieter Bazlamit brothers, spent a little time in the Jordanian army before his mother convinced the military that her son had more important work at home. Zakaria trained soldiers and cooked for them in Abu Tor. He led neighborhood patrols and invited soldiers to dinner at his home in No Man's Land—an action that could set off alarms for Israeli soldiers up the hill keeping watch on any suspicious military moves by the Jordanians.

One of the Jordanian officers in charge of the area, a man they called Abu Hani, took a special liking to the Bazlamits. Occasionally, he would risk sparking an international furor by slipping under the fence and into Israel to pick some fruit or vegetables.

Abu Hani patrolled the area, so he knew what was growing in the fields along the border. He watched the Israeli chickens, oblivious of the international border, crossing into No Man's Land to lay their eggs. He rescued the Palestinian sheep that sometimes got trapped in the barbed wire and had to be untangled.

One quiet morning, Abu Hani stepped over the low stone terrace walls on the hillside, crept through the fence and chased down a wild turkey wandering through the Israeli brush. Nearby, he saw some ripe tomatoes growing in someone's garden. He picked some, stuffed them in his pockets and rushed back into No Man's Land before anyone could see him.

Abu Hani slit the turkey's throat, gutted it and brought it, along with the tomatoes, over to the Bazlamits.

"Courtesy of Israel," he said. *"Enjoy."*

Life in No Man's Land settled into some semblance of normalcy. But it was always a point of contention. Israelis kept close watch on who was coming and going. They had given their OK for some Palestinians to live in No Man's Land, but they wanted to make sure that the Jordanian soldiers didn't use that as a cover to set up new military positions. In the mid-1960s, one of the Bazlamits' old neighbors came to visit. Eid Yaghmour and his family were thinking about coming home.

"Is it safe here?" he asked the Bazlamits.

"Will we be OK if we move back to our house?" he asked the Jordanian soldiers.

Eid Yaghmour's claim to land in Abu Tor went back even further than the Bazlamits'. He and his brother had bought their property, which ran alongside the Bazlamits', in the 1930s. The family wanted to see about coming back to the place they'd fled in 1948, thinking at the time that they'd be able to return soon. Sixteen years later, when Eid Yaghmour was 80 years old, he returned to the family's two-story gray stone home, just up the hillside from the Bazlamits, close to the well. The house was little more than a chilly shell. The windows were open holes. The floors were covered in a thin layer of red sand, created by years of dust storms.

"The only things living there were birds and snakes," said Eid's grandson, Ziad, who was 12 when his family moved to No Man's Land in 1966.

1967: "WE HAVE TO GO"

It wasn't long after the Yaghmours moved back to the border that tensions started rising again.

The recently formed Palestine Liberation Organization was sending more and more militants over the borders from Syria and Jordan into Israel for sneak attacks. Israeli forces were carrying out more reprisal raids. Shooting incidents along Jerusalem's border began to intensify. More Jordanian soldiers turned up in Abu Tor.

"Do you have enough food and water?" Abu Hani asked the Bazlamits one day when another battle with the Jewish soldiers seemed inevitable. *"You should make sure that you do."*

When the fighting started in June 1967, the Bazlamits pulled their shutters closed and hid inside a home that was about to be caught in the cross fire of another war.

Busloads of Jordanian soldiers rumbled into the valley below. They set up new sandbagged positions in homes as families packed up clothes, food and water before fleeing from the border. Though they couldn't have been in a worse position—framed by border posts—some of the Bazlamits decided to stay.

At first, it seemed like the Jordanian soldiers might have the upper hand in the battle for Abu Tor.

The Jordanians hit the Israeli soldiers on the upper hillside with mortars and machine-gun fire. Soon the fire coming from above grew heavier. The Bazlamits could hear the mortars whizzing overhead and the crack of bullets slamming into stone. Even if they wanted to get away, it was too dangerous now to go anywhere.

By the second day, the shooting outside the house had come to an end. It sounded like the battle had been won. But the Bazlamits didn't know who had come out on top.

Abu Tor was choked with hazy, sweet, pungent smoke rising from charred wood, rubber, uniforms, hair and muscle. Zakaria could still hear fighting across the valley, but it seemed too far away to be dangerous. The big conical roof of the Christian church inside the Old City walls had been burned away, creating an apocalyptic, smoldering, pencil-top frame silhouette on the horizon.

Zakaria quietly stepped out of the house and made his way toward the Jordanian army post down the way. He checked house after house. They all were empty. Abu Tor seemed to be a ghost town. He saw the bodies of bloodied, broken Jordanian soldiers behind garden walls. The hillside was peppered with bullet casings and shrapnel.

As Zakaria got closer to the Jordanian position, he could see soldiers and thought all was OK. Zakaria waved to them. When they waved for him to come over, Zakaria realized something was wrong. They weren't Jordanian soldiers. He ducked away and cut through the homes until he finally found some friends hiding in their home.

"What's happened?" he asked them.

"Don't you know?" they replied. *"The Jews have been here for two days."*

Zakaria rushed home and told everyone the news.

"We have to go," he told them.

Zakaria hustled the family down to the neighbors and then went back to get some food and supplies. As he approached the house, he saw a soldier shooting at the shuttered homes trying to get inside. Zakaria quietly crept away.

From the streets below, the Bazlamits and other families watched as Israelis looted their homes. There was nothing they could do.

Armed with guns and tire irons, the looters walked away with jewelry and embroidered wedding dresses. They took sheep and chickens. Homes were torn apart and picked clean.

Then the Israeli soldiers came for the Bazlamits. The soldiers told the men to put their hands up and walk in a single-file line to the Israeli command post up on the crest of Abu Tor.

One of the Israeli soldiers, probably from the country's minority Druze community, turned to Abdullah, a good-looking teenager with thick, wavy hair.

"How old are you?" the soldier asked him.

"Nineteen," Abdullah replied.

"You don't look 19," the Druze soldier told Abdullah. *"If anyone asks how old you are, tell them you're 14."*

Then they took Zakaria and several other men to the top of Abu Tor. They questioned Zakaria for a few hours and set him free when they figured he wasn't a threat. Abdullah was waiting nearby. On the way home, the brothers ran into another group of Israeli soldiers with more questions.

"Hey, where are you going?" they asked the brothers.

Home, they told the soldiers.

"How old are you?" they asked Abdullah.

"Fourteen," he told them.

"You're not a soldier?" they asked Abdullah.

"No," he said. *"I don't know how to do anything."*

The Israeli soldiers didn't believe him. So they took him off to the Russian Compound, where he was questioned for days at Jerusalem's central police station before being released.

"ISRAEL IS A WONDERFUL COUNTRY"

While the men from Abu Tor were being interrogated, the women were crossing the old border to meet the people they'd seen for years over the fence.

One of the first to come over was Leyla,* a young Israeli mother, originally from Morocco, who still spoke Arabic and tried to allay their fears.

"Don't worry," she told them. *"Israel is a wonderful country."*

Leyla and other Israeli women came to offer help to the mothers across the way.

"What do you need?" they asked. *"Do you need bread? Do you need milk? Whatever you want, we will get it. We're neighbors."*

It seemed like things might not be so bad for the Bazlamits. Then Israeli thugs descended on Abu Tor. They were looking to take over empty homes and planned to drive out any families that were trying to stay. Like the Bazlamits. Like the Yaghmours.

Among these thugs, police and residents said, was Shlomo Baum, the burly, combative former Israeli commando with a shaved head and bushy mustache.

The Israeli soldiers turned the marauders away. But a gang came back the next morning and surrounded the Yaghmour home next to the Bazlamits.

"What are you doing here?" the Israeli thieves asked the Yaghmours. *"This isn't your house."*

The Yaghmour women, trapped inside their house, screamed for help.

Abdullah Bazlamit stood in the trees with some other neighbors and watched the armed men from afar. The men were wearing civilian clothes,

---

* Leyla's real name has been changed.

but they had a curt, decisive military demeanor. It was impossible to tell who they were and who they were with.

"Who speaks English?" one of the men in the gang asked the growing group of onlookers.

No one spoke up. Finally, Abdullah raised his hand.

"I do," Abdullah told them.

The man ordered Abdullah to serve as their translator.

"Ask them what they are doing here," the man said.

"It's their home," Abdullah replied as more people gathered to see what was going on.

The gunmen had a short chat in a language Abdullah didn't understand. Then they backed off. The Yaghmours thought they had been spared. But that night the gang returned. And this time the men weren't going to be scared off. They strong-armed their way into the homes and took men out one by one. They grabbed Abdullah, two of his brothers and one of the Yaghmours and dragged them into an abandoned house nearby where they threw the Palestinians to the ground. Then they started drinking.

"They took us to an empty house and they tried to kill us," Abdullah said. "From midnight until five in the morning, they beat us with everything. Our faces were swollen. They beat us with sticks, with the handle of their guns, with their hands."

Throughout the night, the men threatened to kill the Arabs and their families if they didn't leave.

"Take your stuff and go to Jordan," they told Zakaria. *"If we see you here again, we will kill you."*

As the sun came up, the men gave them all a warning.

"It is now five," they told their captives. *"You have until seven to leave your houses. You can't stay."*

Abdullah didn't know what to do. He walked over to see if Leyla, their Jewish neighbor from Morocco, might be able to help them.

Leyla was startled when she saw Abdullah's cuts and bruises.

"What happened to you?" she asked when he turned up at her door. *"We have to call the police."*

Zakaria went home and told his family they had to leave.

"Let's pack up and go," he said to his wife.

Zakaria was ready to go. He was prepared to give up the land where his father had been shot dead. Leyla came by to talk him out of it.

"No, don't go," she told them. *"Don't worry, this is a gang. This is not the army."*

The Bazlamits didn't know how to get in touch with the Israeli police; they didn't even have a telephone. And they didn't speak Hebrew. Leyla made the call for them. She told the Israeli police the whole story and pleaded with them for help. Before long, police officers tracked down one of the men involved in the home attacks and told the Bazlamits that the gangs wouldn't be coming around again.

"I promise you, nothing will happen," the police officer said. *"We took them far away."*

The Israeli police took the injured Bazlamit men to the hospital and vowed to keep the goons from returning.

"We will deal with the gang," the Israeli officer said. *"Don't worry."*

Not long after the beatings, Israeli prosecutors accused Shlomo Baum of seizing homes in Abu Tor and threatening a Palestinian family living there. The courts barred Baum and two other men from entering the neighborhood—an order the men unsuccessfully challenged. The men, prosecutors said, sought to justify taking the homes by arguing that "Arabs should not be allowed to live in the area," according to a *Jerusalem Post* article at the time.[17] Israeli courts kept Baum in check—for a little while anyway.

The threats and beatings rattled the Bazlamits. They weren't sure what to make of life under Israeli rule. Their neighbors seemed kind, and the police appeared to be fair. But they clearly weren't welcomed with open arms by all.

Perhaps the strangest thing of all was seeing their new neighbors wearing the Bazlamits' clothes and using the things they'd looted from the family's homes.

One afternoon, Dawlat saw a Jewish girl wearing one of her embroidered dresses from Hebron. She had no doubt the intricately sewn dress was hers. The elaborate stitching and vibrant colors were clearly from Hebron.

"Shalom," Dawlat said to the young woman.

"Shalom," she replied.

"Your outfit is beautiful," Dawlat told her. "Where did you get it?"

The woman didn't hesitate. *"I got it in Hebron,"* she said.

Dawlat didn't say anything. She didn't want problems with the new neighbors. She just asked a Palestinian seamstress to make her some new dresses.

As they adjusted to life in a new country, the police officer who helped the Bazlamits asked Zakaria to go on patrol with him across the hillside. He pointed out all the empty homes and encouraged Zakaria to take advantage of the situation.

"There's plenty of stuff," the officer told him. *"Take what you want."*

To help the Bazlamits, the officer gave the family a big tin of white cheese to fill the cabinets that had been stripped by the looters.

"I got this from a house where they have two tins," the man said. *"You seem like you have a lot of kids, so . . . eat."*

Zakaria took it with thanks. Then he told his wife not to open it.

"We have to find out whose it is," he said.

Two days later, Zakaria and Leyla found the original owners when they went to visit a pregnant woman whose husband was still being held by the Israelis.

"If your husband's not home by the time you have your baby, all the women from the neighborhood will be there to help," Leyla said. *"We'll take care of you."*

"The soldiers also took a tin of cheese from us," the pregnant woman complained.

Zakaria smiled.

"Don't worry," he said. *"We have it."*

For the Bazlamits, Leyla became their lifeline to Israel. She introduced the Bazlamits to all the Jewish families living along the fence and told them to stop by whenever they needed help, day or night.

"Whatever you need—for food, for your children, for whatever—I will bring it," she said. *"We are neighbors."*

"THE COURTING PERIOD"

When things settled down in Abu Tor, Leyla took Nawal shopping in the heart of West Jerusalem. Nawal was amazed by how much the city had changed since it had been split. As they made their way through Jerusalem, Nawal noticed the strange colored light boxes at some crossroads. Nawal didn't understand why people were stopping in their cars and Leyla had to explain how street lights worked.

"I had never seen anything like that in my life," Nawal said decades later.

Along with Leyla, the Bazlamits finally got to meet the scrawny man and his wife: Haim and Rachel Machsomi. They were immigrants from Iran. And the families quickly became two of the closest on the hillside. Endearingly, the Bazlamits started calling Haim *Abu Ibrahim*—father of Avraham, his oldest son. They referred to Rachel as *Imm Ibrahim*—mother of Avraham. It was a sign of intimacy, a mark of honor, for the Jewish families. The Palestinian families saw the Machsomis as neighbors with a common Middle East identity, people who understood the importance of culture, tradition and history.

"He had the qualities of Arabs," Nawal said of Haim. "Every week he would invite his sisters over. Every week he would invite his family."

Nawal and Rachel met at each other's homes to knit together. They shared fresh tomatoes, peppers, lemons and mint. The Bazlamit men started going by to ask Haim for advice and counsel on everything from getting a job in Israel to dealing with their neighbors.

The Machsomis taught the Bazlamits how to speak Hebrew. The Bazlamit kids started going to the Machsomi home on Fridays to turn off their Jewish neighbor's lights, becoming *Shabbos Goyim*—non-Jews helping observant Jews during the day of rest when they are not permitted to do anything considered to be work, be it turning off a lamp, driving a car or heating up soup.

At the beginning of Passover, the Bazlamits and other Palestinian families on the opposite side of the road would buy all the bread from the Jewish families foregoing leavened food to commemorate the flight of Israelites to freedom from the pharaohs. At the end of Passover, they would bring the Machsomis big platters of breads and cheeses, fruits and jams. When Nawal gave birth to a new son, Rachel brought over some baby clothes and a blanket for the newborn.

Zakaria and Nawal Bazlamit's oldest son, Hijazi, named after his slain grandfather, looks back on those years as "the brainwashing period."

"It was the courting period," said Hijazi. "That's when we were deceived." Hijazi was seven years old when Abu Tor was taken by Israel and the Jewish neighbors rushed down to say hello.

"That's the period when they showed you brotherly love," Hijazi said.

No one in the family seemed to be more seduced by the new country than Hijazi. He learned Hebrew and quickly became friends with the Jewish neighbors. He didn't really understand what the Israeli victory meant. He didn't understand that he was now living in Occupied Jerusalem.

"To us, it was simply that the Jordanian army left, and a new government came," Hijazi said. "We thought at the time that whomever was in the Jordanian army could just go into the Israeli army. We were not aware of the consequences of our ignorance."

When he was old enough to get a job, Hijazi knew what he wanted to be: an Israeli police officer. He'd seen the police in Abu Tor and knew what they could be, what they could do. When he was old enough, Hijazi took a government intelligence test, walked away with a score higher than many Israelis, and soon had an open door to join the police department.

At 21 years old, Hijazi proudly wore his police uniform when he worked in East Jerusalem. He wore it when he worked at the Dome of the Rock and al Aqsa mosque. Hijazi thought he had found his calling.

The allure didn't last long.

"We thought the pasha was a pasha," Hijazi said. "He turned out to be a rascal."

In time Hijazi came to see his fate as a modern-day morality tale, one with echoes of a story—a legend—he told about a Palestinian shoeshine boy who worked in the Old City when England ruled the region after World War I:

One day, a British army officer went to check on things in the Old City. As he walked through the crowded streets, he came across a young man shining shoes. So he stopped to have his shoes cleaned. As the young man buffed the British officer's shoes he kept quietly saying under his breath, in Arabic: "Tomorrow you will leave. Tomorrow you will go."

The British officer was cunning. He understood what the shoe shiner was saying. And he knew the trouble it could mean for the British. So he told his aide to invite the shoe shiner to his office.

The shoe shiner was afraid.

"What did I do?" he asked.

"Don't be afraid," the aide told him. "Come, and something good will come out of the meeting."

When the shoe shiner went to the British man's office, the officer had a proposal for him.

"I see your potential to become more than a shoe shiner," the officer told him. "I want you to do better. We want you to become a policeman."

The shoe shiner was wary.

"I don't have any education," he told the officer.

"Don't worry about that," he replied. "We will educate you."

So the shoe shiner took the job. And the first thing the British police asked him to do was to go into the market and get rid of all the illegal stalls.

He went off and did as he was told. He kicked people out of the streets. He pushed them out. His harsh ways earned him promotion after promotion until he became an officer. They eventually put him in charge of all of Jerusalem. But people hated him left and right. Because of his new wealth and prestige, he forgot where he came from.

He kept up his tough ways—until the British came to talk.

"People are complaining about you," they told him. "People are protesting. You have defamed Britain's reputation. We have no need for you and you should go."

The man knew what that meant for him.

"Where should I go, my lord?" the man asked.

"If you are no good to your own people, what good are you to us?" the British officer replied.

And so the people killed him.

Hijazi told the story one afternoon in the fall of 2014, between long drags on cigarettes that filled his low-ceilinged living room with smoke. He kept the wall-mounted television on mute and glanced up every now and again to read the scrolling news headlines running across the bottom of the screen. Unlike his father, Hijazi had kept his silver mane as he got older. His bushy mustache shadowed darkened, nicotine-stained teeth as he thought about the story he'd just told.

"People thought about me like they thought about the shoeshine boy," Hijazi finally said.

For years, Hijazi saw his job in noble terms. He would sit with his friends, his family or anyone else who questioned him, and explain why he was working for Israel.

"As an Arab policeman, I can help you," he told people. *"We have the same language, the same culture."*

Most people weren't convinced. "People felt like I was helping the Israeli occupation, not helping them," he said.

When Hijazi started to rise in the ranks of the Israeli police, he began to see more of what was going on and started questioning his decision. When he looked around, he noticed that Arab police officers all seemed to hit a glass ceiling.

"Why do I just reach one stage when the Israelis can go further?" Hijazi wondered.

Hijazi started questioning his superiors more and more. Then the Palestinian *intifada*—the popular uprising—upended things for Hijazi and the region.

It was December 1987, and Hijazi had been working for the Israeli police for seven years. Israeli forces in the occupied West Bank and Gaza Strip seemed to be facing stone throwers more often. The hostility was growing. On December 8, Israeli soldiers driving a truck through the Jabaliya refugee camp in the Gaza Strip smashed into a car, killing four Palestinian civilians.

Rumors that the crash was intentional fueled demonstrations that spread across Gaza, the West Bank and East Jerusalem. Israel's immediate efforts to contain Palestinian protests only seemed to make things worse.

The following month, Yitzhak Rabin, then serving as Israel's defense minister, vowed to quell the uprising with "force, might, and beatings."[18] Rabin encouraged soldiers to use clubs instead of live ammunition, a policy that earned Rabin the nickname "Bone Breaker."

A few weeks after Rabin outlined the new Israeli response to the Palestinian intifada, Hijazi saw the end result of Rabin's orders. Hijazi was in London when he was startled to see stomach-churning footage on TV. A CBS cameraman had captured footage of four Israeli soldiers using stones to beat two Palestinian teenagers in a West Bank field.

The video sparked international outrage over Israel's heavy-handed response to the Palestinian uprising. The footage haunted Hijazi when he returned to Jerusalem. And things at the police station seemed to be going from bad to worse. Hijazi and his Palestinian colleagues were left out of meetings held to come up with new plans for confronting problems in East Jerusalem, a place Hijazi knew better than most.

Hijazi noticed that Israelis arrested for throwing Molotov cocktails seemed to be set free quickly while Palestinians arrested for similar things faced harsh interrogations and long jail terms. He heard about Israeli interrogators putting sacks filled with dirt and shit over the heads of Palestinian prisoners. As the Palestinian uprising rolled into its third year, Hijazi quit.

"I never felt the democracy that they claimed," he said. "I studied the police laws and I felt that the discrimination was embedded in them. The general law is punishment for all, but implementation of it was only directed towards Palestinians."

Like the Jerusalem shoeshine boy from his story, Hijazi realized that he'd been manipulated.

"They were using me," he said. "Even though the nine years were hard and long, I learned a lot. I learned about their internal sense of discrimination against the Palestinians. To them, Palestinians are slaves."

Hijazi could see little difference between the British and Israeli rulers of Jerusalem, both of whom used divide-and-rule tactics with the Palestinians.

"This is the colonial thinking that we are living with," he said. "Those nine years were the hardest of my life."

"A BULLET BETWEEN THE EYES"

Hijazi's disenchantment grew as the sense of community on Assael started to erode.

Leyla and her family moved away soon after the fence came down. In the early 1980s, Rachel and Haim Machsomi packed up their family and moved out of Jerusalem. The Bazlamits' connections to the other side of Assael were shrinking. And Abu Tor became one of the flashpoints for Palestinian defiance in Jerusalem.

Protesters used burning tires, cinder blocks, boulders and trash to set up makeshift roadblocks in Abu Tor to face off against Israeli forces. Demonstrators set cars on fire and threw stones through windows of Jewish homes. For the most part, the clashes took place down in the valley, far below Abu Tor's Jewish hilltop homes. But the demonstrations weren't contained. Protesters used the network of connecting stairs cutting up the hillside as strategic routes through the neighborhood.

To deal with the tumult, the Israeli police hired a controversial Abu Tor resident to organize a civil guard in the neighborhood: Shlomo Baum.

Baum had a reputation for being an unapologetic advocate for an aggressive Israeli military. His confrontational demeanor and military gait helped him stand out in Abu Tor. Baum had zero tolerance for the street riots spilling into his neighborhood. To him, the stone throwing and car burning were symptomatic of a much larger problem that had to be forcefully confronted.

"Burning cars is only one stage," he told a *Jerusalem Post* reporter in a 1989 interview, soon after he was named to lead the Abu Tor neighborhood watch. "The next stage is torching apartments. It's not that much more difficult, especially in the summer, when a petrol bomb can easily be tossed through an open window."[19]

At the time, Baum lived in a home down the valley in an area of Abu Tor that, like the Bazlamits' neighborhood, had been part of No Man's Land between 1948 and 1967. Baum took over the house as a squatter in 1955 and refused to leave, the *Post* reporter wrote.

"They won't come here," Baum said. "If they do, they will get a bullet between the eyes."[20]

Baum took to the new job leading armed patrols with his usual flair. He started walking the streets of Abu Tor with intimidating dogs, a special insult to Muslim residents, who usually view dogs as unclean animals.

"I don't plan on beating the intifada myself," Baum told the Israeli reporter. "But if I was in charge, it would have ended in three days. You wouldn't have had Israeli soldiers being stoned."[21]

Many Israelis in the area joined Baum. More than two dozen people signed up to take part in armed patrols of Abu Tor. At the time, more than 2,000 Jewish residents were living in Abu Tor, mostly on the top of the hillside, above 9,000 Arab residents increasingly crowded into the valley below.

The head of the Beit Nehemiah community center in Abu Tor, Maya Tavori, showed solidarity with the Jewish residents and banned Arabs from using the playground.

"I'm very skeptical about the idea of living together," Maya said at the time. "We can live side by side and maybe after 1,000 years the cultures will change and we can live together."[22]

Some Abu Tor residents saw Baum's armed patrols as a dangerous move that could make things worse. They quickly drafted a petition calling for Baum's removal.

"We residents of Abu Tor strongly protest the creation of a special unit of the Civil Guard under the command of Shlomo Baum, well known in the neighborhood as an advocate of violence and coercion against the Arab population, and an inciter of hatred and fear among the Jews," the petition read. "A unit under his command could only increase tension in the neighborhood, if not lead to unnecessary violence."[23]

Judith Green, an Israeli-American archeologist who lived on the street above the Bazlamits, told the *Jerusalem Post* reporter that Baum was "violent," "aggressive" and "provocative."[24]

Baum, she said, painted an ominous picture of Arab residents of Abu Tor as poised to "break into our homes and rape the women."[25]

To counter Baum's armed patrols, Judith organized meetings between Arab and Jewish residents of Abu Tor. Judith and her allies convinced the city to lift the ban on Arab kids at the Abu Tor playground. But the Arab kids could tell they really weren't wanted, so they stayed away. It would be a feeling that lasted for years.

"Every time we would go to the park, people would let their dogs loose to scare the children," Nawal said 15 years later.

The divisions in Abu Tor that at one point seemed small were starting to get wider.

"Abu Tor is kind of a test case," Judith said in 1990. "I don't see how people can say Jerusalem is a united city when people pay protective services to watch their cars and houses, and the Arabs are afraid to come to our youth center."[26]

Baum left no doubt that he was among those who wanted to see the Arab families leave.

"Most people hate them," Baum told a visiting American journalist.[27]

Among the Palestinians, the animosity was also building.[28]

"My hatred for them grows every day," Samia, a 19-year-old from the neighborhood who didn't want her last name used, told the reporter. "They treat us as if we were not human beings and we were animals."[29]

Judith Green saw Baum as a provocateur whose main contributions to Abu Tor were to fuel divisions and intimidate those who disagreed with him.

"He considered himself Lord of Abu Tor," she said years later. "He was a bully."

Jewish families living on the western side of Assael Street started shoring up their homes with higher walls and stronger doors. Even as the walls went up, the Bazlamits tried to keep their eyes on their Jewish neighbors. One of the Abu Tor stairways ran right along the edge of the Bazlamit compound. Up above, the next flight of steps ran between the Machsomis' old home and the Joudans' place. It became a regular route for the stone throwers, whose whistles and shouts could be heard echoing off the tin and tile roofs.

One day while hanging laundry on the Bazlamits' roof, Nawal saw some kids throwing stones at Malka Joudan, an Iranian immigrant she called *Imm Ismael,* across the way.

"I rushed down, pushed the kids and screamed at them," Nawal said.

The kids scattered and, when the police turned up, Nawal told them that the stone throwers had come from somewhere down in the valley.

"They are not our children," Nawal told the police.

"Our prophet calls on us to take care of our neighbors," Nawal said. "It is my duty to protect Imm Ismael."

Malka's religion didn't matter to Nawal.

"Our prophet said even if your neighbor is Jewish, you must protect them," she said.

By the time Prime Minister Yitzhak Rabin signed an historic 1993 deal with Palestine Liberation Organization chairman Yasser Arafat as US president Bill Clinton looked on, the walls on the western side of Assael Street were a little higher. Judith and her group eventually managed to put the brakes on Baum's patrols. But the fabric of the street was seriously frayed. The Oslo Accords helped bring quiet back to Assael, but not a renewed sense of community.

Judith tried to capitalize on the new era of optimism by organizing neighborhood dialogue groups and community concerts. Four or five Jewish families from Abu Tor agreed to get together with four or five Arab families in the area. The summer after the Oslo Accords were signed, Judith teamed up with some Palestinian musicians from Abu Tor. With a little support from the city, Judith and the group organized a short series of concerts featuring Arab and Jewish performers. Three were held in the Abu Tor community center where, years earlier, the director had backed segregating Arabs and Jews. The last concert was held on a Friday afternoon on the stone promenade running through the nearby Peace Forest.

Dozens of people came to the park: couples, women with strollers, families from both parts of Abu Tor. Israeli musicians performed South American tunes. The Palestinians played the pear-shaped, stringed oud instrument and drums for more than 100 people. A couple of Palestinian men were so inspired that they got up for an impromptu traditional dabke folk dance performance. Judith was thrilled by the turnout.

"It was really a high point of all the things I had done," she said. "But it's the kind of thing that you can't do forever."

A MARTYR AT AL AQSA

It didn't take very long for tensions to return to Jerusalem.

The year after the Abu Tor concerts, a religious Jewish extremist killed Rabin as he left a peace rally in Tel Aviv. Six months later, Israeli voters turned to the right by backing Likud leader Benjamin Netanyahu, a skeptic of the peace process who played to the country's anxieties about a rise in Palestinian suicide bombings.

The 46-year-old "peace through security" politician became Israel's youngest prime minister, narrowly beating incumbent Shimon Peres, an ally of Rabin and an architect of the Oslo peace deal.

Netanyahu took a tough stance with Arafat and resisted concessions pushed by Clinton. Three months into Netanyahu's term, he gave the go-ahead to open a new exit for archeological digs running along the base of the Western Wall, below the Dome of the Rock complex. Israel's archeological excavations in the Old City were seen by Palestinians as a covert effort by the government to gradually take control of the religious site where the first two Jewish temples once stood. While Rabin and Peres had decided that it would be too provocative to open the tunnel exit, Netanyahu decided the time was right.

On Monday, September 23, 1996, just before midnight in the Old City, scores of Israeli police kept watch as archeologists and construction workers opened the new tunnel exit, which emerged in the Muslim Quarter on Via Dolorosa, the main pilgrimage route known as the Way of Sorrows to Christians, who retraced Christ's steps as he carried his cross through hostile crowds on the way to his crucifixion. The tunnel route also ran underneath an elementary school in the Muslim Quarter, stoking Palestinian suspicions that Netanyahu was trying to steal the contested Jerusalem ground from underneath them. Netanyahu's actions led to a predictable response: Palestinian activists poured into the streets across the West Bank and Gaza Strip, where Arafat had started to build the foundations for what he hoped would eventually become an independent Palestinian state.

The protests started in the streets of the Palestinian refugee camps, but they quickly devolved into deadly gunfights between Israeli soldiers and members of the young Palestinian Authority security forces. Palestinian lawmaker Hanan Ashrawi, a seasoned negotiator viewed by many as one of the more pragmatic voices in the new Arafat-led government, called the tunnel the "tip of the iceberg" of Israel's efforts to covertly extend its authority over the most cherished holy site, one that had been the cause of centuries of conflict.

"What's happening now is not a fight over the tunnel," she said to CNN at the time. "It is a fight over the soul of Jerusalem and the legitimacy of the peace process."[30]

By the time Friday prayers came around that week, at least 40 Palestinians and 11 Israelis had been killed in deadly clashes that quickly became known as the Tunnel Riots.

Thousands of Palestinians flocked to al Aqsa mosque that Friday morning as thousands of Israeli riot police and soldiers fanned out through the Old City to prepare for an inevitable post-prayer confrontation.

Among the 10,000 Palestinians heading to al Aqsa that day was Jawad Bazlamit, one of Hijazi and Wajeeh Bazlamit's many grandchildren. It was a special Friday for the 21-year-old from Assael Street. He was days away from marrying a pretty young Palestinian girl. The Bazlamit house on Assael was filling with relatives coming from as far away as Jordan for the celebration. The women were making stuffed grape leaves and the men were preparing to slaughter fresh lambs to feed the hundreds of people expected to join in the celebration. His father, Abdel Halim, and Jawad's brothers set up a wedding tent in the courtyard to welcome visitors and hung big colorful balloons from the ceiling.

Jawad's 11 brothers and sisters teased him about his marriage and how many kids he was going to have. Because he was one of the younger boys, Jawad was usually quieter than his brothers. He had frizzy brown hair, a thin mustache and a closely cropped beard that wasn't quite full enough to mask his adolescent face.

While his mom cooked Friday lunch, Jawad went off to al Aqsa early to help with a tiling project at the mosque before noon prayers, the biggest of the week, began.

Thousands of Palestinians crowded into al Aqsa for the prayers while thousands more lay out their prayer rugs on the cold stone outside. More than 3,500 Israeli riot police and soldiers had set up an exceptionally large security cordon. Shortly after noon, as prayers were winding up at al Aqsa, scores of demonstrators started throwing stones at hundreds of police positioned along the edge of the mosque compound. Wearing helmets and body armor, the police threw tear gas at the crowds and opened fire with rubber-coated metal bullets and live fire.[31]

"A martyr has fallen!" someone shouted.[32]

Thousands rushed back into al Aqsa and shut the heavy wood doors as bullets zipped through the narrowing entrance. Thousands more scampered up the stone stairs outside and rushed toward the Dome of the Rock as police closed in from all sides.

Sharif 'Abd a-Rahman ran straight into a group of policemen who smacked him to the ground with batons.

"Jerusalem is ours," the Israeli soldiers told Sharif in Hebrew.[33]

Sharif, a 22-year-old from the Arab-Israeli town of Abu Ghosh in the hillsides between Jerusalem and Tel Aviv, asked them for mercy—in Hebrew.

"I am an Israeli citizen with an Israeli passport," he told them. *"Help me."*[34]

His pleas did no good. The police officers kept beating him until he was limp. The clash lasted about 20 minutes. When it was over, three Palestinians were dead, including Jawad Bazlamit.

The coroner determined that he had been shot in the eye—at close range—by a rubber-coated bullet. The bullet was found lodged deep in his brain.[35]

Like his grandfather 45 years earlier, Jawad became a Palestinian martyr.

Friends of Jawad told his family that he hadn't been one of the stone throwers, that he had been shot while praying inside al Aqsa. An investigation by the Israeli human rights group B'Tselem was unable to find anyone who saw Jawad get shot. B'Tselem said he had been killed on a plateau near the Dome of the Rock looking out on the Mount of Olives.[36]

It didn't matter where or how Jawad had been killed. His shooting threatened to ignite new tensions in Abu Tor and across Jerusalem. Scores of Israeli forces converged on Assael Street to quickly quash any problems. Abdel Halim went to talk to the soldiers. He was worried they would make things worse. He assured them there would be no trouble and asked them to leave him to bury his son. They did.

"We don't care for problems like this," he told them. *"God gives and God takes away. This is a lifetime relationship. We're not going to make problems with our Jewish neighbors."*

The Bazlamits served sweet tea with sage and small cups of thick, unsweetened coffee to stunned relatives and friends under the rented wedding tent they'd transformed to shelter mourners. Jawad's mother, aunts and sisters wept in the street. Jewish and Muslim neighbors came to pay their respects.

"He was a nice boy," said Rafi Goeli, whose father had stretched the borders of No Man's Land for their home in the 1950s. "I'd known him since he was a baby."

Although they didn't know Jawad, Herman Shapiro and his son, Alex, also came to say sorry and sit with the family in the tent. The father and son took a seat on red plastic stools the Bazlamits had borrowed for the wedding and sat near Abdel Halim as he came to terms with the loss of his boy.

"Even though I didn't know the deceased, it's a shock," Alex told a CNN reporter.[37]

An ultra-Orthodox Jewish father living on the street above the Bazlamits didn't know the family, but still felt badly for their loss.

"I have strong right wing political views, but this death is so sad, I feel it personally," he told CNN.[38]

Jawad's mother was inconsolable. Her surviving sons supported her, kept her from collapsing to the ground, and washed the tears from her face with handfuls of water.

"How, I ask you, would Netanyahu feel if he had lost a son?" Abdel Halim told the CNN journalist who came to his house. "In that, we are all the same."[39]

Abdel Halim told journalists that he had decided not to play verses of the Quran over loudspeakers at his home to avoid upsetting the Jewish families on the other side of Assael Street who were observing Sukkot, a weeklong holiday commemorating the 40 years of Jewish wandering in the desert.

"They did not harm us," Abdel Halim told an Associated Press reporter. "Why should we provoke them?"[40]

Not everyone in Abu Tor felt badly about Jawad's death.

Shlomo Baum, the former Israeli commando and onetime leader of the Abu Tor neighborhood community watch, told the AP reporter that he shed no tears for Abdel Halim or his son.

"If his son had not rioted, he wouldn't have been shot," Baum said.[41]

To Baum, Jawad was an agitator who got what he deserved. To the kids growing up on Assael Street, he became a hero: a Palestinian who had died while protecting *Haram al Sharif*, the Noble Sanctuary. Palestinian children in the neighborhood started calling Assael "Martyr Jawad's Street."

A NEW WALL DIVIDES FAMILIES

Shortly before Jawad was killed, the Bazlamits had bought a small piece of land just outside Jerusalem in al Azariya, the town on the eastern stretches of the Mount of Olives where Christian tradition says Jesus Christ performed his most transformative miracle: raising one of his followers—Lazarus—from the dead. The town, known to Christians as Bethany, was a short drive from Abu Tor.

The family was getting too big for the compound on Assael. They were running out of land in Abu Tor and Israeli officials never seemed to approve their requests to build anything, no matter how small. So the Bazlamits found three-quarters of an acre of land in Azariya, not far from the Tomb of Lazarus. The property sat just below a Catholic convent and its groves of olive trees.

The family spent years working to make the money they needed to construct a three-story apartment building on a wide, open slope.

Mohammed Bazlamit moved to the building with his wife and four kids in 2000. He'd gone into debt to build the place, but it was worth it. They had space for everyone. The family set up a small carpentry business on the ground floor. Their business profited because the town was on the road running between Jerusalem and Jericho, near the Dead Sea.

The Bazlamit boys and their families were settling into their new home outside Jerusalem when the city started burning. On the last Thursday in September 2000, hundreds of Israeli riot police protected opposition leader Ariel Sharon and a group of Likud Party members as they walked up to the 35-acre compound above the Western Wall and across the site that once held the first two Jewish temples—the Temple Mount.

Palestinians were outraged by what they saw as another attempt by Israel's right wing to reclaim the plateau for Judaism, to build a new Jewish temple and destroy Islam's holy sites in Jerusalem. After 45 minutes, Sharon and his allies descended amid volleys of stones, trash and chairs.[42] Dozens of people were injured as the protests grew.

"The Temple Mount is in our hands—and will remain in our hands," Sharon said after the visit. "It is the holiest site in Judaism and it is the right of every Jew to visit the Temple Mount."[43]

Palestinian leader Yasser Arafat condemned the visit as "a dangerous process conducted by Sharon against Islamic sacred places."[44]

Sharon saw nothing wrong with his visit and rejected implications that he was stirring up trouble.

"What provocation is there when Jews come to visit the place with a message of peace?" he said. "I'm sorry about the injured, but it is the right of Jews in Israel to visit the Temple Mount."[45]

The clashes that followed only grew in size, scope and intensity. Coming one day before the week's biggest prayers at al Aqsa, Sharon's visit set the stage for a bigger confrontation. Palestinian demonstrators wound up that Friday's prayers by throwing stones at Jewish worshippers praying down below at the Western Wall. Riot police were ready. They fired rubber-coated metal bullets, tear gas and live rounds as protestors spilled out of the Old City and spread across East Jerusalem neighborhoods.

By day's end, at least seven Palestinians were dead—the first martyrs of the second intifada. To the surprise of many Israelis, the outrage wasn't contained to the West Bank and Gaza Strip. This time, it stretched into Israel. Arab-Israelis, who make up nearly 20 percent of the country's population, took to the streets, where 12 were killed. The clashes marked the beginning of a new fissure in Israel. Jewish-Israelis began more and more to look upon the Arab citizens as a potential fifth column, a possible security risk that they couldn't contain with concrete walls and checkpoints.

Two weeks after Sharon's inflammatory visit to the Temple Mount, two Israeli soldiers made a wrong turn and ended up in Palestinian Authority custody in Ramallah. In scenes captured on video and shown around the world, an angry mob stormed the Palestinian police station and brutally lynched the two reservists. The image from that day, seared in the minds of Israelis, was of the large, surging crowd cheering as a young man in a white T-shirt stood in an open window of the police station and triumphantly raised his hands in the air, as the blood of the Israelis dripped from his open palms.

Very quickly, Israelis rallied around a new plan for dealing with the Palestinian problem: Build a wall. A security barrier. Bulldozers and planners fanned out along Israel's border with the West Bank and started walling off the country, regardless of the international line separating the two. Miles of concrete and electronic fencing cut into parts of the West Bank so the walls could protect rapidly expanding Israeli settlements that had already eaten away at land that once might have been part of a Palestinian state.

Israeli leaders characterized the project as an unfortunate security barrier and dismissed all suggestions that it was an attempt to unilaterally redraw the Middle East map once again by taking more Palestinian land.

"They are annexing part of the West Bank to Israel," Palestinian Authority spokesman Yasser Abed Rabbo said in 2002 as the first walls were going up outside Jerusalem. "All of this aims at the same thing: to limit the Palestinian lands."[46]

Initially, the US government expressed reservations about the idea.

"I don't know if you're going to solve the problem with a fence, unless you're solving the underlying problems of the Palestinians feeling disenfranchised," Colin Powell, who was serving as President George W. Bush's secretary of state, said at the time.[47]

At the end of 2003, Israel gave the go-ahead to build a ten-mile stretch of the wall between Jerusalem and Azariya. And these were walls. Not the less-obtrusive electric fencing that ran across some parts of the West Bank. These were 26-foot-tall concrete slabs, rising one by one as the wall snaked through the dense hillside neighborhoods surrounding Jerusalem.

The Bazlamits weren't sure exactly where the wall was going to go. They talked to neighbors in Azariya who told them different stories. They spoke to Palestinians working on the crews building the wall, who only knew so much. The only thing they knew for sure was that the route of the wall appeared to be heading right for their home.

Unbeknownst to them the route had already been decided, with the help of the Catholic nuns living on the hillside above them. The nuns ran a small foster home for Palestinian kids from Jerusalem and the West Bank.

In early 2003, Israeli military officials came to see the sisters to ask them an existential question: Which side of the wall did they want to be on? There wasn't an easy answer. But they had to decide. If they chose to be on the western side, "inside" Israel, then they'd be cut off from Palestinian families they worked with in the West Bank. If they chose the eastern side, "outside" the walls, they would be cut off from Jerusalem and the invaluable social network the city offered.[48]

They choose to be inside the wall.

The Israeli officers came back to show the nuns a map of the wall route that circled around their property. But when the construction crews showed up, the bulldozers pushed through the church land.[49]

Margaret Cone and Deal Hudson, Christian travelers from America who met with the nuns later, said the women were aghast at what was happening.

"What are you doing?" Sister Lodi shouted at the men.[50]

An Israeli soldier pointed a gun at the nun and gave her a curt order.

"Sister, go back in your house," he said. *"We are not to talk to you; we are ordered to come here to do what we are ordered to do."*[51]

The crews pushed through the convent's orchard of olive and lemon trees as the nuns helplessly looked on. At least they could say that they were inside the wall. The Bazlamits weren't so lucky.

When the bulldozers finally came over the ridge, they carved a route right through the Bazlamits' backyard. The construction crews started erecting towering sections of concrete, cutting the Bazlamits in Azariya off from Jerusalem. The new dividing line ran through the Bazlamit land once again.

"We spent all our money and even went into debt in order to have a good life for our kids, and look what happened," Mohammed said.

The wall turned a 25-minute drive from Assael Street into a circuitous trek that could take an hour or longer.

More importantly, even if Israeli leaders wouldn't say it, the Bazlamits knew what the wall meant. Anyone living on the other side—the outside—was no longer going to be considered part of Jerusalem. The wall would create a physical and psychological divide that was likely to be followed by an official revocation of their status as Jerusalemites. It was one way to whittle away at the Palestinian population in the city. But there was nothing the family could do.

"We are undesirable creatures," Mohammed said in 2007. "I feel it, and, now, every Arab is made to feel it."

The Bazlamits first tried to beautify the wall by planting orange, olive and almond saplings at its base. Kids came to paint defiant slogans on the concrete wall: *Ya Sharon, ya kalb.* Sharon, you dog.

Nawal couldn't help but notice a pattern. More walls cutting them off from the life they once knew. Each time, by a matter of feet.

"They kicked us out before," Nawal said during one 2007 visit to the family land in Azariya. "And now they have kicked us out again."

Worse than having Israel's new wall as their backyard fence, the Bazlamits' carpentry business had just been crippled. People from Jerusalem weren't going to drive a traffic-snarled 45 minutes to get to their little family shop. It wouldn't be long before they would have to shut the shop down altogether.

"This closure, this siege, only makes the conflict bigger," said Mohammed.

Dealing with the long drive might have been tolerable. But the thought of losing their Jerusalem residency was not. The concrete walls conveyed an unmistakable message.

"They have us surrounded," Nawal said that afternoon while walking along the concrete wall behind her sons' apartment building.

Dressed in a long black coat with a white scarf covering her hair, Nawal smiled at the graffiti as she walked in the shadows of the gray barrier. There was nothing they could do. So the Bazlamits moved back to Abu Tor, where the families crowded into the expanding warren of squat homes on Assael Street.

Building on the land had always been difficult. Israeli laws made it virtually impossible to get permits. The problems stemmed from Israel's reliance on antiquated laws used to determine the legitimate owner of a piece of land. The constant churn of countries, empires and invading armies made hanging on to authentic property records a challenge.

While the laws made it hard, the government made it harder. Jerusalem officials always seemed to come up with one reason or another for denying building permits. Paperwork problems. Design problems. Construction problems. The rationale for saying "no" seemed to be limitless.

"We feel like they are always trying to kick us out," Nawal said.

So the Bazlamits built without official permission. They had to. The family kept growing, and it needed more space. The kids were spilling out of the compound and taking over the street. The young Bazlamit boys sped down to the dead end on their bikes and did wheelies as the road sloped back toward their house. They used Assael's walls, gates and garage doors to kick balls that very often sailed into people's protected yards. The kids would either climb over the fences to rescue the balls or ring the doorbell and sheepishly ask for the ball back.

The constant sound of kids playing on the street didn't go over well with all the neighbors. Some were annoyed at constantly having to throw balls back into the street. Others were startled to find Bazlamit boys climbing over their fences. One longtime neighbor, Malka Joudan, complained that the "Arabs"—the kids—deliberately screamed and shouted when they went past her house, launching her Chihuahua into a barking frenzy all afternoon.

Each day before dawn during the month of Ramadan, one of the Bazlamit men would walk down the street and through the neighborhood banging a bass drum to wake families up for the big *suhur* meal meant to get them through the day until the *iftar* dinner after the sunset. The pounding of the bass drum couldn't help but wake up everyone in the neighborhood as the echoes thumped across the hillside.

GOD, GRAFFITI AND A NEW DIVIDE

No one on Assael was more bothered by the Bazlamits than Carol, an Israeli-American realtor who lived across the street with her two daughters. Carol's arched, blue iron garden door opened onto three small steps, right across the street from the Bazlamit compound. The steps were a perfect place for the neighborhood boys to sit, drink tea, smoke sticky, apple-flavored tobacco from a tall *shisha* water pipe, and watch what went on down the street.

Carol moved to Assael in 1998 and loved her little cottage, especially the small garden with the white picket fence. She adored Abu Tor, especially Assael Street. Her daughters played with Palestinian girls on the other side of the street. There was something romantically poetic about it: Jewish and Muslim girls living across from each other, playing, laughing, creating a common, guileless bond that could transcend the bitterness and hatred that clouded their parents' lives. Carol stood in her door on Assael Street and smiled with pride as she watched their lives unfolding.

"The thing for me that was so beautiful about that is the girls had no common language," Carol said, "but they would find common language in their play."

Carol imagined being part of the new generation of Jerusalemites who would conjure up a solution that had eluded the city for eons.

"In my fantasy world, people would live together and it would be an ideal world," she said. "It wasn't so much."

At some point, for Carol, things went sour on Assael. She loved the girls right across the street. But not the Bazlamit kids. They seemed unruly and inconsiderate. The boys were *always* sitting on the steps. She could never keep them all straight and remember who was whose son. They were always tossing candy wrappers and soda cans into her garden. They were always bickering over the limited parking spaces—all on the eastern side of the street.

They just seemed to be disrespectful.

"It wasn't a racist thing at all," Carol said. "They were just not good people. Their last name could have been Cohen, and had they behaved the way they behaved, I would have had exactly the same issues with them."

Relations became ever more strained. There were more shouting matches in the street. One time someone vandalized Carol's car with paint. The Bazlamits found Carol to be cool and unkind. Nawal complained that Carol reported her young kids to Israeli police simply because they had sneaked into her yard to pick some fruit. She had very little to say about Carol at all. She dismissed her neighbor with a thinly veiled jab: "One can tell when a person wants to live together and when they don't want to coexist."

Carol started to feel the same way about her neighbors. In 2003, she decided to transform her tiny, unkempt yard into a courtyard so she and her kids would have more space outside their cozy house, which seemed to be getting smaller as the girls got bigger. Carol replaced the small rectangle of dry grass with wide tiles she'd kept in storage. She installed new benches and replaced the white picket fence rising over Assael Street with a cement block wall. Carol painted the inside of the new wall with Southwestern pastels of yellow and blue. She added red, blue and yellow pillow accents, a wood table and dark blue umbrella for shade. Inside, it was serene and beautiful, a little oasis in Abu Tor. From the outside, the whitewashed wall was ugly. It was easy to see where the old wall ended and the new one began. The bottom five feet of the retaining wall was made of rough-hewn stone blocks, cemented in six straight rows. The top five feet, where the white picket fence once protected Carol's home from the street, was smooth, whitewashed concrete that glowed in the moonlight on Assael Street like a tantalizing blank canvas.

In 2006, Zakaria and Nawal took one of the most important trips of their lives. They flew to Saudi Arabia to make their pilgrimage to Mecca, a spiritual journey that is one of the five pillars of Islam.

While the couple was away, their family planned a celebration like no other. They put up strings of lights and balloons. They planned the lamb slaughter and started cooking days before the couple's return. They ordered dozens of plastic chairs and rented a tent for the courtyard. At night, a few of the younger Bazlamit guys carried paint and brushes out into the darkened dead-end street so they could decorate the walls of their compound. Like their neighbors across the way, the Bazlamits had gradually walled themselves off from the street. What was once a low stone wall was now a tall patchwork of cement blocks topped by sheets of corrugated tin. The Bazlamits painted red crescent moons and blue stars to signify the couple's auspicious journey to Mecca.

"Welcome to the pilgrims," they spray-painted in Arabic. "A blessed Hajj."

They painted images of the Ka'aba, the towering black marble cube that the couple joined thousands of other Muslims in walking around seven times as a sign of their unified devotion to Allah.

Underneath the spray-painted Ka'aba, the men wrote: "May all your sins be forgiven."

They used yellow paint to make the image of Jerusalem's Dome of the Rock, the spot where the Prophet Muhammad, led by the archangel Gabriel, ascended to heaven.

But they didn't stop there.

As the paint was drying, they turned around, crossed the street and kept painting on Carol's blank, white concrete garden wall. When Carol woke up the next morning, she was stunned to see the Arabic graffiti on her wall. She didn't know what it said. She had no idea that it was meant to mark one of the most important moments for the family across the way. She thought the graffiti might be something spiteful. Something hateful. She called the city and asked them to send someone out to paint over the vandalism.

A few hours later, Carol saw the small city vehicle pull up outside and went to say hello. It was a cold, gray, drizzly day so she offered them tea or coffee. When she came out a few minutes later, the two Jewish city workers had been joined by a Palestinian guy from the municipality, two Bazlamit men and another neighbor.

The city official seemed irked, but Carol didn't know why.

"Why did you complain?" he asked Carol.

"I didn't complain," Carol replied. *"I made a request for the city to remove some graffiti."*

The men gathered in front of her house talked amongst themselves in Arabic—and they weren't happy. The city official explained to Carol that the graffiti was meant to welcome the Bazlamits back from their pilgrimage to Mecca. He told her it was an honor for the couple and a celebration for the family. Then they told her she shouldn't ask the city to paint over it. Carol was shocked. Someone had written something in Arabic on her wall. She asked the city to come take care of it. And now she was being treated like she had done something wrong?

"It was very threatening," she said. "It was really scary."

Feeling backed into a corner, Carol capitulated. She told the city workers to go. She'd let the graffiti stay. Carol went back into her house and stewed. She'd been intimidated. She understood that the Bazlamits wanted to celebrate. But it was also *her* wall, not theirs.

"Maybe if they had come to me, even though there was no reason to paint on the wall, and said: 'Listen, there was this huge honor etc. etc., we'll paint it and then paint over it in a month,' I most likely would have agreed," Carol said.

The more she thought about it, the more Carol felt like she'd been unfairly coerced. It was her wall, after all. So she called the city and asked
them to send someone back out to paint over the welcome-home graffiti.

"I understood that it is a sign of respect to a family and an honor when
they make the Hajj," she said of the graffiti. "But, from a moral standpoint,
it was wrong to paint on somebody else's wall."

When the city crew came out the next day, they tried again to dissuade
her from having her wall whitewashed. This time she was adamant. They
painted over the graffiti on her side of the street. The next morning Carol
came out to find all four of her car tires had been slashed.

Any neighborly goodwill that might have remained between Carol and
the Bazlamits drained away. Carol was irate. She had no clout on the street,
but the situation was untenable.

"The tension was scary bad," Carol said.

Carol wasn't sure what to do. The Bazlamits called it a terrible shame
and said they had no idea who slashed her tires. Some Palestinian friends of
Carol's suggested that she take part in a *sulha*—a neighborhood reconciliation meeting—with the Bazlamits. Carol had little to lose. One afternoon,
she walked over to the Bazlamits home to try and bring some peace back
to the street. There didn't really seem to be that much reconciliation happening while they drank small cups of hot tea with freshly picked mint
leaves and a coating of granulated sugar at the bottom. Carol expressed her
regrets and the Bazlamits accepted her contrition.

"I didn't think I needed to apologize, but I did because I was kind of
scared," she said.

Though her heart wasn't in it, Carol shook hands with the Bazlamits
and hoped that might end the fight between them.

"I was afraid," Carol says. "I thought, if I do a sulha, then maybe they
won't do something violent, like slashing tires."

The sulha didn't change the way the neighbors really felt about each
other. Carol stopped using the garden door as much as she could. She
stopped parking her car on Assael altogether. Soon, Carol was looking for
another place to live. The charm of living in Abu Tor, the allure of Assael,
was gone.

Before she moved out, Carol took her girls on one last weekend away.
They came home to find their cottage had been ransacked and robbed. The
thieves took pretty much everything that was worth anything. Television.

Stereo. Jewelry. Her VCR and, with it, hours and hours of irreplaceable family videos, including her grandmother's last Passover.

"That was most painful," she said. "They don't have any need for that. It was my family memories."

Carol might have chalked the robbery up to living on the edge of a poor neighborhood—except for the drawing in her bedroom, above her bed. A crude phallic image that was clearly meant to humiliate her.

"I don't believe it was just a random break-in," she said. "In a random break-in you don't have time to paint an obscene picture on the wall."

Once again, the Bazlamits expressed shock. Carol didn't believe it.

"I had a good relationship with people on the street," she said. "I felt safe and comfortable letting my kids walk outside. Things just got out of control with this family. They really misbehaved."

Carol had no idea why the Bazlamits took a dislike to her. Perhaps they looked down on her because she was a divorced mother. Maybe they thought poorly of her because she didn't cover her short, curly brown hair and defer to men.

"I don't think the men in the family liked me because I was an independent, single woman," she said.

Carol did what she could to be neighborly. Sometimes she helped the women across the street to bang the dust out of the big rugs they'd brought into the street to clean. She'd rescue wayward toddlers who wandered down the road toward the busier street at the beginning of Assael.

"Maybe there are just too many people living in the house to know what's going along with everybody," she said. "It's a hard family to get along with."

Years later, that era of Carol's life was still so distasteful that she asked that her real name not be used when telling her story in this book.

DEMOLITION CREWS COME TO ASSAEL

By the time Carol moved away, the Bazlamits had cemented themselves as the street's foundation stone. Permit or not, the Bazlamits had created a three-level warren of seven houses stacked together like Lego blocks. Four generations of Bazlamits, dozens of aunts, uncles, cousins and babies, were living on the land. Nawal was living in a house built on top of the courtyard where her father-in-law had been shot in 1951. Her brothers-in-law built their own homes on the hillside below. Each one had a demolition order hanging over their heads. From one edge of the property to the other, the Bazlamits were swamped by court orders and demands to pay thousands of dollars in fines for illegally building. They handsomely paid lawyer after lawyer to keep the demolition crews away.

The Bazlamits were squeezed. They'd hoped to spread out with the apartment building in Azariya, but they'd been pushed back to Assael so that Israel wouldn't strip them of their Jerusalem residency. And it was pointless to apply for permits from a city bureaucracy that seemed to do all it could to conjure up reasons to reject their applications or, worse still, find reasons to seize the land.

Israel's complicated laws made it easy for the state, when it wanted, to find reasons to confiscate land. The nation's Absentee Property Law gave Israeli officials lots of ways to take control of property. The law allowed Israel to take all, or part, of a piece of land that was owned by anyone it determined lived outside the country. There had been years of battles over whether the law applied to East Jerusalem, but they knew it was always best to assume the worst. Israel had tried to seize part of the Bazlamits' property by arguing that some of the family members who owned the land lived in Jordan.

While they fought the attempt to take the family land, the Bazlamits also had to beat back repeated demands that they tear down their illegal rooms.

Israel held the threat of home demolitions over the heads of tens of thousands of East Jerusalemites. Every year, heavy Israeli construction excavators razed dozens of Palestinian homes in the city, leaving hundreds homeless and keeping countless more wondering if they were next.

When they weren't paying lawyers to stop the attempts to seize their property or demolish their homes, the Bazlamits had to deal with penalties handed out for violating other city laws. One time they were fined for putting solar panels on their home. Another time they were cited for hanging laundry from their roof—a daily routine that the city decided was a physical blight on the neighborhood.

Abdullah built two small apartments for two of his sons and spent more than 15 years fruitlessly trying to get the city to remove them from the threat of demolition.

The only thing that topped the Bazlamits' frustration with the endless series of costly legal battles was their incredulity over the city's approval of a towering three-story apartment building two doors down.

While almost all of the Arab families on the eastern side of Assael had tried in vain for years to get building permits, it didn't escape their notice that the owners of the one big building that got approval to build were Jewish.

"We are fighting the city and the courts every day," Abdullah said. "Now, if I bring a Jewish man to take this house, they will give him a big house, a big building."

In 2012, Mohammad, Abdullah's older brother, finally lost the fight to protect his small house on Assael from demolition. With no other options, Mohammad and his family moved their stuff out of the rooms before the demolition crews came to knock part of their house down.

The Bazlamits got the message. Their property and Assael didn't have any special protection. If anything, it was clear to them that their street, their property, was still on the front line and that they still had to fight, every day, to hang on.

FOUR

THE SETTLERS

They knew it was time to leave when the Arabs kidnapped their queen. Malka. Their little 13-year-old queen. Even her younger sister agreed that Malka, which meant "queen" in Hebrew, was the prettiest one. She had long, wavy hair and always got compliments from people about her beautiful eyes. Malka was three years older than Rachel, who adored her sister's beauty and confidence. Rachel was the dutiful one who helped their mom with the housework. Growing up, the sisters were inseparable.

There was good reason for the girls to cling to each other. They were a minority of a minority: They were the only Kurdish-Jewish family living in a small Arab village in Persian Iran.

Their dad was always traveling for work. To where, exactly, the girls never really paid much attention. To them, Chaima was an absentee father who came around once a week to ask them and their brothers to do their chores and look after their mother while he was gone.

The family came from a small village in a sliver of Kurdish Iran near the country's western borders with Turkey and Iraq. There wasn't much for a father to do there, so they moved around. Their dad didn't have enough money to live in the big city of Tehran, so they settled for a while in the small Arab town. They were the only Jewish family there, something that didn't escape anyone's notice. Though life for Jewish families in 1940s Iran was far from ideal, they were able to light their Friday night Shabbat candles without fear. But Iran's close ties to Nazi Germany and its history of Jewish pogroms meant that the family never felt that comfortable in their own country. The simmering hostility started to boil again when Israel was established in 1948.

And then the Arabs kidnapped Malka.

One day, Malka didn't come home. She was just gone. She had been taken by an Arab man. It took days to get word to her dad and days more for her dad to get home.

"It's time to go," Chaima told his family when he finally returned. *"We're going to Israel."*

In 1950, the family boarded a plane in Tehran and flew to Israel. Rachel Aharoni, then ten years old, arrived on the windy Mediterranean coast with her parents, grandmother and four brothers.

Malka was left behind.

Rachel and her family were part of a growing wave of immigrants from the Middle East and North Africa that was flooding Israel. Although many Jews had lived successful lives in Muslim-majority countries, the establishment of Israel stoked smoldering hostility toward Jewish families across the region.

In response to the growing dangers, Israel launched a series of missions—some of them secret—to spirit the Jews out. Operation Magic Carpet brought nearly 50,000 Jewish immigrants from Yemen to Israel.[1] Operation Ezra and Nehemiah brought more than 120,000 from Iraq.[2] Operation Yachin brought thousands more from Morocco.[3]

More than 260,000 Jewish immigrants from the Middle East and North Africa, including 30,000 from Iran, streamed into Israel during those first few years, swamping the new country and presenting an overwhelming challenge.[4] Many of the new arrivals, like Rachel and her family, were dropped off at Israel's Ellis Island: Sha'ar Ha'Aliya, the Gateway to Immigration. The doorway for the Jewish diaspora to "return" to Jerusalem. It was supposed to be a temporary processing center for the hundreds of thousands flowing into the new country. But Israel wasn't prepared for the surge of immigrants, the *Olim,* and had nowhere to put them all. The numbers at Sha'ar Ha'Aliya just kept growing, and Israel's primary gateway turned into a sprawling refugee camp.

The camp was established on Israel's northern Mediterranean coast, at an old British army barracks in Haifa. When the camp officials ran out of space in the barracks, they moved people into canvas tents. The tents swelled with new arrivals from France and Morocco, Italy and Iran, Germany and Tunisia.

Very quickly, the camp was plagued by overflowing outhouses, rat infestations and endless lines.[5] There were lines for breakfast. Lines for lunch. Lines for dinner. Lines to see a doctor. Lines to fill out the paperwork they needed to get out of there. People had to wait for hours to take showers—when there was enough water to take them. The camp smelled of stagnant sewage from overflowing toilets and acrid smoke from cooking fires dampened by sharp winds blowing over the Mediterranean Sea cliffs.

It was clear from the start that the Farsi- and Arabic-speaking Jewish families from Iraq, Iran and Morocco were different from their Yiddish-speaking cousins from Germany, England and America. The language barriers fueled misunderstandings in the camp. It wasn't surprising to see frustrations over the endless lines boil over into arguments and fistfights.

The fact that the camp was enclosed by fences, barbed wire and armed guards didn't always make people feel welcome in the new Jewish nation.

For those who had survived the Holocaust and lived under Nazi rule, it was a shock to discover that Israel's official gateway looked like it could be a concentration camp. Some became so enraged by the situation that they tried to tear down the fences and escape.[6]

Rachel watched as family after family packed their suitcases and boarded buses headed for new homes somewhere else in Israel. Rachel didn't know where they were going, but she knew it had to be better than that terrible welcome camp. The family shared two small tents for months. Rachel and her brothers were sent every day with buckets to stand in long lines for water. They spent months in limbo while their dad kept looking for ways to get them out.

When their day to leave finally came, Rachel was thankful. Like many others, Rachel's welcome to Israel was a constant reminder of how her family's fortunes could change very quickly. It was a painful lesson that stuck with Rachel as she embarked on the next chapter of her life in Israel.

"The people who emerged from this flawed process were emboldened, often disappointed, vocally and physically defiant, and carried with them a strong sense of entitlement to the goings-on in their state," said Israeli historian Rhona Seidelman.[7]

To deal with the continued flow of immigrants, Israel created more than 100 refugee resettlement camps—*ma'abarot*. In 1951, Rachel and her family packed their things and headed off to one of the ma'abarot near Jerusalem. They were finally able to move into a home with four walls, but they were still living in a refugee camp and wondering if they'd made the right decision to leave Iran.

The Aharonis soon joined a small group of Kurdish and Moroccan families in creating a small *moshav*—a farming cooperative—on a fertile hillside that Palestinians said belonged to villagers who fled in 1948. Rachel began doing odd jobs around the moshav—picking fruits and vegetables, cleaning houses. Her father sent her to an all-girls boarding school, but she and her friends got so bored that they came home after a few months.

There wasn't that much more to do on the farm, but Rachel liked hanging out with her family. When she turned 16, talk turned to marriage. Rachel had lots to offer. She was petite, with long, dark brown hair, and self-assured for her age. One of her second cousins told Rachel she knew just the guy: her brother. Haim was funny and smart. He was witty and adventurous. And he lived with his family in one of Jerusalem's most unsettled neighborhoods—Abu Tor. Haim lived above the barbed wire, between Israeli guard posts, on the edge of the country.

Rachel didn't know much about life on the border; it certainly sounded dangerous. But living in Jerusalem would be the fulfillment of a fantasy. Was this the answer to her prayers? Rachel wasn't sure. Haim's older sister kept pressuring Rachel to marry him. She showed Rachel photos of Haim and told her they didn't do him justice. He had woolly, dark hair and big, boxy, black-rimmed glasses. He had the long, smooth fingers of a guy who liked to read and the deep dimples of a young man who liked to smile. Eventually, Rachel's family agreed. When she finally got to meet Haim Machsomi, after they were engaged, Rachel was kind of disappointed with her second cousin. The Dream Guy fantasy she had created in her mind didn't match the reality.

"He wasn't what I was dreaming of," Rachel said. "But, afterwards, when we had kids, he spoiled me."

LITTLE IRAN IN ABU TOR

Life in Abu Tor wasn't what Rachel had dreamed about either. Living on the edge of Israel in 1957 wasn't easy. It felt like they were always being watched. By the Jordanian Legionnaires across the border. By the Israeli soldiers manning sandbagged positions hidden below tall, skinny evergreens scattered across the hilltop. When the shooting started and the sound of gunfire echoed through the valleys, it was hard to tell where it came from and where to run.

Rachel moved into a small home with her new husband, his sisters and their widowed mother. Haim and Rachel didn't have much privacy. But they were building a community. There were only a handful of Jewish families living on the Abu Tor border. Almost all of them were immigrants from the Middle East and North Africa. Many were from Iran. Avraham and Malka Joudan, who had come from Iran in 1951, had been living there for years. So had the Jacobys, some of whom liked to point out that they were the "real" Iranians—*Persian* Iranian Jews, not *Kurdish* Iranian Jews. Haim's uncle, Eliyahu Goeli, lived a little ways up the hillside, where rebuilding the family outhouse would one day spark an emergency UN investigation.

The Abu Tor hilltop was becoming a Little Iran on the outer edge of Israel.

It was no coincidence that the country's newest, poorest immigrants ended up living on Israel's front lines. There was already a divide between the usually darker-skinned Sephardic Jewish families coming from the Middle East and North Africa and the normally lighter-skinned Ashkenazi Jewish families coming from Europe and North America. Everyone knew who got better treatment.

But living on the edge of Israel had one perk those on the other side of the railroad tracks didn't get: Abu Tor had a panoramic view of the Old City, a chance, every day, to see the Temple Mount, where G-d collected dust to create Adam, where the faithful had once kept Moses's stone-tablet Ten Commandments in the Ark of the Covenant. Every day, they could look out on the place where the High Priest could talk directly to G-d.

They could see their Temple Mount, still out of reach, on the other side of the barbed wire, in Jordan's hands.

Every day, the Jewish residents of Abu Tor would turn toward the Temple Mount with their prayers.

"Return in mercy to Jerusalem Your city and dwell therein as You have promised," they would recite as they looked across the dark divide separating them from the Temple Mount. "Speedily establish therein the throne of David Your servant, and rebuild it, soon in our days, as an everlasting edifice. Blessed are You L-rd, who rebuilds Jerusalem, speedily cause the scion of David Your servant to flourish, and increase his power by Your salvation."

Each day, the words were a reminder of the unfulfilled prayers for construction of the third Jewish temple on the Temple Mount. The biblical prophecy has been the catalyst for repeated clashes with Muslim protesters in the Old City over who has the right to control the small spiritual plateau on which the Dome of the Rock and al Aqsa mosque have dominated the skyline for centuries. One day, the Jews would return.

In 1959, with their family getting bigger every year, Haim and Rachel moved to a larger home closer to the fence. The old stone Palestinian house had a big garden with a balcony that looked out on the neglected orchards, crumbling terrace walls and stone block homes sitting empty in No Man's Land. But their new place had a large living room with mosaic tile and lots of light. Apart from the fact that it looked directly out on No Man's Land, it seemed like a perfect place to raise their kids.

Rachel spent her time taking care of the garden, picking fruit from the trees to make jam, hanging the laundry, and keeping an eye on her children as they scrambled over a hillside that was always within sniper range of the Jordanian soldiers down below.

Some days the border separating the two sides seemed lower than others. One day Haim's mother chased a turkey into No Man's Land and returned to tell her son that she'd heard a child crying in one of the Arab homes. Haim was surprised, and told his mother she couldn't cross through the barbed wire again.[8]

"Why not?" she asked her son. "They're our neighbors."[9]

This isn't Iran, Haim told her. "You could get shot."[10]

Haim's message took awhile to sink in as the neighborhood began to grow and the blurred border became more defined. The Machsomis' immediate neighbors, Avraham and Malka Joudan, had endured the same trauma when they arrived in Israel as immigrants from Iran in 1951. Malka, who got married at the age of 14, was pregnant with her fourth child when she and her husband were loaded into a cargo plane and flown to Israel, where they were immediately sprayed down with some unknown liquid (meant, they assumed, to prevent the spread of one possible disease or another) and subjected to days of bewildering questions from Israeli officials.

The couple arrived at Sha'ar Ha'Aliya with three kids, a few Persian carpets, some gold jewelry, and small satchels of clothes. They were bundled off to one of the dismal ma'abarot 20 miles from Jerusalem where Malka, in the final weeks of a tough pregnancy, refused to get out of the truck.

"They promised to bring us to Jerusalem," she said. *"This is not Jerusalem."*

The camp officials and truck driver tried everything to get her to get out. They tried sweet talk and threats. She wouldn't budge.

The camp workers wouldn't force Malka to stay, so they sent her and her family all the way back to Sha'ar Ha'Aliya, nearly 100 long miles, until they could find something in Jerusalem for the immigrants. They finally found one room for the Joudans in the city. That was enough. The family moved in and used government coupons to buy butter and eggs while they settled into their new life.

In 1952, Israeli officials came to the family with a proposal. They had a house for the family—but there was a catch. It was on the border, right above the Arab and Muslim families on the other side of the barbed wire.

"I don't care," Malka told them. *"I lived among them before. As long as I have a place to raise my kids, I don't care."*

Rachel Machsomi and Malka Joudan quickly became friends. Their kids would play soccer and hide-and-seek together while the women spent hours talking about their kids and their husbands. While working in the garden and hanging up clothes to dry, the women would occasionally see the women on the other side of the barbed wire a few yards away. The water well for the people living in No Man's Land was just down the hill from the Machsomis' house, so Rachel and Malka began to see the other women routinely. Rachel could sometimes smell the scents coming from the Arab houses below, where the mothers and wives would bake fresh pita bread in their wood ovens. It smelled like home.

The neighbors separated by the barbed wire tried their best to create a sense of normalcy for their families. When chickens from one side of the divide scampered over to the other side, people would shoo them back to their homes—most of the time.

But there was no getting around the fact that they all lived in a dangerous neighborhood. Two of Israel's nine Jerusalem guard posts—known as the Palm Tree and the Lion—sat on the high ground in Abu Tor. The narrow band separating Israeli and Jordanian soldiers made it one of the most contentious stretches of the border. UN officials were frequently called upon by one side or the other to step in and mediate disputes.

Over the years, soldiers and civilians on both sides fired potshots that sent people diving for cover. When Israeli forces invaded Egypt's Sinai Peninsula in 1956 to challenge President Gamal Abdel Nasser's territorial ambitions and nationalization of the Suez Canal, Jordanian forces fired shots of solidarity along the Jerusalem border. One bullet slammed into the Joudans' back window, bending the iron bars that faced No Man's Land. The tensions got so high that Israel moved some of the families off the front line with Jordan for six months while the Suez crisis played itself out, ending with Israel withdrawing its forces from Egypt in the spring of 1957.

"It was the most dangerous neighborhood to visit," said Maya Joudan, the daughter Malka was carrying when she arrived in Israel in 1951. "Nobody came there."

ROMEO AND JULIET ON THE BORDER?

Maya and her family shared their one-story home with another family from Iran. The Jacobys rented a small room attached to the back of the house, on the edge of the garden overlooking No Man's Land. The Jacoby, Machsomi and Joudan kids all played together. The older kids looked after the younger ones. Some of the kids were intimidated by Maya's dad, Avraham.

Avraham, a balding man with dark skin and a hawkish nose, could be stern. His kids thought their dad looked like Egyptian leader Anwar Sadat. The Jacoby children could hear the Joudan kids crying after being punished by their dad. And Avraham wasn't afraid to try to teach the neighborhood kids some manners as well.

Shimshon Jacoby, who was born in 1951, used to get in boyish fights with Avraham's sons. Avraham didn't take too kindly to Shimshon's roughhousing. When Shimshon was six or seven, Avraham grabbed him under his knees and shoulders, lifted him up and started carrying him toward the border separating Israel from No Man's Land.

"I'm going to throw you to the Arabs," Avraham told Shimshon, who writhed and pleaded for mercy until he broke free.

The incident scarred Shimshon for years. Avraham meant to scare Shimshon. And it did the trick. Decades later, Shimshon remembered that day vividly.

"For years, I was afraid of Arabs," said Shimshon, a businessman with a tall, broad, Alfred Hitchcock–type build. "Because Arabs were like . . . darkness."

Abu Tor attracted an unusual assortment of characters. In the 1950s, the neighborhood developed an underground reputation on the Israeli side for being home to a number of prostitutes. At some point, some of them may have worked out of the house at the top of the hill, next to the grave of Abu Tor; the house may have once been a mosque or home to a Greek Orthodox patriarch. Others worked out of their homes along the border. The Joudans and Jacobys lived next to a family from Morocco, including a single mother named Leyla who always had a lot of men coming and going.

"There were always a lot of foreigners and UN cars out front," Maya Joudan said of the Moroccan mother who was one of the first to embrace their Arab neighbors when the fence came down in 1967. "When men would come around, her grandmother would wait outside."

Because the residents of Abu Tor lived on the border, their lives were always under scrutiny. Everyone kept watch on each other. Israeli border guards scanned the empty houses in No Man's Land for any sign that Jordan was trying to set up secret bunkers. Jordanian soldiers looked for indications that Israeli forces were trying to sneak in heavy weapons banned under a UN agreement that outlined what kind of firepower each side could have along the border. Nothing was above scrutiny. Not even Pinchas Joudan's pigeons.

Pinchas, Avraham and Malka's eldest son, was obsessed with pigeons. He talked about them all the time. He learned how to take care of them and what they liked to eat. After badgering his parents for months, Pinchas convinced them to install a pigeon coop on their roof.

It wasn't long before a white jeep with a blue-and-white UN flag fixed to its body rumbled down the last dirt road on the Israeli side of the border and stopped outside the Joudans' house. Investigators with the UN Mixed Armistice Commission (MAC) had arrived to carry out a surprise inspection of the pigeon coop.

"What is that on your roof?" the UN inspectors asked the Joudans. *"We need to make sure that you aren't hiding any weapons."*

As the kids from the neighborhood gathered around, the UN inspectors took out their notebooks and began their examination of the pigeon coop. They checked the type of wood and took measurements of its size. They examined the pigeons and looked for any hidden compartments in the coop that might be used to hold weapons. Some residents of Abu Tor saw the UN inspectors as buffoons. Pigeon coops? This is what the United Nations is concerned about? But Itzik Joudan, Pinchas's younger brother, looked at the UN inspectors and saw heroes.

That's what I want to be, 13-year-old Itzik said to himself.

Itzik's younger sister, Maya, wasn't into pigeons or soccer. She was a chubby teen who didn't have many friends at school. Maya was lonely, even at home, and she would spend long afternoons staring out the back window at the garden and the No Man's Land just outside their low stone wall. She would eat fresh oranges and figs and pick handfuls of purple bougainvillea running along the walls. If there hadn't been an enemy army outpost across the way, it would have been idyllic.

One day, Maya spotted a handsome young man on the other side of the border. He had a head of thick, dark hair and an athletic build. Maya was intrigued. She walked out to the edge of her garden and peered over the wall. The boy, who couldn't have been much older than her, spotted Maya. She caught his eye and waved. The boy waved back. They were separated by only a few yards, but they didn't share a common language, and a fence ran between them. If they were spotted by soldiers they might be questioned as potential spies for talking to the enemy. But the two teens weren't afraid. Maya started rushing home from school and creeping to the window where she could peek out to see if the boy was there.

"The curiosity was very deep," Maya said. "It seemed, somehow, that we liked each other."

Very quickly, their cross-border curiosity grew into an unusual friendship.

"He would come and sit there on the ground and he would lean his head on his hand and his elbow and look at me—and I would look at him," Maya said. "It was like a silent movie."

One day, the boy signaled that he wanted to try one of Maya's father's cigarettes. Maya got one from her dad, tied it to a rock with some string, and tossed it over the border fence. The boy took it, tied one of his own cigarettes onto the stone and threw it back into Maya's yard—a thank-you gift for her father.

Maya confided in one of her girlfriends from the neighborhood that she had a secret friend she wanted her to meet. Maya and Dina whispered into each other's ears about the boy across the divide and imagined what his life might be like. After school one afternoon, when Maya and Dina went out back to see the boy, he threw a small, cheap ring over the barbed wire.

"Don't pick it up!" Maya warned Dina. *"Maybe he put a spell on it to make you fall in love with him."*

The girls ran to Dina's grandmother, who had moved to Israel from Morocco and knew a thing or two about spells and witchcraft.

"If you go to the bathroom on the ring before you touch it," she told the girls, *"it will cancel out the spell."*

The girls ran back to the barbed wire and found the ring in the yard where they'd left it. The boy on the other side was gone. Dina looked around, squatted over the ring and peed on it. If there had been any kind of love spell, it definitely had been broken.

THE PRICE OF POPPIES IN NO MAN'S LAND

As the cross-border relationship blossomed, some new neighbors arrived across the way in the fall of 1966. Malka and the families on the western side of the street could hear banging and shouting just down the hillside at two abandoned Palestinian homes in No Man's Land.

A group of men was cutting down mimosa trees and working inside the vacant houses.

Malka listened to the men sawing, hammering and talking all day. She knew something wasn't right. There weren't supposed to be people building things in No Man's Land. Malka kept an eye on the homes below from her garden, where her daughter was secretly flirting with the Arab boy on the other side of the border.

After more than a week of watching, Malka's anxiety boiled over. What were they doing over there? Something was wrong. On day ten of the work, Malka called the United Nations to tell them there was a serious problem on the border.

In September 1966, the UN team, waving its blue-and-white flag, once again drove over to Abu Tor to check out reports of trouble.

"For the past eight years, the two houses in question have been empty," Malka told the UN investigators, army captains from Ireland, France and Belgium. "For the past ten days, I noticed work in the yards of the houses. I heard hammering and the sound of furniture being moved in the house. . . . I am very anxious about the 'new neighbors' that have just arrived."[11]

Malka told them she'd seen the men working day and night. She saw upward of 20 people bringing bedding and other supplies into one of the homes.

"This morning around 10:00, I saw two Jordanian officers entering the above mentioned yards," she told the UN team. "They came into the southern house, but before entering they took off their rank markings."[12]

That raised questions for the UN investigators. Maybe the Jordanian army *was* trying to set up a secret bunker in No Man's Land.

While the men questioned Malka about what she'd seen, a Jordanian major joined two UN officers from Italy and Norway as they drove along the eastern edge of No Man's Land, on the Jordanian side, until they spotted the pair of two-story stone homes at the center of the complaint. They found the gate through the barbed wire and headed up the sloping dirt path past low, crumbling, terraced garden walls in No Man's Land. They walked up to a squat, two-story stone block house where they found a young boy and told him to go get the owner. Out came 80-year-old Eid Yaghmour, *Abu Ali*, a longtime Abu Tor farmer with thick, rough hands, a whitish-gray handlebar mustache and neatly trimmed beard. The UN investigators peppered him with questions.

"I am an old man," Eid Yaghmour told them. "I cannot work. I was only leveling a piece of tin. I was repairing a piece of tin to fit a manhole for sewage."[13]

A sewer cover? The UN team asked him to show them what he was talking about. Eid Yaghmour went to find the suspicious piece of tin and handed it over to the UN officials. The investigators measured the man-made sewer cover and scrupulously documented its dimensions. They took photographs of the homes and the trees, the stone walls and the terraced gardens. They drew detailed sketches of the houses that pinpointed every chicken coop, room and wall on the property.[14]

"How long have you been living in this house?" a UN inspector asked.

"I left my home about 10 years ago," Eid told them. "I returned to live in my house about two weeks ago."

"How long have you owned these houses?"

"I bought the land and I constructed the houses in which I am living approximately 50 years ago," Eid said. He seemed somewhat exasperated. He couldn't move a stone or bang on some tin without the UN coming to investigate.

"The house was visited by the UN two weeks ago, and also a week ago," he said. "Now I request to be permitted to clean the herbs and stones around the house."

The UN officials gave him no answer, wrapped up their questioning for the day and returned to the MAC office to type up their findings. The following morning, the UN officials returned to question the Yaghmours' next door neighbor, Zakaria Bazlamit, the 28-year-old shoemaker living with his family next to the homes under investigation.

"My father, who was killed in this area, built the house and we have been living in this house since then," Zakaria told the UN team. "We have been living in the house for about 26 years."[15]

After looking over the detailed reports, Lt. Col. M. C. Stanaway, an officer from New Zealand then serving as chairman of the UN MAC, rejected Israel's request for an emergency meeting. The investigators concluded that there was nothing nefarious going on in No Man's Land. Despite her protestations, Malka's new neighbors were there to stay.

The following spring, Rachel Machsomi was looking after her garden when she saw Eid, the elderly Arab man, outside his house picking colorful poppies that didn't seem to grow on the upper hillside in Israel. Using a mix of Persian, Arabic, Hebrew and hand signals, Rachel asked him if he would pick some of the flowers for her.

"Could I have some of those pretty red anemones?" she asked the man.[16]

Rachel climbed through a hole in their basement and met Eid at the chain-link fence that had replaced the barbed wire.[17] He came to the border and handed her a bouquet of flowers.

Minutes later, Jordanian soldiers entered the man's house. When they left, the old man came out back and saw Haim.

"I mustn't talk to you anymore," the man whispered to Haim.[18]

Rachel was grateful for the kind act and wanted to say thanks to the old man living in No Man's Land. She kept an eye out for him, but he didn't turn up. When Rachel saw the women across the way at the well, she signaled to ask them where the older man had gone. The women crossed their hands in an "X" and shook their heads. Rachel assumed he had been arrested by the Jordanians. It would be months before she would find out what happened to the old man. But the two families were about to become two of the closest neighbors on the hillside.

A FAREWELL TO NO MAN'S LAND

Stoked by Soviet mischief, tensions between Egypt and Israel were growing in the spring of 1967. Egyptian forces, fueled by false Soviet intelligence about Israeli military moves, massed on Israel's southern border and blocked Israeli ships from getting to and from the country's southern port, a provocative move that cut off Israel's access to the Red Sea and Indian Ocean.

The families in Abu Tor could tell that something was up. Israeli soldiers repeatedly told the kids where to run for safety if another war started. They told the families to stock up on food. Schools started piling extra sandbags around the buildings.

The shooting started around 10 a.m. on Monday, June 5, a few hours after Israeli planes launched a surprise assault that decimated the Egyptian air force. Most of the kids from Abu Tor were at school, but some had stayed home as word spread that war might be on the way. Israeli soldiers watched as buses filled with Jordanian soldiers drove into the valley below and echoes from loudspeakers rippled up the hillside.

"The war has begun," the Arabic voices warned. "Now we're going to finish the game."[19]

Malka, who understood the terrifying messages from the Arab soldiers, rounded up her kids and grabbed some things for the shelter, including a razor blade. Malka wasn't prepared to have her or her daughter raped or killed if Israel lost the war.

"If the Arabs get too close, you know what you have to do," Malka told Maya as they ran for the bomb shelter. *"You do it to me. I will do it to you."*

The Joudans scrambled out their door, but they didn't get far. The shooting was getting closer and they had to hide under a narrow set of stone stairs next to a small pigeon coop beside their house. Joining them as they rushed for cover was an outgoing young French woman, Gina, who'd moved into the spare room once used by the Jacobys before the Iranian family moved to a bigger place down the street. Gina had become part of the Joudan family. She took them in her tiny Citroën down to southern Israel to buy a sheep that they put in the back seat for a long, crowded, hilarious and memorable drive back to Jerusalem. Only later would the Joudans hear that Gina might have been a spy.

Across the street, Rachel Machsomi corralled her kids and herded them up the hill to the shelter with their neighbors. When they got inside, Rachel counted her kids. Her stomach churned.

"Pini," she said. *"Where's Pini?"*

Her youngest son, her baby, was missing. As the fight for Abu Tor unfolded, Shimshon Jacoby, then 16 years old, rushed back to find Rachel's infant son. A couple of guys from the neighborhood joined Shimshon on the rescue mission. They scrambled from house to house, climbing through gardens until they got back to Rachel's home. They rushed inside to find Pini sleeping, oblivious to the fact that his frantic mom had left him behind—and that his country was at war.

The fighting intensified the following morning when Israeli soldiers moved in to seize Abu Tor. Relieved Israeli residents greeted the soldiers in the streets with trays of tea and cookies. Jordanian forces pummeled the hillside with artillery and mortar fire as the Israelis hunkered down to plan their counterattack. The Joudans and Machsomis could hear Israeli and Jordanian soldiers fighting furious gun battles in the homes nearby. By the end of the second night, the shooting seemed farther off. Israeli forces had pushed the Jordanians down the hillside and into retreat across the valley. The Israeli soldiers closed in for a showdown in the Old City.

The fight in Abu Tor was costly for both sides. Many Jordanian soldiers and 16 Israeli fighters, including the battalion commander, were killed. By the third day, the shooting in Abu Tor seemed to be over. The Machsomis, Jacobys and Joudans emerged from the shelter and made their way back down the hillside to see if their homes were still standing.

Their stone walls were peppered with bullet holes, but none of their houses had been seriously damaged by mortars or artillery rounds. The families gathered in the streets as Israeli soldiers rounded up Arab men hiding with their families in their Abu Tor homes. Israeli soldiers were on the lookout for Jordanian Legionnaires who had taken off their uniforms and changed into civilian clothes to avoid being caught. Shimshon grabbed his camera and started taking photographs of the captives as they marched past his house. The men walked silently with their hands raised and fingers clasped over their heads. Few of them looked like soldiers. They were skinny, balding men with thin mustaches, patchy jackets, loose-fitting pants and thin-soled black leather shoes. Among the men paraded past Shimshon as he took photos was Zakaria Bazlamit.

PRAYING AT THE WESTERN WALL

As the Israeli soldiers solidified their hold on the city, Shimshon and other guys from Abu Tor set off to check out the silent houses in No Man's Land. Across the valley stood the Old City, smoke still rising from the cramped alleys where Israeli soldiers were searching for any Jordanian holdouts. The homes in Abu Tor were shuttered and silent. The Israelis peeked into houses and stopped to check out the bodies of Jordanian soldiers shot dead in the streets. They made their way through the neglected groves in Kidron Valley, which once served as King David's escape route when he fled his rebellious son, Absalom. They walked past towering biblical limestone tombs and burial caves carved into the hillside. They looked up at the Mount of Olives and the carpet of Jewish graves filled with ancient souls who expect to be the first to be resurrected when the Messiah returns. The young men passed Gethsemane, the garden where Jesus Christ was betrayed by Judas and taken by Roman guards to be crucified. Then they started the climb toward the Old City walls. They flinched at the smell of charred rubber and flesh coming from a burning Jordanian bus with dead soldiers inside. They stopped to check out a smoldering tank and turned away when they realized it was Israeli, not Jordanian. Finally, they arrived at Lion's Gate, the small, arched entrance to the Old City, where Israeli paratroopers and tanks first broke through en route to triumphantly raising the Israeli flag above the Western Wall on the Temple Mount, site of the first two Jewish temples. Days earlier, Moshe Dayan, the combat veteran who had drawn the lines splitting the city in 1948, and Yitzhak Rabin, who had overseen the war as the Israel Defense Forces chief of staff, had walked through the same gate as

jubilant soldiers celebrated in the streets where Jewish rabbis were blowing *shofar,* ram's horns, as they carried large, handwritten Torah scrolls
to the Western Wall.

Shimshon looked up toward the Temple Mount, closed his eyes and
said a quiet prayer as tears fell from the cheeks of the men standing alongside him.

THE LOOTING OF ABU TOR

While thousands of Israelis flocked to the Western Wall, others took advantage of the power vacuum to descend on the abandoned Abu Tor homes.
Israeli opportunists looted the homes and stripped some clean. They took
handwoven carpets and embroidered dresses. They carried away gold
wedding necklaces and silver bracelets. They hauled off tiled tables and
idle sheep. Some Israelis moved into the houses abandoned by families that
had fled.

At one point, Israeli soldiers turned up and tried to stop the looting.
One soldier, a young man who still had bloodstains on his uniform, stood
outside the hole in the barbed wire as Israeli civilians returned with armloads of stolen goods. He stopped Israelis as they came through No Man's
Land and berated them for stealing. He pointed at the blood on his uniform
as the looters tried to get away.

"This is the blood of my friend," the soldier told them. *"He didn't die so
that you could go and steal dishes."*

One of them, Shimshon said, was Avraham Joudan, the dad who'd
scared him to death when he was young. Shimshon said he watched the
soldier point his gun at Avraham as he tried to bring armloads of looted
stuff into his home.

*"You put those things back, or you burn them, but you will not take
them,"* the soldier warned Avraham.

As one man rushed past with a bedsheet filled with looted things, a
pretty piece of embroidered cloth fell to the ground in front of the Joudan
family's door. Maya said she was immediately attracted by the beautiful,
vibrant, hand-sewn red-and-green flower.

"Don't take that," Malka, Maya's mom, said to Maya as she went to pick
it up. *"That's not yours."*

Maya took it anyway. If she didn't, the beautiful piece of artwork would end up in the trash.

As the Palestinian families returned to see what had happened to their homes, Malka kept watch. She saw an Israeli soldier beating an Arab man on the roof of one of the homes.

"Stop it!" she shouted at the soldiers. *"Don't be a show-off. That's not how you treat Arabs."*

When she saw another Israeli soldier firing on Arabs making their way home, Malka rushed up and gave him a shove. The soldier's rifle shot slammed into a nearby stone wall as he stumbled.

"You almost killed me," the soldier angrily shouted at Malka.

"I know," she shot back at the soldier. *"Watch out."*

Haim Machsomi also tried to stop the looters. He called the police, who confiscated some of the stolen property and asked Haim to look after it until they could return it to their owners. Haim was afraid he'd be accused of being a looter if he kept it, so he agreed only to look after the sheep his neighbor had taken.[20]

As the looting subsided and families began fixing up their war-damaged homes, Rachel and Haim walked down to meet the people who had been so kind to them over the years.

"What do you need?" they asked the Bazlamits. *"We're your neighbors now. Whatever you need, we will get it. Do you need bread? Do you need milk?"*

"We never had a bad day with them," Abdel Halim Bazlamit said of the Machsomis. "Never."

While the women gathered in one garden, Haim took one of the Baz-lamit men aside for a private talk.

"Our neighbor took your sheep," Haim confided to Abdel Halim. *"He stole it."*

Haim returned the sheep he'd been looking after to a grateful Abdel Halim. In a gesture of thanks, the Bazlamits slaughtered it and they had a big post-war party together.

Itzik Joudan did not see a thief when he looked at his dad. His father wasn't a looter who would steal anyone's sheep. His father was the guy who helped the Arab neighbors fill out confusing new Israeli government paperwork filled with questions about their homes and families.

"None of our friends or the people we knew were part of that," Itzik said of the looting. "No, we were the opposite."

When they were sure that the shooting had stopped, Haim and Rachel took out their prayer shawls and *kippah,* looked out on the city walls they had prayed toward for years, and made their way to the *Kotel,* the Wailing Wall.

Haim and Rachel walked into the Old City to see the place they had fantasized about as kids in Iran. They made their way past the stalls and shattered windows, through the streets filled with soldiers and shopkeepers, until they finally saw it.

Rachel was flooded with unexpected joy. Haim joined the men while Rachel joined the women. She prayed for her husband and her family. She prayed for her brothers and herself. She prayed for her sister, Malka, their queen, the one they had to leave behind.

IS THIS ARAB MEAT KOSHER?

After soldiers came to haul away the border fence on the ridge, the Machsomis and Yaghmours became some of the closest neighbors on the newly united hillside.

"We were like family," said Ziad Yaghmour, Eid's grandson, who was 13 when the dividing line was erased in 1967.

At long last, the Machsomis were able to talk to Eid Yaghmour—Abu Ali—the family patriarch who had handed the poppies over the fence. Haim saw Abu Ali carrying a stick with a white flag. He walked down to meet the elderly man, who drew back in fear.[21]

Haim reassured the man and extended his hand.

"Finally," he said. "We've been neighbors for so long and at last we can shake each other's hand."[22]

The two men talked about the flowers and the Jordanian soldiers who had harassed Eid. The old man was defiant. He'd had his fill of people coming to ask him about flowers and home repairs.

"Why are you harassing me?" he'd told the Jordanian soldiers. *"I only threw her flowers."*

With the barbed wire gone, there seemed to be little separating the families on the upper side of the hill from those down below. Ziad's mother, who Rachel called *Imm Ziad*—the mother of Ziad—brought fresh baked bread. Imm Ziad and the other women across the way took to affectionately calling Rachel *Imm Ibrahim*—the mother of Avraham, her firstborn son.

Imm Ibrahim would go across the street to knit with Imm Ziad and Nawal Bazlamit, *Imm Hijazi*, the woman who had thrown bread over the barbed wire to Haim.

The Jewish mothers cherished their new nicknames. It was a sign of the intimacy the families shared in Abu Tor. Rachel's kids taught Ziad some Hebrew and Ziad taught them some Arabic. Imm Ziad taught Rachel and Malka how to make spicy stuffed squash. The girls from the neighborhood played hopscotch on the open patch of dirt on top of the hill where they'd hid during the Six-Day War. They climbed trees together and tossed rotten fruit at each other. The older boys—the "bad" boys—walked down the hillside to a small clubhouse where they shot pool with Arab kids in their part of the neighborhood. Sometimes one or two of them took a drag from a cigarette.

On Friday nights, when Haim headed to the neighborhood synagogue for Sabbath prayers, his kids would rush across the old barbed-wire line to the Yaghmour house where they would gather around the TV to watch the weekly Arabic language movie on Israel's Channel One. Sometimes Rachel would come watch too.

The Bazlamits and Yaghmours would make hot, thick, sweet, cardamom-infused coffee for Haim on Fridays after the sun went down and religious dictates prevented him from making it for himself. Some Saturdays, during the Jewish Sabbath, Ziad would turn on the TV for Malka— the mother they called Imm Ismael—when she wanted to watch an Arabic language show that reminded her of home.

"My mother always said: 'They are not Muslim,'" said Malka's son, Yanki, of the Yaghmours. "'They have Jewish blood.'"

The trust between the families grew quickly. Then the Yaghmours and some of the other Arab neighbors extended special invitations to the Machsomis and the Joudans: Please come join us for lunch with our families in Hebron.

The Machsomis were elated. There was no greater sign of respect. It was an invitation they were happy to accept. They piled into a couple of cars and drove south to Halhoul, a small village near Hebron, near the Cave of the Patriarchs holding the tomb of Abraham, the prophet revered by Muslims, Christians and Jews as the father of their faiths.

They arrived to a massive feast. The Palestinian families laid out freshly made *labneh* yogurt and olives. They brought out steaming lamb, slaughtered just to welcome their special guests from Jerusalem. The Machsomi kids looked at each other, all thinking the same thing: *Is this meat Kosher?* Haim and Rachel had never said anything to their neighbors. It hadn't crossed their minds to say something.

"What do we do?" Haim asked Rachel.

"We have to tell them," she replied.

Haim walked up to the men and explained the problem. Their embarrassed hosts huddled to talk about the culinary crisis. Then they quickly took the meat away and brought more fruit and vegetables for their honored guests. There were still lots of things the families had to learn about each other.

The visit solidified the bonds the new neighbors were building in Abu Tor. Eid started gardening for the Joudans. Unbeknownst to Eid, he was working for the woman who had complained to the United Nations about his return to No Man's Land a few years earlier.

One day, Israeli police turned up at the Joudan home with some concerning questions. They were looking for Gina, the friendly French tenant who had become a big part of the Joudans' daily lives before the war. But Gina was gone. She was missing. And Israeli officials wanted to speak to her. The Israelis told the Joudans she was wanted for questioning. They wouldn't say why. But the Joudans figured that she had to be a spy for Russia or some other enemy of Israel. It would become one of the war's unsolved mysteries.

WHEN MAYA MET ABDULLAH

The break in the fence also created an opening for Maya Joudan to finally meet the handsome boy with his cigarettes and love-spell rings. His name was Abdullah Bazlamit. He was 19, just three years older than Maya. He called her *Mazal*.

They met on the edge of what had once been No Man's Land for an awkward first hello. They didn't know what to say to each other. Even if they did, they didn't speak the same language. But the curiosity was still there. In fact, it had definitely grown. Maya wanted to know everything about Abdullah and his life. What was his home like? What did he do with his days?

At the time, Abdullah was working at a barbershop in the Old City's Armenian Quarter. Maya wasn't supposed to go to the Old City on her own. But she was so taken by Abdullah that she wanted to see Jerusalem through his eyes. Maya and one of her friends put on baggy Palestinian dresses to conceal their identities before they walked with Abdullah to his shop. The visits seemed dangerous and daring. Maya was sneaking away from her home—*and* doing it with a boy from across the old border. If her parents found out, she'd be in big, big trouble. But Maya wasn't afraid. She wanted to spend time with Abdullah. Maya picked up Arabic quickly. She prided herself on having a sharp enough ear to distinguish Arabic spoken by Jerusalemites and that spoken by Hebronites. Maya got to know Arabic so well that she could get Abdullah and his friends laughing by telling classic jokes about dumb Hebronites—with a Hebronite accent. Maya and Abdullah became minor neighborhood celebrities when an Italian journalist came to write about their unlikely friendship. Their photos were splashed across pages of an Italian magazine, Maya said.

But the more time Maya and Abdullah spent together, the more it became obvious that there would always be a divide between them. Religious. Cultural. Social. There were so many obstacles. At the end of the day, both of them knew what it would mean to be more than friends. It wasn't going to happen.

"We became very good friends, but I knew it would never become a romance," Maya said. "I knew enough that Jews didn't get romantic because of the religious differences. It was like we were buddies."

Over the next year or two, Maya and Abdullah drifted apart. Maya went off to study in Canada. Abdullah got married, had kids and moved to Abu Dhabi.

"We really had a great time," Abdullah said. "But it was superficial. That innocent relationship had no place in my new life."

While Maya and Abdullah's friendship dissolved, the families on both sides were getting ever closer. At the start of Passover, when the Machsomi family had to get rid of all the *chametz,* or bread, in the house to commemorate the rushed flight from Egypt, they sold it to the Yaghmours. On the last day of Passover, the Machsomi family would go to a nearby park for an afternoon picnic and come home to find that the Yaghmours had laid out a huge spread of freshly baked breads and homemade cheese, jam and fresh olives.

They weren't just neighbors. They were becoming friends. Haim did what he could to help all the Arab men who came to ask him for advice. But there was only so much one person could do. Haim wanted to do more for Abu Tor. So he took his case to City Hall. In 1969, Haim drafted a petition asking Jerusalem mayor Teddy Kollek to fix up the neighborhood. More than two dozen Arab and Jewish residents signed the appeal for the city to deal with the sewage and poor lighting in No Man's Land.[23]

The letter, believed to be the first of its kind signed by Arab and Jewish residents of a united Jerusalem, asked the mayor to help them "complete the blessed work which has begun in our quarter. . . . We are happy to be pioneers in bringing together the hearts of the two people."[24]

The bonds kept getting stronger. The Machsomis all walked across the road to celebrate Ziad's wedding. The Yaghmours piled into cars to go to Avraham's 1977 wedding at a Jerusalem wedding hall.

"The center of our life was with them," said Rachel's son Pini, the baby left behind during the 1967 war. "It wasn't like there were Jews *and* Arabs—it was Jews-and-Arabs."

The Machsomis would buy shoes for their kids from their neighbor Abed Mujahed's shoe shop in the Old City. Ziad and Avraham worked together for years at a Jerusalem printing press. Rachel brought Ziad's wife, Randa, ointments for their son's dry skin from the small medical clinic where she worked. Randa learned how to make ice cream and cakes with the Machsomis. And the Machsomis took their shot at learning to make spiced chicken and rice. When Randa's father in Hebron wanted to reach his daughter, who didn't have a telephone, he would call the Machsomi home and ask for Randa.

"[Rachel] would shout across the street that my dad was on the phone and I'd run over to talk to him," Randa said.

At times, the Machsomis' living room became an informal neighborhood music hall. Rachel and Haim would host big holiday parties and birthday celebrations. There always seemed to be music and singing coming from their home. Their cousins would come and play the sweet sounding oud, the Middle Eastern string instrument with the bent handle. The songs reminded Rachel and Haim of Iran. They reminded Rachel of her sister, Malka. Rachel always wondered what happened to her. In the late 1970s, two Iranian men came to Rachel with a message.

"We know where your sister, Malka, is," they told her. *"We can make contact if you want."*

It seemed too good to be true. She sent word: *"If you can make contact, we want to know how she is."* Rachel waited for word about her sister. But it never came. The chance to reconnect was cut short when the Shah of Iran was toppled in 1979.

"WE'RE MOVING"

Life in Abu Tor in the early 1980s for the Machsomi kids was idyllic. There were plenty of places to get lost for the afternoon and lots of friends to play with. They could go anywhere and knew everyone.

"There was no difference between Jews and Arabs," said Rivka, Rachel's seventh child, a daughter who was born, perhaps not uncoincidentally, nine months after the Israeli military victory in 1967 that brought down the fence outside their house.

"We didn't have the need for luxury like people today, but we lived really well, and we didn't lack anything," Rivka said one night at her home in 2014.

The kids would go get their hair cut in the Arab shops. Ziad's mom sold them newspaper cones filled with warmed nuts they would eat while walking home.

"The place was magical," said Liora Machsomi, who was born four years after the Six-Day War. Liora only knew about the Abu Tor dividing line from her older siblings. To her, the Arab girls across the road were just her friends on the other side of the street. Then, one day in 1983, when Rivka was 15 and Liora 11, the girls came home to find boxes in the house.

"We're moving," Rachel told them.

Rivka was shocked. It's a moment that still causes her to go a bit white when she thinks about it.

"They uprooted me from there," she said, using a blunt Hebrew word to describe leaving Assael Street.

Rivka was just starting high school when her parents decided to leave Abu Tor. She was shattered. They were moving. Not only that, they were moving out of Jerusalem to a desolate, uninviting hillside where a few thousand Israelis were setting up a new community with panoramic views of the Jordan Valley. They were calling it Ma'ale Adumim—the Red Ascent. It would become one of the country's most controversial West Bank settlements.

Israel's settlement movement had been gathering momentum since the 1967 war. Religious Jews in Israel argued that they had a G-d-given right to the newly seized West Bank. It was part of the Promised Land. They referred to the West Bank as "Judea and Samaria," embracing the biblical names for the area. Construction of what was to become the West Bank's first major settlement began three months after the Six-Day War. The following year, a small group of ultrareligious activists drove to the West Bank, rented rooms at a Hebron hotel to celebrate Passover, and refused to check out. The Israeli military responded to the protest by moving the group to a nearby military compound that eventually expanded to become Kiryat Arba, another of the most contentious West Bank settlements.

Despite international condemnation it received for building new towns on occupied land, Israel stepped up the effort. In December 1975, without official Israeli government approval, a small group of settlers drove up a hillside between Jerusalem and the Dead Sea, set up a couple of simple huts, and declared it home.

The Israelis were part of *Gush Emunim,* the "Block of the Faithful," a new, aggressive settlement group that challenged the government by repeatedly trying to seize land in the West Bank for Jewish families.

They were forced off the West Bank hillside several times but kept returning to rebuild until the Israeli government relented. In 1977, Israel's new prime minister, Menachem Begin, anointed Ma'ale Adumim as one of Israel's official settlements. By 1983, 3,500 Israelis were living in Ma'ale Adumim. Another 20,000 were living in dozens of other settlements built on confiscated and disputed West Bank land.[25]

Like Israeli general Uzi Narkiss in the 1950s, Israeli politicians in the 1980s knew that what mattered most was not the border itself "but the number of Israeli civilians living permanently on the line,"[26] so they kept moving families into Ma'ale Adumim. Toothless denunciations from friends and foes around the world didn't matter much as long as the building continued.

In 1983, the Israeli Ministry of Construction and Housing released a special promotional video to entice families interested in Ma'ale Adumim. Architect Thomas Leitersdorf stood on the rocky, treeless hillside overlooking the Judean Desert and sketched out his vision for transforming the barren land into a "garden city."[27] The Machsomis were sold. They had gotten an offer they didn't think they could refuse.

A developer offered to buy their home on Assael Street and build them a better one in Ma'ale Adumim. At the time, Israel was offering various incentives for people to move to settlements: tax breaks and benefits that made it much more affordable to build and live in places like Ma'ale Adumim. The Machsomis decided to move to the red hilltop four miles outside Jerusalem.

The Yaghmours cried as they said good-bye to the Machsomis. No two families on opposite sides of Assael Street had been closer.

"She was the best one for us as neighbors," Randa said of Rachel, Imm Ibrahim.

The Machsomi girls and boys hugged their friends and set out to start a new life a few miles away as part of the burgeoning settlement movement.

For the Machsomis, the move was more practical that political, more economic than ideological. They could get more for their money in this new Jerusalem suburb. Moving to the hilltop right outside Jerusalem, with rows of uniform red-tiled homes, didn't feel like being a settler.

As a teenager, Rivka was more concerned about making new friends than figuring out the geopolitical implications of her new home. Although she was born and raised on the old borderline in Jerusalem, Rivka hadn't spent much time learning about the changing geographic realities of the region.

"When I first came here, I didn't understand [what] the idea of a Green Line was," she said over coffee one night in 2014 at the family home in Ma'ale Adumim. "I didn't even know what the Territories were. I didn't know there *were* Territories."

To Rivka, Ma'ale Adumim was a boring Israeli frontier town, far from her friends in Abu Tor. The family spent six months in a temporary home in the settlement while construction crews finished building their new modest, one-story, four-bedroom home.

Rachel and Haim got to know their new neighbors and embraced their religion more strongly. Rachel wrapped her head in a scarf to cover her hair and started spending more time at the synagogue.

"I like it better here," Rachel said of living in Ma'ale Adumim. "I loved it when I lived there, but when I came here I like it more."

Rachel decorated the home with tall vases of plastic flowers and photographs of revered Sephardic rabbis, including Baba Sali of Morocco, a leading figure in Kabbalism, a mystical branch of Judaism that won Hollywood notoriety when pop star Madonna started studying it. Between her big goldfish tank and a living room couch, Rachel placed a large framed photograph of the son she'd lost to leukemia when he was barely 40. Right above her living room couch, Rachel hung an elongated photograph poster of the Western Wall with G-d's commandment written below: "Return to me, and I will return to you."

A NEW WAR FOR ABU TOR

The Yaghmours tried to keep in touch with the Machsomis. The first Passover the Machsomis spent in Ma'ale Adumim, the Yaghmours drove out to the settlement with big trays of breads, fruits, cheeses, olives and sweets for their old neighbors. Randa Yaghmour drank coffee with Rachel at her Ma'ale Adumim home. But it wasn't the same—for any of them. Though Ma'ale Adumim was a 25-minute drive from Abu Tor, the divide between the two was already growing.

"The kids became soldiers," Randa said of the Machsomi children.

By Israeli law, one after the other, the Machsomi kids signed up to join the army. Pini, the son Rachel had left behind in the house during the Six-Day War, started his military service soon after the family moved to Ma'ale Adumim. He eventually joined Israeli military intelligence—Unit 8200, a secretive group known for picking up everything from embarrassing phone calls from Jordanian queens to orders from Arab leaders to attack Israel. To do his job well, Pini learned Arabic. Avi never seemed to miss an opportunity to tease his younger brother about it.

"Your Arabic is better than your Hebrew," Avi told Pini more than once in their lives. Avi was the classic oldest brother who had embraced his role as the man of the family when Haim passed away at the young age of 59. Avi's sisters and brothers turned to him for perspective, direction and laughs. Avi was the only one of the Machsomi kids to stay in touch with people on Assael Street after the family moved to Ma'ale Adumim. Perhaps because he was oldest, he had the deepest connections to Abu Tor. Even after he married in 1977 and moved to Gilo, a West Bank settlement on the southern edge of Jerusalem, Avi came back to Abu Tor every Friday to play soccer at the field behind the hilltop community center.

When the Palestinian uprising gathered strength in the late 1980s, Avi stopped going down into the Arab streets in Abu Tor where he'd once played pool, gotten his hair cut and bought milk for the house.

"You couldn't get anywhere close to there," he said. "They started throwing stones. Then it was war."

Like the Machsomis, the Jacobys cut a deal with an aspiring developer and some of the family moved to a different part of Jerusalem. The Joudans stayed on in their home. And it wouldn't be long before they found themselves in the middle of a new fight for Jerusalem.

Young Palestinians in Abu Tor used the narrow stairways running between the houses during their cat-and-mouse confrontations with young Israeli soldiers, who chased them through the neighborhood. The Joudans were right on the front lines once again. Everyone knew where the Jewish part of Abu Tor really began: right outside the Joudans' door, where the barbed wire once ran. Their home was repeatedly hit by stones during the first Palestinian uprising.

"Every day we were attacked," said Yaacov, the neighbor known as Yanki who used walks with his Chihuahua, Timmy the Sixth, to keep an eye on things. "They were coming up and down and it was scary. They would break the windows and run. They'd kick the door. Every night."

Though the Palestinian stone throwing didn't touch Ma'ale Adumim, it hardened the views of the settlers living there. Palestinians from nearby villages and towns were stoning Israeli settlers and soldiers as they drove along West Bank roads. If Rachel had ever really thought there could be peace between Israelis and Palestinians, the intifada solidified her belief that it was impossible.

"I don't have faith in them," Rachel said in 2007. "They were throwing stones for no reason. They were killing people for no reason. They were killing innocent people—for no reason."

The disillusionment grew in the years that followed the first intifada. Sporadic bursts of peace talks and diplomatic progress always seemed to be the small respites between the fighting.

The lynching of two Israeli army reservists at the start of the second Palestinian uprising in 2000—the brutal mob attack whose ferocity was captured in images of one Palestinian attacker showing his bloody palms to a cheering crowd—came to encapsulate many Israelis' perception of relations with the Palestinians.

"When you get close to an Arab village, you don't want to go in because you don't know if you're going to come out," Rivka said in 2014. "It's just a few people, not one, two, three, but it's a few that are causing all this trouble. I know people who are Arabs and they're really good and you see that they want peace, too. Nobody wants this, but those people are ruining it for people on both sides. It's a pity."

By the start of the second intifada, Ma'ale Adumim's continued expansion made it seem inevitable that it would never be handed over to Palestinians in any peace deal. Israel declared Ma'ale Adumim its first official city in the West Bank after its population hit 15,000 in 1991. A decade later, its size had nearly doubled.

There always seemed to be new construction in the settlement. Red-tiled single-family homes rose in clumps alongside multistory apartment buildings. Israel built a highway link with a special tunnel to connect Ma'ale Adumim to Jerusalem. Ma'ale Adumim created everything its residents could want: malls, cafés, health clubs, pools, libraries, even its own art museum.

Developers transformed the "Founder's Circle," where the original families set up camp in 1975, into a major industrial zone that eventually housed hundreds of businesses, including SodaStream, the Israeli company that would create an international celebrity controversy by hiring American actress Scarlett Johansson as its public face.

For the most part, the Machsomis in Ma'ale Adumim were isolated from the violence outside. The armed settlement security made sure no suicide bombers got into Ma'ale Adumim.

Rachel was getting used to life in Ma'ale Adumim when she received another surprising message from Iran: Her sister Malka was alive. Rachel's relatives had tracked Malka down in Iran. They brought Rachel pictures of her sister and her two kids: a boy and a girl.

The photos brought tears to Rachel's eyes, and she thought about that day in Iran when the direction of their lives diverged forever. She wondered if she'd ever see her sister again. It seemed impossible. Malka was a citizen of a nation whose leaders saw Israel as a cancer in the Middle East that needed to be removed.

"It's just a pity that we couldn't save her," Rachel said in 2014. "We couldn't get her out."

"DEPORT THE TROUBLEMAKERS"

Rachel and her family were forever grateful that they'd left Iran. To them, Israel was a beacon of opportunity in a region filled with tyrants, dictators and kings who used fear, intimidation and ignorance to keep a thumb on their citizens. At the Israeli tax authority where she worked, Rivka saw Israeli equality day after day. She saw the Arab workers brought in under the country's affirmative action programs.

"There is that equality between Jews and Arabs," she said. "They are given opportunities to integrate into our society."

In small measures, Rivka tried to build bridges with the Arabs who worked in her office.

"We have a cleaning lady who is Arab, and I even give her my bank card so she can take out money for me," she said. "She goes in the morning and buys bread and milk for the office because we can't get out."

Rivka and her husband moved in with her mom in Ma'ale Adumim, a decision driven by financial constraints and a desire to be there for her mother as she got older. Rivka inherited her parents' hospitality gene. She always made sure her guests in the busy house—visitors, brothers, sisters, husband, nephews, nieces—had something to eat or drink: homemade soup, kibbe, warm bread, some more juice or soda, sweet tea or coffee, honey-soaked baklava . . .

When Rivka looked at the Palestinians, she saw people who appeared to be doing better than she was, people who didn't seem like they had much to complain about.

"It's not that I'm jealous, but they have everything," Rivka said. "Look at the universities. They study. They get degrees. They're doctors. They have everything. So what are they lacking? Just to rule themselves?"

So they didn't have the right to vote. Rivka wondered what more the Palestinians wanted.

"They are the best car mechanics," she said. "They are the best laborers in construction. The best builders. They're also in medicine. Manual labor. So what happens in their villages? They're dealing more with explosives there."

After decades at Ma'ale Adumim, Rivka came to see the settlements as important security buffers, especially at a time when Islamic extremists from groups like the Islamic State seemed poised to turn their sights on Israel.

"This is for our security," she said ruefully, thinking back on those days on Assael Street. "It would be so much better if there was that wonderful neighborliness, that harmony among Jews and Arabs. It was so much more fun. Today, it's really not. I remember my childhood, when we were neighbors with them, and I really miss those days. It's lacking in my life. As a child, I wasn't scared to walk around the village that was all Arabs. Today, there's no way that I would go into an Arab village."

Weary of another spiral of violence, Rivka wondered if it wasn't time for the Israeli government to start expelling troublemaking Palestinians and their families—a controversial idea known as "transfer" whose popularity has waxed and waned over the years, depending on the levels of anxiety and violence.

"The people that make problems, they need to be deported with their families so others can see and be an example," she said. "That way they'll start getting scared and then we'll live the way we should—in peace. As soon as we use power against them and deport all these problematic types, then it will be quiet."

Rivka didn't see the point of giving the Palestinians any land for a state.

"It doesn't matter how much we give them, it will never be enough," she said. "Even when we're not here, we'll always be a bother. Even if we're somewhere else, we'll always be a nuisance: because we're Jews."

Of Rachel's kids, Pini, who spent his career in the Israeli military, grew up to be the most conciliatory. Pini saw the inequities. There was no question: Jews living in West Jerusalem had it better than the Arabs in East Jerusalem.

"If we compare the infrastructure in the Jewish and Arab neighborhoods, I also wouldn't accept that type of discrimination," Pini told his oldest brother and sisters one night in 2014 at their mother's home in Ma'ale Adumim. "You see the differences very clearly. It's logical that there will be bitterness."

Pini's military intelligence work in the occupied West Bank led him to the Jordan Valley where he met regularly with people like Saeb Erekat, one of the Palestinians' leading political negotiators. There seemed to be plenty of common ground between them when they met. Perhaps because he knew Arabic well and spent so much time in the West Bank, Pini saw Palestinians as more than bloodthirsty extremists scheming to destroy Israel.

When tensions were low, Pini took some of his siblings into Jericho for lunch at a local restaurant run by some Palestinians he knew from work.

Jericho was one of the first places freed from direct Israeli military control after the 1993 Oslo Accords set the stage for the rise of the Palestinian

Authority. To the Machsomis, the humid town, surrounded by miles of date palms, was a city of legend, the first target Moses chose for attack when he sent Joshua and his army to conquer biblical Canaan as the Israelites fled from slavery in Egypt.

For days, according to the Bible, Joshua and his soldiers marched around Jericho's walls with priests carrying the Ark of the Covenant. On the seventh day, the priests blew their ram's horns, the shofar, until Jericho's walls came tumbling down. Joshua and his army slaughtered almost everyone in the city, man, woman and child.[28]

The Machsomis were excited and anxious to be driving into Jericho. It was like putting their heads in a lion's mouth. They trusted Pini, but they knew things could always go bad very quickly. When they arrived at the restaurant, Avi was stunned to hear Pini talking to the owners in flawless Arabic.

"I felt for a second that it wasn't my brother," Avi said of Pini. "He spoke better than the Arabs."

Because of his sympathies, because of his command of Arabic, Pini had always been something of a black sheep in the family. His younger sister Liora became one of the most religious kids. She got married at 18, had eight kids by the time she was 40, and became a grandmother at 43. She started wearing a tight wrap to cover her hair and long, plain skirts—a style often associated with religious settlers. In time, she became one of those who believed that Jews had a biblical, G-d-given right to the land. To Tel Aviv. To Jerusalem. To Hebron. To Nablus. To Jericho.

"It's our land," she said. "They need to understand that it's ours."

A little bit of freedom emboldened the Palestinians, she said, giving them the courage to create chaos.

Liora's animosity increased in the summer of 2014 when three Israeli teenagers hitchhiking in the West Bank were kidnapped and killed.

"They came from Halhoul, by the way," said Avi, who found no small irony in the fact that the killers came from the same village in which he and his family were treated like royalty by their Arab neighbors from Assael Street in 1967.

The kidnapping of the three teens was followed by the abduction and murder of 16-year-old Palestinian Mohammed Abu Khdeir, a seven-week war in Gaza, and a spike in lone-wolf attacks in Jerusalem that ignited concerns that Israelis and Palestinians were heading for a third Palestinian uprising.

"They run over little girls, they run over soldiers," said Liora, who backed Israel in 2014 when it resurrected its controversial policy of demolishing the family homes of Palestinian assailants. "If we don't do something to them when they murder us, then they will continue. It's a contagious disease."

Liora lampooned the Israeli government for not cracking down hard enough on the troublemakers.

"They are the wise men of Chelm," she said, harking back to the Jewish folkloric image of fools. "They are not dealing with the root of the problem."

"How do you solve the problem?" Pini asked his sisters in Ma'ale Adumim at the end of a long night talking with his siblings about their childhood in Abu Tor.

"Deport them," Rivka said.

"Deport whom?" Pini asked. "Whom?"

"I am telling you, this land is ours," Liora told Pini. "I have no problem taking care of their infrastructure. They should live. They have children too. They should have property, because it's hard to live. But this land is ours, and they should not give even a little piece of it to them."

If Liora was in charge, Israel would expel the troublemakers and allow only the few who risked their lives to protect Jewish people, the modern-day "righteous gentiles," to remain. Asked if that would include her childhood friend from Assael, Samira, Liora was noncommittal.

"I'd have to see her first," said Liora, who liked to remember Assael as she'd left it.

"I want it in my imagination to be the way it was when I lived there," she said. "I was really happy there. Now it's not the same, even if Jews and Arabs do live next to each other."

THE NEXT DIVIDING LINE

That was certainly true on Assael, where the Joudans walled themselves off from their old friends and neighbors across the street. They encouraged the city to install a thick iron door to close off the stairway that ran past their home. The barrier prevented Palestinians from lower Abu Tor from using the path as a shortcut through the neighborhood. It cut off the only path on Assael Street connecting the Jewish hilltop to the Arab hillside.

Yanki gained a reputation as the guy who "kept an eye" on his Arab neighbors. Like his mom, Yanki didn't think twice about calling Israeli authorities to report Arabs across the way whom he suspected of illegally building on their own property. The Abu Tor of today, he said in 2014, was not the Abu Tor of yesteryear. Too much had happened since then to bridge the divide: years of stone-throwing; Palestinians cheering for Iraqi leader Saddam Hussein in the first Gulf War; suicide bombings; rockets from Gaza; a guy from Abu Tor, Mu'atez Hijazi, trying to kill a right-wing Israeli. It all made one thing clear to Yanki: You can't trust Arabs.

"My mom helped a lot," Yanki said. "My mother and father helped so many times. But, you know what? When I see the bombs explode, when I see my fucking neighbor here killing a guy in the city, Hijazi, when my neighbor was clapping and singing 'Bomb Tel Aviv,' I hate them all."

Yanki didn't see his neighbors across the street as people who wanted peace. He saw an ungrateful community that had forgotten who brought them electricity, who brought them paved roads, who brought them running water, who brought them jobs and medical care and a life better than anything they could have dreamed of under Arab rule.

"They don't know," Yanki said. "They grew up like this, so they want America. But they don't know that their parents already got America—from Israel."

If they weren't happy in Abu Tor and they wanted to live under Palestinian rule, Yanki said, his neighbors could move to the Gaza Strip and deal with its militant Hamas government.

"They don't know what it is to suffer," he said of his Arab neighbors. "So that's why I tell them: 'Go to Gaza. That's the way you're supposed to live until now. Then, appreciate it: Israel.' They don't. They don't want to live like me. They want to take over me."

Like Yanki, Avi Machsomi lost faith in peace talks. He came to question the idea that giving up land would really solve fundamental problems. But he was willing to let go of some areas—those places where Jewish people didn't go. Avi ticked off the impoverished East Jerusalem neighborhoods he'd be willing to give to the Palestinians: Shufat. Jabal Muqaber. Issawaya.

"I don't want them," he said. "They can stay there. We can put a fence up."

It was a plan with practical benefits for every Israeli driver.

"There will be more space on the road," he said. "It's not because I am a racist. There are Arabs that I work with that I really love. But there are other Arabs, let them stay there."

Avi was ten when the fence came down in Abu Tor and the neighborhood underwent its renaissance. But that environment, he said, was almost impossible to re-create. He especially felt the divide with the neighboring Palestinian town of Azariya, on the hillside between Ma'ale Adumim and Jerusalem.

"When we grew up in the neighborhood it was Jews and Arabs, living together," Avi said. "Now I can't be friends with those in Azariya. I work with a lot of Arabs and we get along. If it was us and them trying to make peace, we'd have peace in a week. There would be no problems. No problems. Because we talk. We talk like friends and we work together. When I talk to them I ask: 'Why? We can do it this way. You eat with us. We're together.' If we, Arabs and Jews, the simple people, would sit, there would be peace. It would be completely different. I don't see any problem when we talk—Jews and Arabs. The problem is the hatred and the incitement. If I go to Azariya, I don't know if I will come back. On the other hand, if they come here, it's great for them. They have a nice time. They have fun."

In 2014, Avi figured he'd probably be OK if he went to Azariya, but he wasn't certain.

"There are Arabs, even if I go to Azariya, they will help me," he said. "But we can't trust them, because we don't know who we will run into over there."

Unbeknownst to the Machsomis, their old neighbors from Assael Street were living in Azariya. It was where the Bazlamits built their small apartment building on the edge of town, where Israel built the 26-foot-tall concrete walls that cut them off from Jerusalem. The wall that had cut the Bazlamits' property in Azariya out of Jerusalem just kept growing. The line was gerrymandered to run a jagged route across the rocky hilltops of the Judean Desert and enclose Ma'ale Adumim and the Machsomis.

Eventually, the wall was supposed to grow to put the Machsomis on one side, inside Israel, and the Bazlamits in Azariya on the other.

By and large, the Machsomis came to see the new dividing line as an unfortunate necessity. And if the Palestinians wanted a state, they were going to have to accept the new realities. For the Machsomis, Ma'ale Adumim and the other settlements in the West Bank would always be part of Israel.

"There's nothing they can do," Avi said. "This is the situation."

Avi dismissed claims from Palestinian farmers in Azariya that parts of Ma'ale Adumim were built on their fields.

"Here it was just desert," he said. "There wasn't a house here, so why didn't they do anything here before? Now we've built here. It is what it is. There's nothing you can do."

Whereas his sisters were uncompromising on what they would be willing to give up to resolve decades of tumult, Avi was not. If push came to shove, he said, he'd be willing to give up Ma'ale Adumim. Really.

"They can have Ma'ale Adumim," he said as his incredulous sisters showered him with friendly insults. "Do I really care? My real hope is that we live in peace and that they can come to our house. That's the dream. My dream is that we live in peace and that we'll live together, without hatred. No slogans."

While the Machsomis stayed close to Jerusalem, Maya Joudan moved to Canada, where she and her brother Itzik both settled with their families. Like Pini Machsomi, Maya took great pride in her knowledge of Arabic and the relations she'd forged on Assael Street.

"I had more trust in them than my own people," she said. "I will do anything with them with huge trust in my heart."

Unfortunately, Maya said, it didn't run both ways. If Jordan had won the war in 1967, how would they have treated the Israelis?

"If it was the other way around, for one moment do you think that they would come to our home and help us?" she asked. "Do you think that they would stop the donkeys going to the well and put running water in their homes? That they would put lights in the street? Do you think they would come and introduce us to proper lighting? That they started having stoves? They went above us so quickly. Do you think they would have done that?"

No, she said. They had much to be grateful for. So did she. Maya looked back on her childhood in Abu Tor and saw a certain kind of paradise.

On one visit home, Maya came across the beautiful Palestinian embroidery stolen from one Arab house in 1967. The cloth sat for years in a closet at her childhood home in Abu Tor. Maya decided to bring it back to Vancouver. It had been sitting in the darkness long enough. Maya carefully ironed the hand-embroidered flower and put a cut-out photograph of her son when he was three years old in the middle. She put it in a frame and hung it above her bed in Vancouver. Something, she said, to remind her of her heritage.

"This is my past," Maya said. "And you need to surround yourself with things that mean something to you."

FIVE

THE COLLABORATOR

A *meel.*

The slur followed him everywhere he went.

Friends would whisper it behind his back with a hiss.

Ameeeeel.

Assailants would shout it from the street as they tossed Molotov cocktails at his house. Guys would spray-paint the warning, the implied threat, on the stone walls outside his home on Assael Street:

Collaborator.

*Beware of the collaborator: Abu Fadi.**

To call someone a collaborator in Jerusalem is to make them a marked man. Abu Fadi wore it as a badge of honor. He wielded it as a weapon. He used the fear his neighbors on Assael Street had of collaborators to intimidate. He was not cowed. He was proud.

Sitting in his dimly lit living room smoking cigarettes and playing backgammon with a friend one afternoon in 2007, Abu Fadi said he didn't care what his Arab neighbors thought of him. As far as he was concerned, they could move to some other Middle East nation and live under one Arab tyrant or another.

---

*The names of Abu Fadi and his family have been changed.

"Israel is the best country in the world," he said between rolls of the dice. "Period."

If someone asked Abu Fadi whether he preferred to be called an Arab-Israeli, a Palestinian-Israeli or a Palestinian, he would choke on the question.

"I'm Israeli," he said, again and again. "One hundred percent Israeli."

With the thick living room curtains drawn, Abu Fadi sat on the edge of his couch in dress pants and a sleeveless white T-shirt that showed off a heart-shaped tattoo on his shoulder. His den felt claustrophobic, and the smoke choked the room. It seemed like Abu Fadi had embraced his reputation as a small-time thug. He silently sized up strangers while sitting on his chocolate-colored fabric couch set with fake gold frames.

Abu Fadi pointed to a wood carving hanging on the living room wall.

"See that?" he asked.

It was the shank-shaped map of Palestine as it existed under British rule until 1948, the land meant at that time to be split so two new countries—Israel and Palestine—could live side by side. The image is ubiquitous in Palestinian iconography. It serves as a reminder that there was once, not so long ago, a place called Palestine. Uncompromising Palestinian nationalists hold up the old lines as borders they hope to reclaim someday by eliminating Israel from the map. Abu Fadi looked at the image and saw something else.

"That," he said, "is Israel."

Not Palestine. Not Israel and Palestine. Just Israel.

It's a view not even Israeli moderates imagine when they look at the image. It's the view of the most uncompromising of Israelis who see the land—*all* of the land—as the G-d-given property of the Jewish people. It's the kind of thing you hear from armed Israeli settlers living in illegal West Bank trailer park compounds where they have defied their own government to seize more land.

Abu Fadi didn't care that Jews didn't consider him one of G-d's Chosen People. He was Israeli. A full Israeli citizen, unlike most of his neighbors on the eastern side of Assael Street. That gave him a right most of them didn't have: to vote in Israel's national elections. For him, that was more than enough.

Abu Fadi didn't just cast his own ballot in Israel's national elections. He helped get out the vote for the party he loyally backed: Likud. The political party that gave life to Israel's settlement movement. The party of Ariel Sharon, known as the "Butcher of Beirut," who was forced to resign as Israel's defense minister after being held personally responsible for the 1982 massacre of thousands of Palestinians in the city's Sabra and Shatila refugee camps. Likud was the party of Yitzhak Shamir, who helped kill British officers ruling Palestine in the 1930s, rose to become prime minister and helped champion the settlement movement that methodically gobbled up parts of the West Bank and Gaza Strip. More than anything, for Abu Fadi, Likud was the party of Benjamin Netanyahu, the man who sent Israeli spies to Jordan in 1997 to try to kill Hamas militant leader Khaled Mashal, and the prime minister many held responsible for sparking the 1996 "Tunnel Riots."

Abu Fadi's modern political hero was Netanyahu: *Bibi*. Abu Fadi's truth-teller. An Israeli Ronald Reagan who believed that the only way to peace was through strength.

"Likud is the only party that can bring peace," he said.

Abu Fadi was a Likudnik through and through. He religiously attended Likud Party meetings. He collected photographs of himself shaking hands with Likud's luminaries as if they were baseball cards of his favorite players. He had an autographed picture from Bibi. He had photos with Ehud Olmert, the Jerusalem mayor who became prime minister in 2006. Abu Fadi faithfully voted Likud. And he made sure that his wife did too. Abu Fadi proudly called himself a "son of the state." A son of Israel.

"What I like is the freedom," he said. "Only in Israel can you say what you think."

THE POLITICAL PUGILIST OF ASSAEL

Abu Fadi was the political pugilist of Assael. He bulldozed people with views so extreme his neighbors didn't know what to say. He was to the right of most Israelis when it came to the idea of a Palestinian state. Although much of his family lived in Hebron, although his youngest brother became a member of the Palestinian Authority police force, Abu Fadi was opposed to the creation of an independent Palestine. Sometimes he even pushed the extremists' argument that the Palestinians were an invented people with no historic claims to a land once called Palestine.

He was aghast at the Hamas takeover of the Gaza Strip after Israeli forces removed all of the country's settlers from the Mediterranean enclave in 2005. To him, the 2007 takeover was a sign that Palestinians should never be allowed to govern themselves, that they would always pose a risk to Israel.

"I have not recognized the Palestinians as a people, let alone their state," he said. "They have Gaza—that's enough for them. It's even too big for them."

Abu Fadi wasn't willing to cede more ground to Palestinian politicians for any proposed peace deal. He saw it the way uncompromising Israelis saw the landscape.

"There are 22 Arab countries," he said. "They have a lot of land. Israel is small."

Abu Fadi arrived on Assael Street with a fearsome reputation—one he did little to dispel.

"It was known at the time that he was a collaborator," said Judith Green, who moved to the street above Assael in the 1980s, shortly before Abu Fadi arrived in the neighborhood. "We found out that he was planted there as a scout, a kind of lookout, to keep an eye on the streets below."

Abu Fadi became part of the neighborhood when he married Imm Fadi. He was 21. She was 17. Imm Fadi's family was woven into the fabric of Abu Tor, from the ridgeline to the valley below. Her father bought the property on Assael Street when it was being used as a temporary sheep stable. When Imm Fadi got married, her new husband paid the property taxes and transformed the shell of a building into their new home.

By the time he moved to Assael Street in the 1990s, Abu Fadi's thick, wavy hair was beginning to give way, leaving behind small brown patches above his ears and random strands that did nothing to conceal his baldness. Abu Fadi seemed suspicious, wary of people's intentions and always prepared to defend his views.

Before Abu Fadi and his family moved to Assael, their neighbors said, they had been run out of two other communities.

In the late 1970s, Abu Fadi and his wife moved to Al Ram, a small West Bank town between Jerusalem and Ramallah. Abu Fadi started working with the town's Israeli-backed Village League, a move seen by Palestinian nationalists at the time as working for the enemy.

The Village Leagues were Israel's equivalent of South Africa's Apartheid-era Bantustans—they were efforts to prop up co-opted allies in constrained positions of power meant to retain Israel's political and military dominance over the Palestinians.

The Village Leagues were created during Likud's first years as Israel's ruling party. Israel picked the members of the Village Leagues and chose people it thought would be malleable allies who could counter the influence of Yasser Arafat and the Palestine Liberation Organization.

Members of the Village Leagues were given enough power and support to clamp down on their fellow Palestinians. They grilled drivers at checkpoints. They acted as the security arm of the Israeli government. They were textbook examples of collaborators.

It was an accusation that Abu Fadi was willing to fight over. Again and again. Abu Fadi's views didn't win him much favor with his neighbors. Neither did the stories that came to Assael with him.

No one on Assael sowed more confusion than Abu Fadi. He quietly reported his neighbors when they tried to build new verandas for their houses without securing building permits from the city. He argued with them over parking and politics. People on the street heard shouts and screams from Abu Fadi's house that hinted at violent fights inside. They got used to seeing Abu Fadi wave his gun when things on the street got tense.

"Abu Fadi scared everybody," his wife said. "They would fear him."

Abu Fadi spent hours smoking and drinking coffee at his neighbors' houses. Though they saw Abu Fadi as a collaborator, the families on Assael repeatedly turned to him for advice. They asked for help getting construction permits from the city. They asked him how to prevent the city from demolishing their homes. Sometimes he'd help. Sometimes he wouldn't. He could be mercurial in deciding when and for whom he would step in.

"He would control them," Imm Fadi said. "He had a controlling personality."

"THE ANACONDA OF ASSAEL"

For many, Abu Fadi was like a dark cloud hanging over the street. When there were problems on Assael, they were more often between Abu Fadi and his Arab neighbors than between Arab and Jewish residents of the street.

"Abu Fadi is the black snake of the neighborhood," said one of his Arab neighbors on Assael. "The Anaconda."

Unlike the other Arab homeowners on the street, Abu Fadi had no problems getting the permits he needed in the 1980s to build a new house for his family to replace the abandoned ruins on his wife's family land. That only fueled suspicions that Abu Fadi was a collaborator. Abu Fadi did little to dissuade his neighbors from having that notion.

"If there was a problem, Abu Fadi could fix it," Imm Fadi said.

It was better to be on Abu Fadi's good side. Those who weren't, those who knew his reputation, made sure that Abu Fadi didn't feel welcome on Assael Street.

In Jerusalem, there could be no greater disgrace for anyone—Palestinian or Israeli—than to be called a collaborator. A traitor to your country. To your people. To your religion.

Jerusalem has been the setting for some of history's most epic betrayals.

King David's son Absalom betrayed his father and stole his throne. The Abu Tor hillside is said to be the place where David's spies waited for word from allies inside the city walls about the fate of the kingdom.

Down the valley from Abu Tor, Judas betrayed Jesus Christ with a kiss in the Garden of Gethsemane. Some say Judas then hanged himself in the Valley of Slaughter below Abu Tor.

Like the Bible, history is rarely kind to collaborators.

French women who collaborated with Nazi occupiers during World War II had their heads publicly shaved before they were paraded through a dangerous gauntlet of men spitting taunts and threats. In the fight to create Israel, Jewish militants killed dozens of Jews accused of helping British rulers in Palestine.

The fate of small-time collaborators could be just as unforgiving.

During the fight against South Africa's racist Apartheid regime in the 1980s, black activists would fill rubber tires with gasoline, force them over the heads of suspected collaborators and set them ablaze. The deadly tactic was known as "necklacing."

Palestinian collusion with Zionists working to establish the state of Israel was so controversial that religious scholars issued a decree in 1935 meant to stop Muslims from selling land to Jewish buyers. The *fatwa* declared that anyone who sold land to Jewish buyers was not only taking land from Muslims, they were "a traitor to Allah."[1]

Collaborators were deemed heretics who should be shunned, if not killed, even if the collaborator was your son, father, sister or mother. Their crimes were so great, the scholars declared, that they were to be denied a Muslim burial.[2]

The stigma only got worse after 1948. Palestinians developed different terms for collaborators: Agent. Informant. Land dealer.

They all became targets. They were ostracized and demonized. They would be killed in the cruelest of ways. Lynch mobs pulled them from their homes and hanged them from lampposts. Their bodies were dragged through the streets behind slow-moving motorcycles for all to see.

Ameel.

During the first intifada, when Abu Fadi and his family moved to Assael, more than 700 suspected Palestinian collaborators were killed in the West Bank and Gaza Strip. The backlash against those who sided with Israel increased during the second intifada.

In 2001, as the al Aqsa Intifada was intensifying, Yasser Arafat oversaw the execution of two accused Palestinian collaborators. One was shot dead in Gaza City. The other was killed in Nablus, one city at the center of the uprising. Thousands gathered in the West Bank town's square to watch six masked Palestinian Authority police officers shoot the man. Palestinian leaders justified the killings as unfortunate outgrowths of the fight for freedom.[3]

"The collaborator betrays his own people either because he is in a position of weakness and suffering (i.e., under torture or in need of health care during detention, etc.) and/or perceives the occupying power to be invincible, and he and his people are hopelessly weak," wrote Palestinian historian Saleh Abdel Jawad in an article at the time of the second intifada titled "The Classification and Recruitment of Collaborators."[4]

"This is why if we look today it is difficult to find Israelis who collaborate with Palestinians," he wrote. "However there are many cases of Jews who collaborated with the Nazis, because at the time, the Jews were also in a position of similar weakness."

Jawad's piece was part of a one-day conference held in 2001 to discuss what participants saw as the insidious role of collaborators in undermining the Palestinian uprising.

"The Palestinian collaborator is an expression of Israel's larger 'defense' policies," he wrote in his presentation. "Israel is one of those preeminent countries, whose interest in acquiring information has historically acted as a main part of its military power and as a means of control. Collaborators are a part of this process of information gathering alongside the satellites, sensitive listening equipment, wiretapping, unmanned drones, not to mention access to data from schools, banks and other bureaucratic paper trails.

"The Palestinian collaborator in the Israeli strategy also serves the purpose of creating mistrust, spreading confusion and undermining collective self-confidence within Palestinian society."[5]

Ameel.

"THEY SLAUGHTERED US"

More than once, Abu Fadi's home was hit by Molotov cocktails. Abu Fadi enclosed the front of his house in iron shutters that made it look like a movie-sized armored tank. But the attacks still kept coming.

Some nights the family would be awoken by the sound of shattered glass and stones slamming into their roof, a reminder of the hatred and hostility right outside their door.

Some mornings they would come out to find new graffiti scrawled on the stone walls of Assael Street: *Beware of the collaborator: Abu Fadi.*

Perhaps the biggest confrontation on the street took place when Abu Fadi's family got into a feud with one of the neighbors over borrowed holiday lights.

Abu Fadi had loaned strings of lights to the Mujahed family a few doors down so they could hang them for a wedding. It was a common courtesy on a street where someone always seemed to be hosting a celebration of a wedding, birthday or religious holiday. This time, the lights didn't come back right away. After a month of waiting, one of Abu Fadi's sons went by to find out where they were. Ramadan was coming up and his family wanted the lights back to decorate their home. The young Mujahed searched his house and found a bag of lights. But they weren't the right ones.

The two young men started arguing. Their voices rose as they threw insults at each other. The younger Mujahed said something about Imm Fadi, an affront about his neighbor's mom that he probably knew might trigger a neighborhood brawl. And it did. Curses gave way to pushes, pushes turned into punches. Then came the bats and stones. Blood spattered the stone stairs and iron gates as the brawl spilled out onto the cobblestone street. The families issued calls for help—for reinforcements. Dozens of friends and relatives rushed to Assael to join the fight. Abu Fadi waved his gun around as assailants forced their way into his house and rampaged through the rooms.

"They slaughtered us," Imm Fadi said.

Stones smashed into metal gates and car windows. The shouts, screams, curses and accusations woke the neighborhood. Israeli soldiers and police eventually turned up and people scattered. They brought out their dogs to search Abu Fadi's home for weapons. Abu Fadi and his sons were hauled off to jail, along with some of the neighbors.

"It was terrible," said Sara Arnold, who was at her home on the western side of Assael as the feud cascaded down the street. "I heard shots. I didn't know if it was firecrackers or not."

Sara, a prim, short-haired blond with glasses that accented her schoolteacher demeanor, counted herself one of Israel's liberals. She backed the idea of a Palestinian state and worked with young Palestinian students in poor Jerusalem neighborhoods like Beit Hanina. She opposed Israeli settlements in the West Bank and didn't think much of Netanyahu. She'd moved to a small place on Assael Street in the late 1990s when things with Israelis and Palestinians seemed to be heading in the right direction. Netanyahu and Arafat signed peace deals—and violence appeared to be on the wane.

There was a sense that Israelis and Palestinians might not have to live their lives in perpetual conflict. Maybe. Sara and other Jewish residents of Abu Tor would walk down a few blocks to buy things from the Palestinian shops where boys from Assael would hang out.

After the street fight, Sara ran into a couple of them at the store. She wasn't sure which families they came from, but her teacher instincts kicked in.

"You don't know what you're doing to your little brothers and sisters," she told them. *"You don't know what you're doing to all the little kids on the road. I saw them running into their houses. They're going to have nightmares for years about that."*

The boys laughed at Sara and blew her off. That only fueled her frustrations. To her, Assael was an ideal place to live. The street brawls made her think twice.

"Stupid," she said of the brawl. "That is a terrible part of their culture."

Sara wasn't willing to accept that kind of violence as a normal part of neighborhood living.

"It shocked me," she said. "I worked in Bethlehem and Beit Hanina and I hadn't seen that kind of violence. That was just really a childish kind of violence."

It didn't matter much what people like Sara thought. Abu Fadi and his sons weren't afraid to settle a problem with a street fight. The neighbors would get into confrontations over the smallest of things. One American couple living on the street took to calling them the "Friday Night Fights." One of the biggest triggers was parking—something that was always in short supply on the street.

Because it had once been little more than a ridgeline trail, Assael was so narrow that it was impossible for cars to park on both sides without blocking the street. Most of the families on the western side of Assael had off-street parking garages. And street parking on the west side of Assael was banned. The best place to park was at the end of the cul-de-sac, where about a dozen cars could park in a line under a 15-foot-tall pink stone wall on the western side of the street, below the Goeli home where the UN had prevented the Great Toilet Fight of 1966 from becoming the trigger for a bigger problem. But the lot was often full, especially at night when everyone was home.

Everyone on the eastern side of the street jealously guarded the parking spots outside their homes. Families hung hand-painted "No Parking" signs from their fences and rushed out to shout at people who ignored the warnings. As surveillance technology evolved and the prices for high-tech equipment dropped, families on Assael installed cameras outside their houses. One after the other, the residents of Assael Street set up security cameras with the lenses trained on their parking spaces and front doors. Some families ran the live feed on their television sets while they did other things around the house. So it's no surprise that one of the biggest battles on the street between Abu Fadi and his neighbors started as a fight over parking.

One afternoon in 2009, one of the Mujahed boys parked outside Abu Fadi's home. One of Abu Fadi's sons came out to tell him to move it—and things quickly got out of hand. The bad blood between the two families had thickened. Neither guy was willing to back down. Abed Mujahed came out to defend his son. Abu Fadi came out to protect his boy. Abed said he was thrown down his front steps by Abu Fadi when his neighbor stormed into their house. Abu Fadi's sons said they were pelted with stones and left with bloody gashes on their faces. Israeli police arrived and hauled men from both families off to jail.

When tempers cooled, members of a neighborhood reconciliation committee, a sulha, tried to mediate. They heard from both families and decided that Abed was in the wrong. They told Abed to pay Abu Fadi $2,500. For Abed, it was the final indignity. He stopped talking to Abu Fadi's family altogether.

SINS OF THE FATHERS AND THEIR SONS

Though most of the people on Assael Street only knew Abu Fadi by reputation, there was one man who knew his history intimately: Hijazi Bazlamit, the grandson of the man shot dead on the Abu Tor hillside in 1951. The younger Hijazi and Abu Fadi shared a common history in more ways than one. Their past went back much further than this street. Back to the days when they were both young men, about the same age, trying to figure out how to adjust to life under Israeli rule.

Like Abu Fadi, Hijazi had cast his fortunes with Israel as a young man. More than anyone else on the street, because of his work as an Israeli policeman, Hijazi knew what it felt like to be called a collaborator. But the two had met even earlier. Hijazi had hired Abu Fadi to work with him at a small vegetable market. The partnership soured when Hijazi accused Abu Fadi of stealing from him. That set the tone for the two men's tangled, lifelong relationship. Although Hijazi had spent years enforcing Israeli laws, he had no sympathy for what he considered to be Abu Fadi's betrayal.

"It is well known that the Israeli occupation seeks to find people who are vulnerable, and he was the perfect case," Hijazi said.

Hijazi traced Abu Fadi's corrosive life to his childhood, from a sober young boy who was beaten by his father to a young man who fled an abusive home and found a new beginning working for Israel.

"They started giving him money," he said of the Israeli government. "They started asking for information. They found out that he had the perfect appetite for that kind of work."

The two didn't cross paths again until the late 1980s, when Hijazi started moonlighting as a part-time security guard for the editor of a small East Jerusalem newspaper.

"My first day on the job, they came to me and said: 'We'd like to introduce you to the head of security,'" he said. "I was shocked to see [Abu Fadi], because I knew he wasn't a clean man."

The two men didn't talk about their past as they worked out security for the editor. When the newspaperman had to get around town, Hijazi would drive in the front of the convoy and Abu Fadi would provide security in the back.

After a few weeks on the job, Hijazi said Abu Fadi came to him with a proposal. Abu Fadi was worried that the editor would get rid of his security, so he came up with a plan to stage an attack on his convoy. Hijazi wanted no part of it. He told the editor of the plan, but his boss wanted proof. When the day of the planned ambush arrived, Hijazi said he thwarted the attack by leading the convoy down another route. He was fired by Abu Fadi that day. But that wasn't the end of the incident. Not long after he was fired, Hijazi said he was heading home from work when a car pulled up alongside him and opened fire. The shots missed, and Hijazi sped off after his attacker. He knew who it was before the cars pulled up outside Abu Fadi's home.

"I chased him, I hit him, and I hit him some more," Hijazi said. "His wife and children were begging me to stop."

Hijazi said he left Abu Fadi bruised and beaten in his home. Hijazi thought that might be the end of it—until Abu Fadi moved to Assael Street a few years later.

"I couldn't believe it," Hijazi said. "How has he moved into this house? On my street?"

Their history clouded their families' relations. And it soon carried over into their sons' relationships as well.

"He found an excellent opportunity to take revenge," Hijazi said.

The hostility between the two men constantly simmered. Abu Fadi accused Hijazi's young sons of spray-painting the threatening "beware of the collaborator" graffiti on Assael Street.

"If you think my sons did it, then take it to the police," Hijazi defiantly told Abu Fadi.

Things came to a head one day in 2010 when Hijazi's son, Ahmad, confronted Abu Fadi's oldest son about an unpaid debt. The argument quickly got physical and Ahmad took a swing at Fadi. The two families agreed to take part in a neighborhood sulha, but it did almost nothing to defuse the situation. To the Bazlamits, it was a neighborhood fight over money. To Abu Fadi, it was a politically motivated attack. Israeli prosecutors accused Ahmad of plotting to kill a collaborator, Hijazi said.

"They made it into a political issue, but my son didn't intend to escalate things," Hijazi said.

Disputes kept breaking out and the two families wound up on opposite sides of a courtroom more than once. One time, the Bazlamits asked an Israeli judge to kick Abu Fadi off Assael Street. They accused Abu Fadi and his sons of spreading rumors and lies about the Bazlamits.

"Please, Your Honor," Hijazi asked the judge. *"For the sake of our family, for the sake of our neighborhood, please remove them from the area. We aren't the ones creating the problem. They are."*

The courts tried to keep the two families apart by telling them to steer clear of each other on the street, Hijazi said. But Assael was so small that it was impossible to do. Abu Fadi and his family couldn't drive to their home on the dead-end street without going past the Bazlamits.

When Abu Fadi died of cancer in 2011, Hijazi thought that might be the end of it.

"None of us went to the mourning when he died," said Hijazi, who saw Abu Fadi as a traitor to his people, someone unworthy of a Muslim burial. "We're not supposed to drink with him. We're not supposed to eat with him. He harmed his people, so we refused to have anything to do with his farewell."

Hijazi wasn't the only one who was silently grateful that Abu Fadi was gone. Abed Mujahed was also thankful to be rid of a man who had been the source of so many problems for him and his family.

"When he died, the neighbors came and said: 'Let's offer some condolences,'" Abed said. "I refused."

Abu Fadi's wife and kids tried to repair some of the rifts with their neighbors on the street. But the underlying hostility continued to resurface.

"I told my children to be careful," Hijazi said.

When Israeli forces came once again in 2013 to arrest Ahmad and accused him of being part of a plan to kidnap a soldier, Hijazi figured he knew who had informed on his son.

It didn't matter that Abu Fadi was dead; fairly or not, Hijazi still feared the family. Every day his son is in an Israeli cell, Hijazi is reminded of the absence in his home. He keeps photos of Ahmad, shaved head, dressed in a dark-blue track suit, on the mantle near the television. Hijazi spends his days watching TV in his living room, right outside Ahmad's empty bedroom where Israeli police broke through the window during their second house raid. Ahmad's wife and young son sometimes sleep there, on the twin bed with the thin mattress, below a silver frame with wavy rays of sun emanating from a picture of the young couple.

The Bazlamits visit Ahmad in the high-security Israeli prison whenever they can. But it's a long trek. And they can't stand seeing Ahmad through the thick prison glass, knowing that Israeli intelligence officials are listening to every word they say, looking for evidence to keep Ahmad behind bars even longer.

"There is a state of quiet, and sometimes a state of quiet scares you more than the other way around," Hijazi said. "It's like the sea. You can see when a sea is tumultuous. But it's the sea that appears calm that might drown you."

A SECOND LIFE IN ABU TOR

Abu Fadi's final years were painful and private. As the cancer spread through his body, Abu Fadi spent more and more time in his home office going through his papers. He started getting rid of everything. Photos. Letters. Memos. Abu Fadi made sure that he took most of his secrets with him when he died.

"I don't think he wanted people to know who he was," his wife said. "He didn't want me to know very much either."

When Abu Fadi was gone, vandals stole two of the three security cameras he'd installed to keep watch outside his house. Mostly, Imm Fadi stopped paying attention to the live video feeds. But she didn't feel entirely safe. One afternoon she saw a young man who'd scaled the front wall and the iron shutters to get onto their tile roof. She thought the guy was Jewish, but she couldn't be sure. Whatever the case, she later had coils of razor wire strung out along the edge of her roof to prevent anyone else from climbing over. The barbed wire returned to Assael. And Imm Fadi launched a new chapter in her life. She stopped constantly wearing the head scarf her husband always told her to wear when she went out. She learned the Hebrew her husband had prevented her from studying. She started looking after elderly Israelis and made some money to support her family. Imm Fadi packed what was left of Abu Fadi's political paraphernalia and gave it to one of her sons. She did what she could to move on.

But Abu Fadi's presence still loomed over the house. Imm Fadi hung a large portrait of her late husband above the television in the living room, right below a pair of exposed fluorescent lights that cast his stern, unsmiling gaze in an unflattering yellow pallor.

Every time she or her kids sat down on the leopard-print-covered couches to watch the flat-screen television mounted on the wall, Abu Fadi looked down on them with the same dour look he had flashed at people his entire adult life.

"No one accepted him as he was," his wife said one night in her living room. "When people needed him, he was a good man. When they didn't need him anymore, he wasn't important."

Imm Fadi thought the trajectory of history had proven her husband right in choosing the Israeli side of the fight.

"A long time ago, whoever sent their son or daughter to study on the Jewish side would be thought of as a collaborator," she said. "Now, everyone sends their son or daughter to study on the Israeli side."

After years of acceding to her husband's demands, Imm Fadi cut her own path. One of the first things she did was distance herself from her husband's politics.

"The Likud choice was imposed on us," she said. "If I were to go vote now, I would maybe leave it blank. I feel different now."

Still, Imm Fadi felt a certain responsibility to vote since she was one of the few Arab Jerusalemites who had Israeli citizenship that gave her the right to cast a ballot in national elections.

"I think, because I'm an Arab and I have the opportunity to vote, I should vote for somebody who will help us," she said. "We should look for a party that represents our ideas and vote for them. Had Abu Fadi been alive, I wouldn't have been able to discuss who serves us as an Arab."

Imm Fadi figured they were doomed to eternal war with the Jewish people. She was just tired of it all. After so many years of fighting, Imm Fadi just wanted to work, to look after her family, and take off her shoes at the end of the day knowing she'd done some good.

"It is written in the Quran that we will always fight with the Jews," she said. "Now we have given up. We have surrendered. I don't see any good coming out of all the protests."

Imm Fadi saw nothing to be gained by dwelling on her husband's life. As she got older, the slurs aimed at her and her husband stung less and less.

"Before I used to hate it," she said. "Now, I don't care. Fadi says: 'My father was a collaborator. He's dead. No one on their last day will be held accountable for another person's sins.'"

"OUR FATHER PROTECTED ASSAEL"

Perhaps the only thing worse than being branded a Palestinian collaborator in Jerusalem is being the son or daughter of someone who has been tarred as a traitor. The schoolyard taunts are biting and relentless. Nothing can stir up a street fight faster.

In 2005, Arab-Israeli director Hany Abu-Assad's Oscar-nominated movie, *Paradise Now*, brought the issue of Palestinian collaborators to a global audience. The film traced the decisions of Said and Khaled, two young men from the West Bank city of Nablus who had been chosen to carry out suicide bombings in Tel Aviv.

As he tries to justify his plans to the woman he has fallen in love with, Said reveals that his father was an ameel—a collaborator.

"The crimes of the occupation are countless," Said tells her. "The worst crime of all is to exploit the people's weaknesses and turn them into collaborators. By doing that, they not only kill the resistance, they also ruin families, ruin their dignity, and ruin an entire people. When my father was executed, I was ten years old. He was a good person. But he grew weak. For that, I hold the occupation responsible. They must understand that, if they recruit collaborators, they must pay the price for it. A life without dignity is worthless. Especially when it reminds you day after day of humiliation and weakness."

The film won a Golden Globe for Best Foreign Film and was the first film representing Palestine to be nominated for an Academy Award. The same indignities depicted in the film played out on Assael Street for Abu Fadi's kids, especially the older ones. They were constantly being taunted and getting in fights at school or on the street. Abu Fadi sent his two oldest kids to a school across town so they wouldn't have to face the heckling from mean-spirited kids in Abu Tor. But there was no way for any of them to really escape their father's reputation. Mahmoud repeatedly came home from school and wept in his room.

"I don't have one friend on the street," said Mahmoud, one of Abu Fadi's three sons.

By the time he was 30, Mahmoud was divorced and remarried. His first marriage had been tumultuous. When he was alive, Abu Fadi would drive to his son's house to try to defuse tensions. After he died, there was no one to help keep things together, and the couple fell apart.

Arab families refused to let their daughters marry into Abu Fadi's family because of his reputation. Abu Fadi's kids found the treatment they received from their neighbors to be duplicitous and hypocritical. None of the neighbors had any problem asking Abu Fadi for help when they had issues with the city. None of them called him a collaborator when they needed something.

"The word collaborator is used to put people down," said his oldest son, Fadi. "Because he was able to solve their problems with Israel, they think he's a collaborator, even though solving their problems is in their benefit."

Mahmoud rejected the suggestion that his father had embraced an Israeli identity. Mahmoud saw his dad as an unsung hero who had suffered the slurs of his neighbors while he did all he could to help them.

"Instead of having an Israeli identity, my father protected the whole neighborhood," he said.

None of the kids was more protective of their dad's image than Abeer, the eldest of three daughters. Among Abu Fadi's kids, Abeer was the most successful. She studied law at Israel's prestigious Hebrew University, worked in the Israeli Justice Ministry and went into private legal practice before she was 30. She dyed her hair blond and wore stylish skirts and jackets that accentuated her figure. As the eldest daughter, she was closest to her father. Abeer saw nothing to be gained by talking about her dad.

"It's private," she said one evening at their house when she came home from work in late 2014. "I don't want to share this with anyone."

Like her brother, Abeer bristled at the suggestion that her father had embraced an Israeli identity.

"Why are you talking about these things?" she asked her mother and brothers. "It's private."

When pressed to talk about their lives on Assael Street, Abeer got visibly angry and walked out of the living room. Her mother chased after her and the two got in a heated argument before asking their visitors to leave them alone. Abeer wanted nothing to do with people picking apart her family's lives. Her father had been misunderstood. It seemed like their family had been forever scarred, physically and emotionally, by Abu Fadi's decisions. If any of them were ever going to have a chance to define their lives for themselves, they had to get out from under Abu Fadi's shadows.

"He's dead," said Abeer, who appeared to be on the brink of crying as my Palestinian colleague and I left the family home for the last time. "What else is there to say? Abu Fadi is dead."

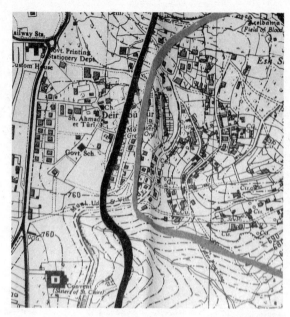

A UN copy of the cease-fire lines through Jerusalem's Abu Tor neighborhood, as drawn with grease pencils by Israeli general Moshe Dayan (left, in red) and Jordanian officer Abdullah El-Tell (right, in green) in 1948. Modern-day Assael Street runs through the middle of the two lines. Photo by Dion Nissenbaum.

A French officer holding a white flag and an Israeli soldier watch in May 1956 as nuns from a French hospital in West Jerusalem search for a patient's dentures that had fallen from a window overlooking No Man's Land. Photo by David Rubinger.

Israeli and Jordanian officials set up a makeshift court in No Man's Land north of Jerusalem in May 1957 to decide the fate of cows that farmers on both sides of the border claimed were theirs. Photo by David Rubinger.

Photograph from the UN investigation in September 1966 into the return of the Yaghmour family to No Man's Land. Malka Joudan, an Iranian immigrant to Israel whose house on the edge of modern-day Assael Street is identified by the faint arrow, called to alert officials to the Palestinian family's return. Photo via UN Archives and Records Management Section.

A UN photo from 1966 shows No Man's Land in Abu Tor from the Jordanian side. This photo was part of a UN investigation into the Yaghmour family's return to their home between the barbed wire separating Israel and Jordan. Photo courtesy UN Archives and Records Management Section.

A Scottish officer working for the United Nations and an Israeli paratrooper lead a joint Israeli-Jordanian medical team tossing poisoned meat in No Man's Land in December 1957, along the "Barbed Wire Alley" that later became Assael Street in Jerusalem. Photo by David Rubinger.

Palestinian residents of Abu Tor, Jerusalem, march off for questioning by Israeli soldiers at the end of the June 1967 war. Photo by Shimshon Jacoby.

Members of the Joudan family gather with other neighbors outside their Abu Tor home right above No Man's Land at the end of the June 1967 war. An Israeli soldier keeps an eye out for Israeli looters carrying stuff from Palestinian homes in No Man's Land. Photo by Shimshon Jacoby.

Israeli and Palestinian boys play pool at a lower Abu Tor community center some time after the 1967 war. Photo by Shimshon Jacoby.

Eid Yaghmour (left) serves tea to Haim Machsomi (right) on Assael Street in May 1969 after the barbed wire came down and the men were able to shake hands for the first time. "We are happy to be pioneers in bringing together the hearts of the two people," Haim wrote in a petition at the time for better city services. Photo courtesy Werner Braun/Jerusalem Post.

A sign in Hebrew, Arabic and English marks the beginning of Assael Street. People who live here disagree on where the street gets its name and how to spell it in English. Photo by Dion Nissenbaum.

Nawal and Zakaria Bazlamit stand outside their home on Assael Street in 2007. Until 1967, their property marked the edge of No Man's Land with Israel. Photo by Katherine Kiviat.

Rachel Machsomi talks to visitors at her home in the West Bank settlement of Ma'ale Adumim. Rachel and her late husband Haim were some of the first people to move to the edge of No Man's Land on what became Assael Street. Photo by Seema Jilani.

Marchers carrying Israeli flags and weapons walk down Assael Street in June 2008 to celebrate Jerusalem Day, a national holiday to commemorate Israel taking control of all of Jerusalem in 1967. Photo by Dion Nissenbaum.

Alisa Maeir-Epstein (right) stands in front of her house in 2007 with Asaway Bazlamit, one of the girls who lived across the way on Assael Street. Photo by Katherine Kiviat.

Khaled Rishek takes a break in the West Jerusalem YMCA, where he works full time. As part of his work, Khaled serves as dialogue supervisor for an Arab-Jewish youth choir that is based at the YMCA. Photo by Seema Jilani.

Amjad Rishek sorts through stacks of papers documenting his long fight with Jerusalem over his family home on Assael Street. He has spent years trying to prevent the city from demolishing their house. Photo by Seema Jilani.

Nawal Bazlamit stands in front of Israel's separation wall in 2007 on the outskirts of Azariya, outside Jerusalem. The wall runs through the backyard of her sons' apartment building, placing them outside the barrier, separated from the rest of the family on Assael Street. Photo by Dion Nissenbaum.

The wall on Assael Street that became the focal point of a bitter neighborhood feud over graffiti painted on the outside. The graffiti welcomes a Palestinian resident home from making his pilgrimage to Mecca, Saudi Arabia. Photo by Dion Nissenbaum.

A woman walks down Assael Street past the widely derided building built by Israeli developers on the side of the street that used to be in No Man's Land. Many Abu Tor neighbors tried unsuccessfully to prevent the contractors from building the apartment complex. Photo by Dion Nissenbaum.

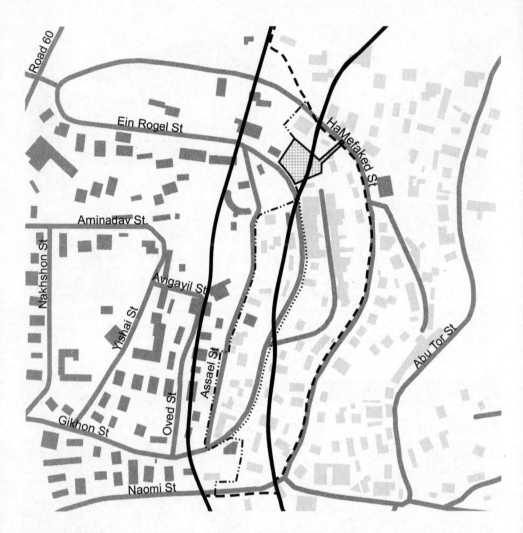

Abu-Tor

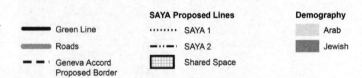

Green Line	SAYA Proposed Lines	Demography
Roads	⋯⋯ SAYA 1	Arab
Geneva Accord Proposed Border	–·–· SAYA 2	Jewish
	Shared Space	

0 12.5 25   50   75   100
                                Meters

N

A graphic of Abu Tor shows the potential borders separating Israel and a future Palestinian state. The dotted line for one route runs down the center of Assael Street, the old path that marked the edge of Israel until 1967. Photo courtesy SAYA Architects.

SIX

THE PEACENIKS

t took the hands of a healer to secure a breakthrough in modern-day Israeli-Palestinian relations on Assael Street.

Alisa Maeir-Epstein could see that the psychological walls dividing East and West were thick and high. Alisa knew she would have to summon all her energies to bring some healing to Abu Tor.

A rare window of opportunity had opened: Alisa had a chance to bridge the divide by using her New Age Reiki healing skills to infuse her Arab neighbor's body with soothing energy.

It was as if her life had led her here, to this dead-end street on the front lines of Jewish-Muslim relations.

Before she arrived on Assael in 2005, Alisa lived a nomadic, spiritual life. She'd ventured into the most remote valleys of Pakistan to live with a marginalized tribe in the shadows of the Khyber Mountains. She spent countless nights on the Red Sea desert beaches in Egypt with Bedouin friends, not far from Mount Sinai—the rocky range where Moses received the Ten Commandments.

Alisa had traveled north to Israel's captured Golan Heights to offer prayers at the Middle East's version of Stonehenge: a mysterious 5,000-year-old monument of concentric stone circles that some consider one of the earth's "energy fulcrums."

But the most significant journey came when Alisa was in her 20s. While exploring America one summer, Alisa found her way to South Carolina where she sought spiritual guidance from an East German healer, a Reiki Master, who showed her how to use the power in her hands to heal.

Renate Sorensen wasn't what Alisa expected to find when she went looking for a spiritual guru. Renate was in her 50s and frumpy. She wore large, thick, purple-rimmed glasses and talked about spiritual energy with a quiet, lyrical German accent. Her hair shot out at different angles—like an ungroomed cat. She wore unflattering button-down sweaters over checkered shirts.

"She looked like a funny old lady, walking down the street with a big pocketbook to buy cottage cheese," Alisa said. "But she turned out to be this incredibly enlightened, great being."

Alisa didn't exactly command a room with her physical presence either. She was about five feet tall, with a petite frame that made her look younger than she was. She kept her thin, silverish hair cut pixie-short, then started dying it blond as she got older. But she'd served as an officer in the Israeli military and knew how to take care of herself in a way that only a woman who has traveled around the world alone knows how to do.

Renate taught Alisa something else: the skills she needed to tap into universal spiritual energy—the Reiki—and use her hands to heal the sick. A Buddhist monk developed Reiki in Japan in the 1920s as a way for people to fill up on that invisible energy when it got low. He taught Reiki students how to "lay their hands" on a patient and infuse them with healing power. Alisa learned how to use special hand movements to clear the body's chakras—the body's spiritual energy spots. Reiki devotees raved about it. The International Center for Reiki Training basically says Reiki teachers can perform miracles. It's a claim not that uncommon in a place like Jerusalem. Reiki treatments, the center says, create a "wonderful glowing radiance that flows through and around you." Reiki "treats the whole person, including body, emotions, mind and spirit, creating many beneficial effects that include relaxation and feelings of peace, security and wellbeing. Many have reported miraculous results."[1]

It made sense to Alisa. She'd felt the invisible energy flows. So it seemed logical to her that, with proper training, she could harness that power. Anyone could tap into it. But the ability has to be passed from teacher to student in a Reiki "attunement" ceremony. When Alisa was ready, Renate "attuned" Alisa so she could tap into the healing powers. After lots of lessons and practice, Alisa became a young Reiki teacher.

Reiki has long been dismissed by Western medicine as New Age ho-cus-pocus, but Alisa believed in it. She had seen its power. Now Alisa had the chance to put all her training to use in Jerusalem.

It wasn't what she expected to be doing with her life: Alisa was a reluc-tant spiritual warrior.

She'd spent much of her life wandering the planet, exploring its hid-den corners and contemplating the world's mysteries; she'd always been restless. Perhaps it was because she was a "military brat," born on a US Air Force base in central California to an Air Force doctor and a civilian psychologist who moved around. Maybe it was growing up in the Bronx, a New York neighborhood filled with different accents and friends who were always on the move. Whatever the case, Alisa seemed most at home when she was somewhere else.

Like many Jewish Americans, Alisa's life straddled Israel and the United States. On July 20, 1969, the day Apollo 11 landed on the moon, 13-year-old Alisa arrived with her family in Israel, where they settled into their new lives. The move was jarring for Alisa, who thrived on New York City's miniskirt, rock-music culture and chafed at being thrown into a more sedate all-girls religious school in Israel.

"I was going to be a New York Jewish-American princess," she said. "When I got to Jerusalem, it wasn't like that at all. I wasn't glad at the time, but my parents did me a great service moving to Israel."

Alisa studied Jewish history and geography at Jerusalem's Hebrew University before returning to the United States to get a master's degree in education from Harvard in 1982. Then she veered off the traditional path to get an alternative degree in holistic education. She studied psychology and art, movement and meditation. She'd found her true path.

"Touchy-feely," she said. "That's my stuff."

"WHAT AM I DOING HERE?"

Alisa found her home in Israel, but she still felt unsettled. She felt a spiri-tual connection to the land and an emotional one to the country, but Alisa couldn't understand why she was so rooted in a place that seemed to thrive on perpetual turmoil. On one particularly emotional visit to her "spiritual rabbi" in South Carolina when she was seeking some guidance through her 30s, Alisa asked Renate the simplest of questions: *"Why am I here?"*

"I am somebody who pursues spiritual development and meditates and all I want is for people to be in peace," she told her mentor. *"What am I doing in Israel?"*

Alisa felt the weight of the Middle East conflict taking a spiritual toll. She was tired of having to wear psychological armor, even on the best of days, in Jerusalem. She was wondering if she was meant for something else. Renate told Alisa that living in the Holy City was her calling.

"They need people like you there," Renate told Alisa any time she thought about leaving Jerusalem. *"That's your destiny: to be in a place of strife."*

It was hard for Alisa to accept.

"I find it very difficult on an emotional level to be there sometimes," Alisa told her teacher. *"Why do I need to be in this place where it's so difficult for me emotionally, to be where people have such hatred, and, if there isn't a right reason to fight, they go out and make one?"*

"Places like that need people like you," Renate replied.

Eventually, Alisa came to see her new life on Assael as part of her spiritual journey.

"Maybe on some deep level, I believe; I'm not sure, but I believe, maybe that's why I'm here," Alisa said one day between sips of organic green tea. "Maybe that's what I'm doing on this street."

By nature, Alisa was an extrovert. She seemed to flourish when she put her values to the test. So when the opportunity presented itself, Alisa put her healing hands to work on her Palestinian neighbor.

The opening came one afternoon in 2006, soon after she'd moved with her family to Assael, when she saw a woman picking lemons in a well-tended orchard across the way. Alisa always wondered about the homes on the eastern side of Assael. This place stood out because it was the only one with a big orchard. The deep lot, a rare open space on the hillside crowded with homes, was sprinkled with orange and lemon trees. The rectangular two-story stone house rising above the trees was set back from Assael and slightly down the hill. Alisa looked down from the street at her Palestinian neighbor picking fruit. The woman in the yard, her hair covered in a plain scarf, caught a glimpse of Alisa watching her from the street above and offered her some lemons. Alisa gratefully accepted—and not just because the ones in her own yard weren't ripe. The woman, Ihsan, invited Alisa into the house for coffee where she introduced her sister-in-law, Khulood Salhab.

Alisa didn't really speak Arabic and her Arab neighbors didn't know much Hebrew. They couldn't say much more than *shalom* and *salaam* to each other, so they had to rely on other ways to connect. They struggled through their first conversation and turned to Khulood's English-speaking daughter for help translating.

Khulood was disarmed by her new neighbor's willingness to come into her house for coffee. She couldn't remember the last time someone from the west side of the street had come over for a friendly visit. Usually, Khulood kept to the Arabic-speaking wives she knew on the eastern side of the street. Those women didn't look down on her for covering her hair and wearing long, formless dresses—as some of the neighbors on the opposite side of the street seemed to do. Alisa seemed right at home from the start. Khulood was charmed by her petite new neighbor with her funny American accent. She wasn't sure whether Alisa would ever come back, so she didn't think about it too much after she said good-bye.

But Alisa kept reaching out, kept stopping by, kept saying hello. Though they didn't share a common language, they used a mix of English, Hebrew, Arabic and hand signs to get to know each other. When one of Khulood's English-speaking kids was around, the mothers would rope them in to translate.

Eventually, like the wives and mothers on Assael who had first met when the barbed wire came down 40 years earlier, Alisa and Khulood found common ground at the kitchen table.

One day when Alisa came over to visit, Khulood was cooking *maqluba*, a mainstay in Palestinian homes, made with layers of spiced lamb or chicken simmered in a pot under rice and vegetables that are flipped maqluba—upside down—when served. The smells of cinnamon, cardamom, allspice and pepper steaming in the kitchen swept through the house.

"*I really want to learn how to make maqluba,*" Alisa told Khulood.

"*Oh, it's easy,*" Khulood said. "*Yallah, let's do it.*"

While they cooked, Khulood's shields came down. She confided in Alisa that she was having some aches and pains that weren't going away. Alisa knew how to help: Reiki. Khulood was skeptical. But her kids and her husband encouraged her to give it a try. So Khulood and her eldest daughter walked over to Alisa's house one afternoon to see what it was all about.

Khulood took off her head scarf, a sign of how comfortable she felt with her neighbor, and lay down on Alisa's Reiki treatment table.

With an Arabic-Hebrew dictionary placed next to her aromatic oils, Alisa placed her hands on Khulood. She infused her body with universal energy, giving her more strength to heal.

It seemed to work.

When she got home Khulood felt better. Lighter.

"It was a bit strange," she said. "But it felt good."

Khulood was sold. She went back for more Reiki treatments. Then her oldest daughter figured she would give it a try. Then her only son went around to see if Reiki could help him get rid of his migraines. The intimacy of the connection with the Salhabs gave Alisa some hope that people could find common ground, no matter what political, religious, cultural or linguistic differences there might be. It reinforced her belief that she was on the right path, that there was a larger reason she had found her way to Jerusalem, to Assael.

"I've always felt that it was very hard to be here, but this was my destiny, and there was a reason that I was here, beyond my personal Jewish family history," Alisa said. "It was deeper. Like I was sent here spiritually."

FROM STREET WORKER TO STREET FIGHTER

If Alisa was the spiritual warrior of Assael, her husband, David, was the street fighter.

"I believe change has to come from within, from spirit," Alisa said. "He believes in political and social action."

David Epstein grew up in a blue-collar Pennsylvania town where he was entranced by the brand of Social Justice Judaism he saw unfolding all around him. He was captivated by the Jewish rabbis marching with Martin Luther King Jr. in Alabama and antiwar activists who were giving the Establishment the middle finger. When he got to Brandeis University (alma mater of yippie activist Abbie Hoffman) in the late 1960s, he marched in Boston's anti–Vietnam War protests and lived by the motto "don't let school get in the way of your education." He grew shaggy dark hair and a stringy beard that made him look a bit like Cuban revolutionary and antiestablishment icon Che Guevara.

When the US military called his name for the draft, David cited his religious objection to what he saw as unjust American aggression in Vietnam and refused to go fight for his country, declaring himself a Conscientious

Objector. Instead, David studied Hebrew at Brandeis, joined the campus Nonviolent Direct Action League and got thrown in jail for blocking a bus carrying military draftees heading to training camp. When one American soldier decided to go AWOL to protest the war, David stood guard with other activists in a building where they offered the soldier "sanctuary" from arrest. One of his fellow antiwar activists at Brandeis was Katherine Ann Power, a quirky student who distinguished herself by walking shoeless and braless around campus. David and Katherine both served on the student council and marched together in rally after rally.

One day in 1970, she disappeared from campus and turned up on the nightly news. Katherine and some friends had decided it was time to overthrow the government. But they needed money to do it. So they decided to rob a couple of banks. Things didn't go quite as planned. While Katherine waited as the getaway driver, one of her accomplices shot and killed a Massachusetts policeman trying to stop the bank robbery.

Three of the five radical robbers were quickly arrested. The fourth managed to live under an assumed name for a few years. Katherine was the only one to get away. Though she was on the FBI's Most Wanted list, she created a new life for herself on the West Coast. She took a new name, got married, had a son and tried to work out her demons with a therapist who encouraged her to come clean. In 1993, after decades of living with lies, Katherine finally turned herself in to face her past.[2]

David wasn't that kind of activist. He was against the war. But he wasn't a bank-robbing radical like Katherine. He had other plans. For his junior semester abroad, David decided to go to Israel. It was 1969 and Israel was still living off the euphoria and adrenaline of winning the 1967 war. David's mom couldn't understand why her son wanted to go. To her, Israel was an unappealing backwater.

"Why Israel?" she asked David. *"Why not a cultured country like England or something?"*

David was undeterred. He spent six months traveling the Mediterranean coast, praying at the Western Wall and trying out his witty pick-up lines on the aloof but alluring Israeli girls. By the time he left, David contracted what he called the *haidak alim*—the Israel bug. It would take a few years—and a girl—to get him back to Israel.

And, when he did come back, it was more for the girl than the country. It was 1971. David had an acceptance letter from Northeastern University

Law School and a beautiful girlfriend who was moving to Tel Aviv. He chose the girl. It lasted about three months, tops. The fact that the girl dumped David for the guy she eventually married offered him some consolation. But he was still brokenhearted and adrift in Tel Aviv. So David took a job as what was then known as a "street worker."

"That's not as bad as it sounds," he said.

David was paid to go hang out in Rosh HaAyin, a depressed town on the outskirts of Tel Aviv, where he played pool with high school dropouts who had nothing better to do. Many of the people living in Rosh HaAyin were part of Yemenite families flown to Israel as part of Operation Magic Carpet, one of Israel's early airlift campaigns for Jewish families living in Arab and Muslim nations. The Yemenite boys laughed at David's American-accented Hebrew and helped him get some of the kinks out of his new language.

David lost a lot at pool, but he helped the guys learn some English and get some training. Some got factory jobs. Others went back to school. It wasn't glamorous work. But he liked it. He could see himself making a life helping people. David returned to the United States to get a degree in social work from Case Western Reserve University in Cleveland, Ohio. By the time he was done with his casework, he'd found a new girl who wanted to move to Israel with him. This time, he said, "she didn't dump me."

David and his new girl, Judy, got married and made the move to Israel in 1979. This time, the haidak alim was stronger. David dove back into social work. He got a job helping run urban renewal programs in Jerusalem's poorest neighborhoods. Very quickly, it became clear to David that, if he was going to keep doing social work in Jerusalem, he needed to learn some Arabic. Knowing some would help him better communicate with the city's poorest residents, both Arab and Jew.

So he took a three-week intensive Arabic course and studied, off and on, on the side after that. It was one of David's ways of showing that he was willing to do some serious work to bridge the divide between Arab and Jew.

"I was able to begin the process of, at least symbolically, demonstrating that I was into communicating," he said.

David kept up his work on antipoverty programs and officially immigrated to Israel—making *aliyah*—in 1983. David and Judy had three children together, but the couple starting drifting apart as their kids got older.

Alisa met the couple in 1989 when she joined their Jerusalem syna-gogue, but they didn't socialize all that much at first. In 1997, David hired Alisa to do some part-time grant writing for his business. Outside of work, David and Judy's efforts to save their marriage were going nowhere, and the couple finally separated in 1999.

"Sometimes parents choose their own happiness over that of their kids, which is what I think happened here," Judy Feierstein said of the couple's separation. "It's not nice, but it's the truth. It really was not a good marriage by the time it ended, and we both knew that. Sometimes you need to end it. We probably waited too long, but OK."

Though David and Judy were able to untangle their lives without too much acrimony, the divorce hit their three children hard. So did David's decision to marry Alisa after his divorce from Judy was finalized two years later. And Alisa didn't come to the marriage by herself. In 1999, Alisa had flown to Romania to adopt a nine-month-old girl she named Avital. David's son and two daughters had a hard time adjusting to their dad's new wife and her daughter. Avital went from being the only child of a single mother to the youngest of four kids in an unusual nuclear family.

David held the family together with a staple of eye-rolling "dad jokes" and white-water rafting trips. He was the kind of husband who'd make risqué comments to Alisa about their sex life during the filming of an Israeli television documentary about their Israeli Brady Bunch–style family. He was the kind of father who'd turn Friday night Shabbat songs into a performance on the main stage at one of Israel's premiere outdoor folk festivals. Soon after Alisa and David got married, they went look-ing for a new home in Jerusalem. They checked out dozens of places, but nothing seemed to fit. Some homes were too pricey. Others were too small. Then they heard about a little house in Abu Tor that was about to go up for sale.

For David and Alisa, the place on Assael was perfect. First off, it was cute. Built sometime in the 1970s as a backyard addition to an apartment complex, it had a small garden, natural light and an enclosed garage. Sec-ondly, because it was on the dividing line, the price was right. Because they are in Abu Tor, because they are on the cusp of Arab East Jerusalem, the houses on Assael are far cheaper than the ones in the neighborhood across the train tracks in the trendy German Colony.

"I'm so glad most Israelis are, you know, racist," David said sardonically. "They hear our neighborhood has Arabs. As a result we were able to get something nice, nearly our dream house."

The place had a big living room with mosaic tile floors and vine-covered windows that sometimes made the place feel like a sheltered cave. Alisa planted purple kale and basil in the tiny garden squeezed between their front door and the blue iron gate leading out to Assael. They filled their home with family photos and mementos from their travels—clay Moroccan cooking tajines and a metal sculpture of Shiva, the dancing Hindu god often associated with yoga. Alisa hung a quote by sixteenth-century Renaissance poet Ben Jonson in their bathroom:

> *In small proportions we just beauty see; And in short measures life may perfect be.*

Assael proved to be the ultimate proving ground for David's beliefs, training and skills.

As he biked to and from his job in the German Colony, where he ran a two-room business helping nonprofit groups raise money, he began to see the divide on his street. It was easy to see where Israeli Jerusalem ended and Palestinian Jerusalem began. The eastern side was a series of flat, low stone houses with stone walls and corrugated tin covered with spray-painted Arabic graffiti scrawled above red crescent moons, blue stars and golden images of the Dome of the Rock. The western side was an unbroken series of locked gates, stone walls and dented, metal electric garage doors. Unofficially, the place where the border fence once rose still marked the edge of Jewish Abu Tor.

Where others saw a yawning divide, David saw potential common ground.

This place, he thought, *could be utilized much more as a bridge for coexistence.*

David imagined coexistence block parties and bilingual social workers coming to Assael to organize street art competitions.

Of all the places in Jerusalem where it could grow naturally, he thought, *this is one of them.*

As a community organizer, David looked at living in a "mixed" neighborhood as an opportunity. "Obviously there are some degrees of risks and potential negatives, but both of us kind of took a certain degree of responsibility for trying to make sure that possible negatives would actually work out to be a positive," he said.

David had a special calling card he used to break the ice: a joke he knew—that worked best in Arabic—with a punch line that went, "The big dog is just a dog, but the little dog is a son of a bitch." More often than not, it did the trick. David kept the joke in his holster of icebreakers and pulled it out on Assael Street as he got to know the neighbors. David accepted every invitation he could to visit families living on the other side of the street. He went to the Bazlamits to congratulate Zakaria and Nawal when they returned from Hajj in 2006. David's subtle offers of respect didn't go unnoticed by the Bazlamits.

David watched as the other visitors kissed Zakaria's hand when they greeted him as *Haji* and figured he'd do the same. It was a small gesture from their Jewish neighbor that the Bazlamits remembered for years. When Zakaria passed away a few years later, David went by to sit with the family and pay his respects. For David, it was the least he could do.

THE MAYOR OF ASSAEL STREET

By the time David and Alisa moved to Assael, the west side was entirely walled off. Almost everyone with a house on that side of Assael could come and go without actually walking out to the street. David and Alisa's home was one of the few with a door leading out to Assael—and they made sure to use it.

"We're not the kinds of people who barricade ourselves," David said.

David was always looking for ways to break through the suspicion on the street. When the Bazlamits got into the dispute with Carol in 2006 over the Hajj graffiti painted on her wall, David and Alisa thought things might have gone down differently if the neighbors had spoken to each other.

"If that had happened to our wall, I don't think it would have been a problem," Alisa said. "I suppose if they had drawn Hajj pictures on my wall, I probably would have handled the situation in a different way."

David and Alisa knew the language divide fueled mistrust on both sides. Visitors would sometimes ask them if the Arabic graffiti on the street was hateful.

"People come and ask: 'What does it say? Kill the Jews?'" Alisa said. "When you don't have information, it can be deadly."

David saw Carol's confrontation with the Bazlamits as a perfect example of why neighbors needed to find common ground.

"For [Carol], that act was a gross invasion of privacy and an attack on her property," he said. "It was violation of the ABCs of respectful living together. And she wasn't able to go to them and say: 'Jeez, you didn't ask me, you really shouldn't have done that, I want you right away to please paint over it.' They would have done that and they would have said: 'We really didn't know' or whatever, but for [Carol] that was it. She just lost it. With all due respect, she had a decent reason to lose it. She wasn't totally unreasonable."

David had other hopes for that wall. He wanted to see it become a canvas for some authorized street art—legally sanctioned coexistence graffiti. The cement wall was a perfect little billboard in the middle of Assael Street. It would be one of the small dreams deferred time after time by tensions that swept across Jerusalem.

In time, though, David and Alisa's efforts paid off. Their neighbors could see that they were making an effort. But Reiki and hand kisses only got you so far. David decided he should do more. If he wanted the street walls to represent something besides hostility and suspicion, he needed to step up his game. In 2011, with his wife's encouragement, he decided to run for a seat on the city's community council, an advisory group made up of neighborhood advocates. If he won, David would have the power—and, maybe, the money—to implement his vision. David took the campaign seriously. First, he tried but failed to convince one of the other two candidates to drop out so they wouldn't split the secular vote and lose to the ultra-Orthodox contender. So he had to go door to door to get support and explain his plans. On election day, David won 62 percent of the vote. He became the official community advocate for Abu Tor. Now all he had to do was put his ideas to the test.

"I've been walking around with a vision of what needs to be done for ten years," he said in 2014. "I say to myself: 'Why didn't I do this a long time ago?' All of the sudden I found myself in a position where I was more than just one person."

Technically, the district David represented ended right outside his front door—up to the spot where the barbed wire used to define the edge of Israel. The families on the eastern side of Assael were represented by another council member, someone living in lower Abu Tor. David's district was meticulously gerrymandered to exclude most of the Arab residents of

Assael. The line ran down the center of Assael, curved around the Arab homes on the other side of the street, and enveloped a street dominated by a controversial religious Jewish compound that was a popular target for Molotov cocktails and rock attacks when tensions rose.

David decided to ignore it. He wanted to be an advocate for all of Assael Street, not just the Jewish side. But how? It took David quite awhile to come up with a plan. Eventually, he turned to the Jewish families of Abu Tor with a question: Are you interested in building better relations with our Arab neighbors?

Many ignored his e-mail. Some people thought of it as the naïve endeavor of an American-born Israeli who didn't really understand how the Middle East worked. But there was enough interest to get everyone together to see what they could come up with.

In April 2014, more than a dozen of Abu Tor's Jewish residents met at David's place to talk about what they could do to bridge the gap. They drank green tea and talked for hours about crime and speed bumps, yoga and garbage bins, parking and politics. It wasn't much, but it was something. It was more than most people on that side of the road were willing to do. Some people took to calling David the "mayor of Assael Street."

The group decided to go to the Palestinian families in Abu Tor with some suggestions. They wanted to host a coexistence street fair on Assael and thought it would be nice to set up an organic community garden where Jewish and Arab neighbors could share the secrets of their green thumbs. They thought Hebrew-Arabic-English classes might be a hit. And they proposed yoga classes for any and all women and girls from Abu Tor. Ideas in hand, David had to figure out how to get the families on the other side of the street involved. It wasn't as easy as inviting them over for tea. David wanted to help. But he didn't think he could dive into the biggest problems on that side of the street right away. David wanted to start with small things that wouldn't create too many waves.

"One of the things that one has to keep in mind is the political situation, and it was my strategy that it would be important to talk about common interests, neighborly relations, people's lives, and to keep out as much as possible discussion of politics, political parties, political issues, unless they're related to getting something done," he said.

The challenges became clear when David reached out to a group of young East Jerusalem leaders to see if they could work together on something—getting speed bumps, hosting a community meeting, what-ever might work. The group said no. They saw working with David as "normalization." They weren't willing to take part in anything that could be criticized as helping to prop up Israel and undermine Palestinian nationalism.

Eventually, David found people willing to help: the Bazlamits agreed to host a meeting in their courtyard. The small group gathered underneath the family's grapevines, on the same slope were an Israeli sniper killed the elder Hijazi Bazlamit in 1951. The Palestinians had a list of concerns. They wanted dumpsters with lids for the street, so the cats and dogs wouldn't keep dragging trash into the road. They wanted the city to clean the stinky sewer grates that made the street smell, especially in the summer. They thought speed bumps on one of the main roads through Abu Tor might slow down drivers who zoomed past the entrance to Assael at dangerous speeds. They talked about turning the small patch of empty land at the en-trance of the street into a little park. They were small things. David figured he had to start somewhere. Garbage bins and speed bumps seemed to be as good a place as any.

SONGS OF FREEDOM

As the couple found ways to break through the mistrust on Assael, Da-vid and Alisa bumped into unexpected difficulties raising their youngest daughter, Avital. Avital was seven when they bought their house on Assael Street. Any move can be a challenge for a kid. And moving to Assael proved to be an especially trying one for Avital. Though she kept going to the same school—an alternative private "democratic" program where students had complete control of their education—she had to make new friends on the street. Since most of the kids spoke Arabic, that was hard.

Avital was tall for her age and athletic. She liked to wear pink plastic Crocs and zip around the dead-end street on her purple scooter with her long brown hair whipping across her face.

"I like our street," Avital said. "At first I thought it's annoying that there are Arabs here. I didn't know anything about them. I can't under-stand their Arabic. But then my dad helped me to play with them and we would play together every day."

David taught Avital a little bit of Arabic to help her make friends. At night, they would sit and learn basic sentences in Arabic that she would repeat over and over.

"Shu ismek?" David would ask while Avital played *Sims* on the computer. ("What's your name?")

"Ismi Avital," she would respond. ("I'm Avital.")

"Ween inti saaken?" David would ask. ("Where do you live?")

"Ana saaken fil Shayara Assael," Avital would say. ("I live on Assael Street.")

Avital tried it out on the young girls across the street, who giggled at her Arabic. As she got older, Avital became better friends with one of the neighbors who spoke English well: Khulood Salhab's middle daughter, Maha.

Though Maha was six years older than Avital, the two found plenty of things to bond over, like doing their nails together and trading makeup tips. Maha was protective of Avital and liked to spend time with her, even though some of Maha's friends told her that it was a bad idea to hang out with Jewish girls. Avital didn't care that Maha covered her hair with stylish, colorful hijabs. Mostly they just made each other laugh. Avital quickly grew taller than Maha, who had no tall genes from her parents. The biggest things about Maha seemed to be her dark eyes and eyelashes. Where Avital was outspoken, Maha was demure. Maha mothered her favorite kitten like a baby. She took the kitty to the vet when she was sick and drove her around town in the family car when she needed to do errands.

While Avital didn't stick to her dad's Arabic lessons, she loved the nights spent singing while he played guitar. Every Friday night for Shabbat, the family would sing old American civil rights tunes and folk songs from the '60s. They'd sing traditional Sabbath tunes and John Denver hits. In 2007, the Epstein Family Singers—David, Avital, and the three older kids—spent eight hours in a recording studio to produce a nine-song CD. They sang "Leaving on a Jet Plane" and "Oh, Freedom." They were impressive enough to be asked to perform a few tunes at Jacob's Ladder, the country's premier country and bluegrass festival at a hotel overlooking Lake Tiberias, the place where Jesus Christ had gathered his disciples and walked on water before traveling to Jerusalem.

In 2011, an energetic, young redheaded American guy came to Avital's school looking for singers. Micah Hendler, a skinny guy with rectangular glasses who is fluent in Arabic and Hebrew, wanted to create a new youth chorus of high school students from East and West Jerusalem. He was looking for kids who wanted to "transcend conflict through song."

Micah, a one-time member of Yale's famous a capella singing group, the Whiffenpoofs, wanted to build a Jerusalem chorus where Arab and Jewish kids could meet on common ground to sing songs and talk about their lives. Micah enlisted Palestinian girls from Jerusalem's refugee camps and Israeli boys who lived in the West Bank settlements encircling the city. There were Muslim girls who covered their hair and those who didn't. There were Jewish girls who went to ultra-Orthodox school and those, like Avital, who were getting an alternative education.

Each week, Micah and the kids would gather for more than three hours of rehearsal at West Jerusalem's YMCA, in a room with pictures of Martin Luther King Jr. and John Lennon hanging from the walls. The kids would learn songs in Arabic, Hebrew and English. Then they'd sit down to talk. The group sessions were meant to give the singers a place where they could shed many of the misconceptions they brought with them. Micah wanted the private talks to be a place where kids could let down their guards and find common ground in a city that always seemed to be pulling them apart.

The choir became one of Avital's passions. The group got invitations to perform in Japan and London. They joined forces with Israeli singer David Broza for an album featuring covers of "(What's So Funny 'Bout) Peace, Love & Understanding?" and Cat Stevens's "Where Do the Children Play?"

The songs brought the kids together. The talking could be cathartic, and it sometimes left kids in tears. Things with the group got really bad in the summer of 2014, when it seemed like the city might be heading into another spiral of violence.

WAR COMES TO ABU TOR

As the second intifada wound down and the suicide bombings in Jerusalem tapered off, people on both sides of Assael gave thanks that they had all survived, that the intense fighting had passed over their street.

No one could be sure, but many people thought Assael was spared because of the unusual ties that held the street together. That protected feeling evaporated in 2014 when Abu Tor became a flashpoint for what some people saw as the start of the third intifada.

After years of keeping the turmoil at bay, Assael Street was dragged into the tumult. Stinging clouds of tear gas filtered through living room windows as Israeli soldiers battled a new generation of stone-throwing Palestinians in the streets below. The new war appeared to be sweeping through Assael—and it put the Maeir-Epstein's values to the test.

At the start of 2014, the problems in Abu Tor appeared serious, but isolated. In February, the neighborhood was hit by a series of firebombings. That wasn't too unusual. Vandals, criminals and demonstrators occasionally targeted Jewish houses and cars in Abu Tor. They robbed homes and slashed tires. They hurled stones through windows and tossed Molotov cocktails at parked cars. Usually the spikes in trouble passed.

This time, things got worse.

In June, the nation was captivated by the kidnapping of the three Jewish-Israeli teenagers hitchhiking in the West Bank. Everyone was talking about the fate of Naftali, Gilad and Eyal. Israel launched a new crackdown—the country's largest military operation in the West Bank since the peak of the suicide bombings nearly a decade earlier. Israeli forces searched thousands of homes, rounded up more than 400 Palestinians and, for the first time in years, demolished the home of a Hamas member arrested for murdering a Jewish Israeli during Passover.

When the boys' bodies were discovered under piles of stone in a field not far from Hebron 18 days after they were abducted, Netanyahu called the killers "human animals," launched air strikes in the Gaza Strip, and essentially vowed to exact revenge.[3] Hours after the nationally broadcast funerals—for Naftali Fraenkel, a 16-year-old American-Israeli; Gilad Shaer, 16; and Eyal Yifrach, 19—three men, led by an Israeli settler, did just that.

In an abduction captured by security cameras, two men walked up to a scrawny 16-year-old Palestinian teen with a goofy haircut in East Jerusalem, asked him for directions, then wrestled him into a car that sped off as the boy shouted *"Allahu Akbar."*[4]

The three men took Mohammed Abu Khdeir to a nearby forest, beat him with a wrench, poured gasoline over his bloodied body and set him ablaze while he was still alive. Palestinians uttered his name the way Israelis mentioned Naftali, Gilad and Eyal. Both sides saw the killing of their children as a sign of utter depravity, a clear signal that it was impossible to live together with a people who could to *that* to an innocent boy.

The killing of Mohammed Abu Khdeir became a catalyst for new protests. Every night, street fights would break out between masked Palestinian residents of East Jerusalem and Israeli riot police. The evenings were filled with the sounds of shattering glass and of fireworks aimed at Israeli soldiers. The winds pushing through the valleys smelled of tear gas and acrid rubber from burning tires. Israeli forces used high-pressure water cannons to spray protesters with a foul-smelling, yellow-colored, laboratory-designed riot-control liquid called "Skunk."

Four days after Mohammed Abu Khdeir was killed, Israeli police arrested six people and charged three of them with the boy's murder. Israel was shocked by the brutal revenge killing. It forced Israelis to reconsider the country's carefully cultivated image of itself as a benevolent nation. Netanyahu called Mohammed Abu Khdeir's father in order to distance himself and his calls for vengeance from the Israelis who actually carried it out.

"The murder of your son is abhorrent and cannot be countenanced by any human being," Netanyahu told Hussein Abu Khdeir.

As many Israelis expressed revulsion over the unimaginable implications and repeated the mantra, *"That's not us,"* Naftali's mother, Rachel Fraenkel, went on TV to denounce the Jewish attackers.

"The shedding of innocent blood is against morality, is against the Torah and Judaism, and is against the foundation of the lives of our boys and of all of us in this country," she told reporters gathered outside her home at the end of the family's seven-day mourning period. "Alongside the pain of this terrible act, we take pride in our country's zeal to investigate, to arrest the criminals and to stop the horror, and we hope that calm will return to the streets of our country."[5]

Naftali's uncle, Yishai Fraenkel, told journalists "there is no difference between those who murdered Mohammed and those who murdered our children. Those are murderers, and these are murderers. And both must be dealt with to the full extent of the law."[6]

With some prodding from Jerusalem mayor Nir Barkat, Mohammed Abu Khdeir's father, Hussein, spoke with Yishai Fraenkel, who expressed sympathies "from one bereaved family to another."[7]

The small gestures of compassion were soon overtaken by a new war. Two days after the call, faced with a surge in rocket fire from Gaza militants, Netanyahu sent Israeli planes to bomb Gaza. For six weeks, Israel's military pummeled the Gaza Strip. For the first time since 2009, Israeli soldiers entered Gaza where they fought Hamas militants who popped up from hidden tunnels below their feet. Israeli military strikes killed hundreds of women and children in attacks that drew international condemnation. Scores of Western journalists sitting on waterfront hotel patios watched one Israeli strike kill four Palestinian boys who were playing soccer on the beach. Israeli forces hit more than a half-dozen UN schools, killing dozens of Palestinians who had sought refuge from the fighting.

By the time Israel and Hamas agreed to a cease-fire at the end of August, more than 2,000 Palestinians, most of them women and children, were dead. Sixty-six Israeli soldiers and six Israeli civilians were killed.

The series of crises took a particular toll on the Jerusalem Youth Choir.

Even on the quietest of days, group dialogue was a challenge. The day after Mohammed Abu Khdeir was killed, Micah thought about canceling practice.

"No one told me there was going to be a war," said Micah, who knew full well that war was always a very real possibility in Jerusalem.

One of his singers was from Shu'fat, where the Palestinian teen had been abducted. Shu'fat had been engulfed in protest, and Micah figured there was no way the girl would make it. But he went ahead anyway. He sent word to the kids: "If you can make it safely, please come." Partway through the practice, the girl from Shu'fat walked through the door. Micah was stunned.

"How did you get here?" Micah asked her. "I mean, how did you physically get here?"

"I woke up to gunshots this morning and I was sitting in my house listening to all the demonstrations and all the bullets and all the tear gas and I was going insane," she told him. *"I had to get out. I left, walked down the street. The soldiers tried to stop me, but I ran and got away. This is exactly where I want to be."*

The summer of 2014 wasn't the first test for the Jerusalem Youth Choir, but it seemed to be the biggest. Perhaps because Mohammed, Naftali, Gilad and Eyal were the same age as the singers. Some members of the Youth

Choir knew the three Israeli teens who had been kidnapped and killed. Others knew the Palestinian boy and his family.

On their closed Facebook page and in their dialogue groups, the idea of a "safe space" to discuss difficult issues seemed to be dissolving. Members of the choir threatened to walk out over Facebook posts by other singers in the group. Micah organized emergency meetings that devolved into shouting matches, girls weeping and kids storming out of the room. The choir appeared to be coming apart. And the timing couldn't have been worse. The group was preparing for its first major international tour.

"We were about to go to Japan in the summer and then we went to war and had a very hard time—a very hard time—getting along," Avital said.

Because she had grown up on Assael Street, Avital had sympathy for the Palestinians' frustrations. But hearing the anger and hostility coming from some of the other choir members was hard for her to take.

"One time everyone was kind of yelling at everyone in the choir," she said. "I was so shocked it was happening. It's really hard to keep this whole group together, to keep it from not exploding, because there's so much heat and so many other kinds of opinions."

Like many singers in the choir, Avital was conflicted. Her brother-in-law was one of the Israeli soldiers bringing weapons and supplies to units along the Gaza Strip border, so she had an instinctual desire to defend him and the army. But the images coming out of Gaza of dead women and children made it hard for her to justify. Halfway through the fighting, Avital tried to sort through her feelings in an emotional Facebook post.

"what's on my mind?" she wrote,

well my brother in law is in the army and i am so worried about the soldiers. i hear almost ever day someone dies it breaks my heart. also in gaza people are dying. this war is killing so many people from both sides. its taking father/brother away from family's. if we want to live in peace we need to stop this i am NOT saying that our army is wrong but people are dying because of this. we will not have peace until this ends not just war but until they stop wanting to kill us and a innocent people and i am NOT saying its okay im not really saying anything, i am saying what i am reading every day for the past 3 weeks on every news Chanel and papers. what i want to say is i feel guilty every time my phone beeps and says bad news from any sides and i will keep reading and praying that everything will be okay but i know that will take too long. and i will keep praying until it stops for GOOD.

Though the meetings were volatile, Micah knew that the group had to talk things through for the choir to be something more than another superficial coexistence program.

"People cry, people walk out of the room, people threaten not to come back, but it's important because otherwise it's not real," he said. "It's fantasyland where I have all these friends from other places, but I don't know anything about them.

"For me, that gets to the core about why it's important to have singing and the dialogue," he said. "Singing creates the community, and the dialogue enables it to be real. The dialogue makes it not an imaginary space, it enables it to survive in the midst of all the awful things that are going on."

When the fighting was over, Micah got in touch with an old friend from his Whiffenpoof days who had become a minor YouTube musical celebrity to see if he'd be interested in making a video with the choir. Though he'd never been to Jerusalem, Sam Tsui agreed to do a cover of *American Idol* winner Phillip Phillips's hit single "Home."

The inspirational lyrics resonated for Micah, especially after a trying summer. *Settle down,* it urges listeners. *Don't let demons fill you with fear. Trouble might get its hooks in you, but you're never alone. There's always hope.*

Released in October 2014, the four-minute video showed Palestinian teens in the chorus walking through their neighborhoods, alongside Israel's towering separation walls, and a Jewish member of the group praying at Israel's military cemetery. The Arab and Jewish kids eventually come together and celebrate their unity while dancing around a campfire. The video became a viral YouTube hit that quickly got a respectable 250,000 views. One newspaper writer called it "the most optimistic video about Israel and the Palestinians." Though there was plenty of tension and there were cliques in the choir, it managed to thrive. When the time came, they flew off to Japan as planned.

"Truthfully, I was one of the only people I knew who wasn't depressed all summer," Micah said. "And it's because I was working with the choir."

As the fighting intensified that summer, Jewish residents of Abu Tor talked about setting up new neighborhood watch groups. They created escape plans for their families. They placed baseball bats and handguns strategically around their homes.

"Everybody usually tolerates each other, but it's like a temperature gauge," Abu Tor resident Harvey Brooks, an American-Israeli bassist who'd played with Bob Dylan and Jimi Hendrix, told the *Jerusalem Post* that July. "When the temperature goes up, things get bad."[8]

His wife, Bonnie, said the image of Abu Tor as an island of coexistence was exaggerated.

"Arabs and Jews normally live peacefully here, but it's not the way it should be, because when push comes to shove it becomes tribal," she said.[9]

A PEACENIK GOES TO WAR

David and Alisa found their own beliefs tested by the Gaza war. Neither liked to see women and children being killed by the Israeli military, but they didn't think Israel had a choice.

"I'm left of center, but I don't see what alternatives we had," David said. "When Hamas comes out and says it's totally legitimate to be sending rockets, it's totally legitimate to butcher people in a synagogue, you have to consider those people your enemies."

David recognized the irony of being an American antiwar activist growing up to be an Israeli war advocate. To him, the evolution was easily explainable.

"If someone comes to kill you, you have the right to defend yourself and kill them," he said. "I didn't feel that was the case in Vietnam."

David's transformation was so thorough that he had signed up to serve in the Israeli military as a reserve soldier after he made aliyah, even though he wasn't required to do so. During the first Gulf War in 1990, when Saddam Hussein was firing Scud missiles at Israel, David helped run an emergency call center for panicked people who couldn't get their gas masks on their kids or didn't hear the "all-clear" sirens.

"I felt like this was my home," David said. "In Vietnam, where America was calling Communism the enemy and napalming the hell out of an entire country, I just didn't feel that fell in the category of self-defense. But the Israel Defense Forces are on call to prevent things from happening. The actions I was involved with in the Army were defensive—and I have no problem with that."

Both David and Alisa were particularly appalled in the summer of 2014 by the Western media's coverage of the fighting in Gaza, which they both found to be glaringly anti-Israel.

"Where else can you tell me, where else, in what other war zone anywhere in the world in the last 20 or 30 years, are you aware where someone made telephone calls, sent SMSs [text messages], and dropped leaflets to warn people that there was going to be a bombing 20 minutes before there was going to be a bombing?" David asked. "Where? Tell me? I had a problem with the Gaza war, and that is that it happened. If Hamas had said: 'We're willing to stop if you stop,' we would have stopped."

David and Alisa struggled to explain the situation to Avital. On one hand, they wanted to protect their 16-year-old. But it was impossible. They had family and friends who were serving in the Israeli military. And the kids in the choir would talk about it all the time. The singers from East Jerusalem had a much different take on the war than those from West Jerusalem.

"It was very difficult for Avital to kind of hear what she understood to be a war of defense on our part, to be talked about as war crimes by people whom she's singing with," David said.

David and Alisa would talk about the war and tell Avital about their belief in Good and Evil. Alisa posted an animated video on Avital's Facebook wall showing Hamas as a devious schoolyard bully who goads a reluctant Israel into fighting back and then convinces their teachers and the world that Israel was the aggressor.

The two-and-a-half-minute video ends with a black screen, the Star of David, and the words: "The world is not elementary school. Sometimes you just have to defend yourself."

Alisa encouraged Avital not to take what the Arab kids said at face value and to check out the stories they told. But Alisa sometimes appeared to unwittingly rely on Internet conspiracy theories to buttress her views that the world had unfairly demonized Israel during the Gaza war. Alisa seemed to indirectly rely on one American conspiracy theorist's view that Hamas, not Israel, was responsible for the killing of the four Palestinian boys on the Gaza beach—an attack seen by dozens of Western journalists.

While Israeli officials apologized for the shelling and called it a "tragic" accident, one Internet researcher in the United States cobbled together an outlandish theory that the incident was staged by Hamas, that the boys had been executed the day before and that militants had used planted explosives as a distraction while they placed the boys' bodies on the beach in front of the international press corps.

"I remember feeling very, very bad about it and then I remember reading a few months later that the UN or whoever had done an investigation and indeed they weren't killed by Israelis," Alisa said. "That's a picture that a lot of people have in their mind, and I had in my mind: that four children on the beach who were playing ball were killed by Israel. And also I think they were invited there or something strange like that."

The theory reinforced Alisa's own belief that Hamas was to blame for the war and that the group would go to any lengths to paint Israel as a bloodthirsty villain.

"It's very, very hard for me to understand," she said. "If you make the choice yourself, it's one thing. But if Hamas is making the choice for you and they're saying: 'We're going to make the choice for you that your children are going to be killed so that we can show the media, so they'll be more pro-Palestinian, so we'll get more brownie points' or whatever it is they think they'll get, I don't know."

HELICOPTERS OVER ASSAEL

The residents of Assael Street all hoped the end of the war in Gaza would bring a close to a traumatic chapter. But it didn't.

In late October, a group of Jerusalemites gathered at the Menachem Begin Heritage Center—a short walk from Abu Tor—to hear Yehuda Glick, an orange-bearded, right-wing American-Israeli crusader who favored ending Israel's ban on Jews praying on the Temple Mount. While Yehuda was packing up his car after the speech, a man pulled up on a motorcycle and fired four shots into the Jewish activist's chest before speeding off. Israeli police quickly identified the shooter as a resident of Abu Tor.

Before dawn the next morning, the families on Assael were roused from sleep by low-flying helicopters circling over their street. Israeli counterterrorism teams and border police converged on the home of 32-year-old Palestinian restaurant worker Mu'atez Hijazi, an East Jerusalemite who had spent 11 years in an Israeli prison for a series of crimes, from arson to slashing a guard's face with a razor blade. After his release in 2012, he settled in a small Abu Tor apartment building two streets below Assael and got a job at the Begin Center where Yehuda gave his talk.

"I'm glad to be back in Jerusalem," Hijazi told a reporter shortly after his release. "I hope to be a thorn in the Zionist plan of Judaizing Jerusalem."[10]

The counterterrorism unit chased Hijazi to his roof, where he was shot 20 times. Israeli police said they killed Hijazi after he opened fire on them. Residents claimed Hijazi was unarmed when he was shot. His family said he was framed. The shooting triggered street battles that spread across Jerusalem. The turmoil led Israel to temporarily shut down all access to the Old City's central religious plateau, home to al Aqsa mosque and the Dome of the Rock. It was the first time Israel had done so in more than a decade. Palestinian Authority president Mahmoud Abbas called it a "declaration of war."

It was starting to feel more like a new war on Assael Street. The deadly shootout fed Avital's anxieties about living in Abu Tor and fueled her desire to move.

"We never felt directly under threat, but it was very disturbing," Alisa said. "Very, very disturbing. It sounded like they were on the roof. It was hard for me, too, hearing those noises, not knowing what was going on, not knowing what was a safe explosion and what was not a safe explosion."

The shootout in Abu Tor was followed by a series of deadly attacks that appeared to be the work of "lone wolves" from East Jerusalem who drove into crowds of Israelis gathered at trolley stops and street corners.

The attacks created new questions for residents of Jerusalem, who started sizing each other up once again as potential threats. Palestinian parents worried that their kids could become another Mohammed Abu Khdeir. Jewish parents worried their kids could be run down while going to school.

Maha Salhab, Avital's best friend on Assael, thought the "lone wolf" attacks were stupid.

"You don't get anything by killing people," she said one afternoon that fall while hanging out across the street at Avital's place. "You're going nowhere. You're just ending lives. That's not right. That's not your choice."

Maha was more interested in Bollywood hunks like Shah Rukh Khan than Middle East politics. But wearing a hijab around West Jerusalem meant that she couldn't avoid being viewed with suspicion by some people when she went out. In the midst of the string of attacks, Maha (and her

kitty) drove to downtown Jerusalem to drop her fiancé off at his job working in a hotel on Jaffa Street. After saying good-bye to him and getting back
in her car, Maha saw a group of Jewish boys coming her way. She could tell
right away that they were looking for trouble. Maha locked the doors as the
boys surrounded her car. One of them started pounding on her window.
Maha was sure it was going to shatter. Another one started kicking her car.
Maha didn't know what to do. If she tried to drive away, she'd likely be
accused of trying to run over the boys and be swarmed by an angry mob.
Maha was trapped. She knew if she made the wrong move it would end
badly.

I can drive and just screw you, she thought, *but why? I don't want to
hurt you. They're not really men. They're just kids. I'm like their mother. So
what are they doing?*

Before things got out of control, Maha spotted an Israeli military jeep
in her rearview mirror and saw her salvation.

"Help!" she shouted as the boys backed off. *"They're trying to attack
me!"*

The soldiers scared the boys off and escorted Maha back to her house
on Assael Street where she tried to calm down.

"It was really terrifying," she said the next day.

Maha understood the fear Israelis felt from the spike in random attacks. But she didn't see why she should personally be held accountable.

"You can't live someplace that you could wait for a bus and just be
killed," she said. "It would be chaos. It's not fair. I won't hurt you, but you
can't hurt me either. I was just parking. The police, if I didn't see the lights,
I would be dead. I don't know what they were thinking to do really. There
was fire in their eyes. I don't want to hate them. I don't have to hate them.
But it was really scary."

If there was a silver lining, David saw it in Maha's decision to ask Israeli
security for help.

"I'm a citizen too," Maha told David.

"Undoubtedly there are times when the police go beyond what they're
supposed to do, when they're violently carrying out their work when they
could have carried it out less violently," he said. "But, by and large, I think
there is still a general understanding, certainly the Jews believe this, and I
think the vast majority of Arab-Israelis believe it, that there is still a basic
commitment to law and to fairness and to defending civil rights."

Alisa praised Maha for being level-headed.

"The truth is, if I was in that kind of situation I would stay in the car and hit the gas," Alisa said. "I would have hit them."

Maha was rattled. In her 22 years, it was by far the scariest thing that had happened to her in Jerusalem.

"I was born a Muslim, does that mean I am a terrorist or something?" she asked. "No. I am still kind, so why do you judge?"

Maha had little interest in political discussions. But it was impossible to escape the politics on Assael Street. Even her social life became political. Her Muslim friends gave her grief because of her friendship with Avital. But that friendship wasn't something Maha was willing to give up. For years Maha watched the toll politics took on her father as he fought the city's efforts to claim rights to the open garden lot next to the family home. Israel wouldn't accept Moussa Salhab's claim that the land was his family's. The documents Moussa had were never good enough to prove his case. Moussa's fight with Israel consumed years of his life and much of his salary. He took the case all the way to the Israeli Supreme Court—and lost. Any day, the family expected Israel to seize the land and turn it into an expensive new apartment building.

Maha saw everyone on Assael Street as pawns in a big political game she wasn't willing to spend her life playing. She was more interested in planning her wedding and figuring out how to get a good IT job in Israel. She resented being lumped in with Islamic extremists simply because she covered her hair.

"Who would like to be called a terrorist because of their religion?" she asked. "ISIS, they're not even Muslims. We don't kill people just like that. You don't do that. It's politics, not religion."

Maha was just as dismayed as Avital and her family by the string of attacks by East Jerusalemites.

"You don't get anything by hatred," she said.

Maha and her family had Jerusalem IDs, not full Israeli citizenship. She had little interest in defining herself as Palestinian, Arab-Israeli or anything else with a hyphen.

"I'm human," she said. "That's it."

To her, the war between Israelis and Palestinians could be as silly as the fight between Real Madrid and Barcelona, the rival Spanish soccer teams.

"I'm Barcelona. Oh, you are Real Madrid? You should die," Maha shook her head. "It's only a football game. If politics were in the hands of women, well, we are really soft. It would be very good. All the world would be pink. I would make the street pink, like Hello Kitty. And I would put [Bollywood hunk] Salman Khan in charge, as my assistant, of course."

"DON'T TALK TO HER LIKE THAT"

Maha and Avital got together when their schedules allowed. But once they got into their teens, things changed for Avital on Assael. Avital was taller than a lot of girls her age. She let her long brown hair down while the older girls on the other side of the street started wearing hijabs to cover theirs. Though Maha and Avital both wore tight jeans to school, it was Avital who started getting uncomfortable looks from the boys on the street when she walked home. The boys would talk in Arabic and laugh as she passed. Sometimes they would whistle and make crude noises.

"Every time I walk past them with her, they look at Avital," Alisa said one rainy night while visiting David at his cluttered office overlooking Emek Refaim, the "valley of ghosts," the trendy street filled with cafés, courtyard restaurants, bakeries and boutique jewelry stores.

"They don't do it all the time," David replied. "They've done it a few times and, ever since then, Avital has the feeling that if they are looking at her, that's what they are thinking."

"Every time I walk past them with her, they look at Avital," Alisa repeated. "And they look at her—"

David cut her off: "What's wrong? I would too."

"Excuse me," Alisa said firmly, with a sharp look. "They look at her in a way that, as a woman, I would feel very uncomfortable." To David, it was just boys being boys. Checking out girls isn't something only Palestinian boys do.

"But David, you're from a different culture," Alisa said. "I was living in Israel in the late '60s and early '70s and the country was very different than it is now. It was much less Western. It was very, very uncomfortable to walk down the street as a young teenager who was wearing a miniskirt or Western clothes and not religious clothes. It was very, very uncomfortable, and it limited us as young women. And this was Jewish boys."

David didn't see the situation the same way as Alisa and Avital did. To reduce the awkward walks, Avital started leaving her house through the garage and stairs that led up to the street above Assael, giving her an exit that didn't go past the boys sitting on the steps every day.

When the residents on the eastern side of the street suggested that they remove the chained gate blocking the concrete stairway running past the Joudans' home that once connected the two halves of the neighborhood, Alisa worried that it would mean her daughter would be subjected to even more leering.

"If there was a conduit that went from the Arab neighborhood into the Jewish neighborhood and the Arab men hung out there, it would cause much more of an issue for the young women as well, which, for women, is a big issue," she said. "There's nothing wrong with the Arab citizens of Abu Tor walking through the Jewish parts, but once there's this sexual issue, because it's two completely diverse cultures, it's very problematic."

To David, the problem had much less to do with Arab-Jewish relations than male-female relations.

"I probably would engender the wrath of females if I were to say: 'Well, just ignore it, start talking to them, they're saying that because you're not relating to them. You're just kind of walking by, so develop a relationship and you will get past this.'"

Alisa sighed.

"He doesn't get it," she said of her husband.

"It's not a matter of Avital not getting it . . ."

"No," Alisa said. "I said you don't get it. *You* don't get it."

"I was going to say the *majority of women* don't get it," David said wryly.

Alisa ignored her husband's mischievous goading.

"It's a cultural thing," she said. "It's not political, and it's not Mideastern."

Alisa wasn't sure what to do to. She figured she'd have to talk to the boys' fathers and see if she could get them to have a word with their sons.

"The truth is, if she walks through a scuzzy neighborhood in Jerusalem and boys did that, she'd feel uncomfortable also," she said. "It's not because they're Arab."

One afternoon in the fall of 2014, while Alisa was taking out the garbage, she saw a couple of the younger teenage boys who said something about Avital in Arabic that she didn't understand. Alisa walked back to say something.

"Who speaks Hebrew?" she asked the boys.

The boys looked a little scared.

"I do," one of the boys eventually said. *"We were just saying that you were Avital's mother."*

"You know," she told them, *"Avital is very good girl. She doesn't wear a hijab because she is Jewish. She's not Arab. But she's a very good girl. And I don't want you to talk to her like that."*

The kid translated Alisa's words to the other boys, who gave her sweet embarrassed smiles before she said "thanks" in Arabic and went back into her house.

The small confrontation embarrassed Avital, who wanted to draw as little attention to the issue she could.

"That's the beginning of a dialogue that I'm going to have with them," Alisa told Avital later.

"Oh god," Avital groaned before retreating to her room to decompress after school. "Don't keep doing it."

Alisa didn't know how much good it would do anyway.

"They don't listen to women," she said. "They listen to men. It's a cultural thing."

David and Alisa taught Avital not to draw broad conclusions about Arabs because of the leering boys on Assael. And Avital had enough Arab friends to know they weren't all the same. One afternoon when they were talking about life in Abu Tor, Avital told her mom that she wasn't opposed to falling in love with a Palestinian.

"You know what, Mom? If there was a really nice Palestinian person, I would totally marry the person even if he wasn't Jewish," she said before turning to her visitors. "I think I'm less strict than my parents. But they will welcome anyone in my life, because if I love the person, they need to love that person. I don't think it's such a big deal."

The idea made Alisa uncomfortable.

"It would make your life very complicated," she told Avital. "Not because of your family, but because, to be in Israel, in a mixed marriage between two peoples who have a lot of issues, is very hard."

"I think you're more strict than me, I'm saying," Avital told her mom.

"I'm not talking about my reaction," Alisa replied. "I'm talking about any young couple."

Later, Alisa said her concerns about Avital marrying a Palestinian had more to do with culture than politics.

"It's not a national issue," she said. "It's a cultural Jewish issue. If I lived in America I wouldn't be so happy if she married a non-Jewish person. I'm not prejudiced. If she fell in love I'd say: 'I'd really rather prefer that we keep it in the tribe.' But it's not a nationalist thing. And it would be such a hard life. I know mixed couples in Israel. It's such a hard place. Many of them leave the country."

"MAYBE WE HAVE TO WAIT"

The tension on the street made Alisa question how much good could come from her husband's bridge-building work. How, she wondered, could Israel make peace with people who carry out "honor killings" of girls, young women who could be condemned to death for dishonoring their families by doing something as innocent as flirting with a boy?

"There is such a culture gap," she said. "It's not like making peace between the Irish and the British. . . . If I was an objective person coming from space, if I wasn't part of this, I would say: 'How could this group come to any understanding with [that] group if the culture is so different?'"

In all her travels, Alisa tried to find the things that connected everyone. Underneath all the differences, Alisa saw unity.

"I think each culture manifests another facet of who we are," she said. "I traveled in India, Nepal, Tibet, Central America, even when I was in far islands in Scotland, every culture I've been to has taught me more of what it is to be a human being."

Living on Assael forced Alisa to question her own assumptions about coexistence.

"Maybe my sense that we have a commonality is overblown," she said. "Maybe it's very hard for a liberalized, Western society to come to an understanding with people who still think, like 60 percent of them think, honor killings are an appropriate thing. I don't know. Maybe we have to wait until there is some kind of more serious modernization of the Palestinian people. Not that anything's wrong with them now, but maybe that's the only way that we can talk. I don't want to put them down. I don't think modernization is so great. But maybe that's the only way these two societies can meet."

If there was ever a time the two sides of the street could have found common ground, Alisa said, it was right after the fence came down in 1967.

"I think, unfortunately, we didn't solve these problems in the decade after the Six-Day War, and, as we waited, stupidly, things got worse and worse and worse and less and less solvable," Alisa said. "I think if we would have maybe solved the problems in the first decade after the Six-Day War, there was still a ray of hope. There were still people who were willing. And now it's like . . ." Her voice trailed off.

"A friend of mine who saw the video 'Home' that the choir did told me: 'It breaks my heart that it can't be like they show here,'" Alisa said. "For me, it's like a little light at the end of the tunnel, but the tunnel is so dark and so long that I don't know how much of a difference it makes. I really despair over the situation."

After living on Assael for a decade, Alisa wasn't sure whether her relations with her neighbors would save her if things got really bad.

"There are these young Arab boys and the families on the street and I know we receive protection from them, but let's say things got really, really, really bad, God forbid, like one of these medieval scenarios and my house was surrounded by people who threatened the people across the street not to help us, would they protect us?" she wondered. "I don't think they would be able to."

It was a reality Alisa was prepared to accept, much the same way that she accepted that she probably wouldn't risk her life to save them.

"If these people were threatened, would I protect them with my body?" she asked. "Well, maybe if I was single and on my own I would. But would I sacrifice my life for my neighbors for things that I believed in? Maybe it's just because I'm not made of that stuff. Maybe I'm not like a fighter. Maybe I'm not that person at all."

Alisa wasn't the only one to question whether there was enough goodwill in Abu Tor to serve as a foundation for her husband's work. Other residents of Abu Tor who chose not to take part in David's community-building meetings were privately dismissive of his ideas, especially the more unconventional proposals like women's yoga classes.

"Yoga?" said one Abu Tor resident. "I mean, come on. Look, sometimes people who come here from America don't really understand how things work here."

CAN CHANGING ONE BLOCK CHANGE THE WORLD?

As the violence ripped across East Jerusalem and Abu Tor in late 2014, some people started looking for ways to separate the Arab and Jewish neighbors. By that point, the Israeli military was using the Beit Nehemiah community center at the top of Abu Tor to offer leadership courses to its young soldiers. Israeli soldiers were hanging out at the center where Arab kids came most afternoons to play soccer on the dilapidated concrete field out back. Like Judith Green a quarter century earlier, David found himself fighting efforts by the community center to bar Arab kids from playing on the soccer field.

"You have security people saying: 'You have counselors in the army, you have an army presence, and it's not a smart, safe or appropriate thing to do. Let's make it sterile,'" David said. "That goes in direct contradiction to certainly what we're trying to do, but also to the city's own policy, which says that all of its facilities should be open for use of the community, regardless of religion, sex, etc."

It felt like the movie *Groundhog Day* to Judith, who backed David's efforts, but seemed burned out by the endless cycle of turmoil and reconciliation.

"So far it's been kind of discouraging," said Judith, whose neighborhood activism stretched back to the 1980s. Most of the proposals seemed to go nowhere. One of the ideas everyone had agreed to try was a walking tour of Abu Tor. The Arab tour guides were a little wary of walking around the poorer parts of the neighborhood with a large number of Jewish neighbors. They wanted to take them around in small, inconspicuous groups that wouldn't stand out too much. Groups that wouldn't be as big a target. When the day came for the tour, the Arab residents led the small group around the safe parts of Abu Tor and never ventured into places the Jewish neighbors hadn't been.

"It was rather disappointing," Judith said later. "Anything that David or anyone else can do is definitely a plus. You should do it. But I don't know at this point. There's such different feelings in Jerusalem, and in general.

At best, it might somehow give a feeling of a little more security if people along the border know each other. It's sad. It's a very sad situation. I don't feel like it's dangerous, but it's sad. It's a loss of potential. At best, it's keeping things quiet."

David was undeterred. By early 2015 he was meeting with his Arab counterpart on the city community council, and the two were planning to team up to bring more money to Abu Tor.

"I'm feeling a sense of pride and patriotism in doing what I'm doing, because this is my definition of what Zionism is," he said. "Zionism is making Israel a light unto nations. Zionism is treating the stranger with the same laws. Zionism is Judaism. Judaism is social justice, and that's how I interpret both, not as recipes for separation and control, but as recipes for how a society should function, with a majority and minority, Jewish and democratic."

As a young man trying to find his way, David had been critical of his parents' jobs as psychiatric social workers.

"They were working on a case-by-case basis and I thought: 'What a waste of time,'" he said. "Not a waste of time, but it was like you were never going to solve the problem. You were going to solve one person's problem at a time, which is why I didn't become a psychiatric social worker, but a community organization social worker and a social planner social worker. So, I suppose that if I were now 18, I might say to my older self: 'Why are you just trying to work on the interests of Assael Street? You can do that, but it's not going to bring peace. You should work on trying to get the system changed,'" he said.

The young David dreamed about changing the world. By the time he was ready to retire, he'd come to realize that changing his neighborhood was hard enough.

"I have been on a constant diet," he said. "I wanted to change the entire world. Then I wanted to change the Jewish world. Then I just said, 'OK, I'll just change Israel.' At this point, I'm on my block."

And even changing his block isn't easy.

"I don't know how far I'm gonna go," said David, who likes to think that what he's doing matters to more than just the people on his street.

"It's still beyond me and beyond one person," he said. "So I can still say I'm working on the system."

SEVEN

THE GOOD ARAB

They call him *rebbe*.

Rabbi Khaled.

Khaled's Jewish coworkers reverently refer to this balding, clean shaven, middle-aged Muslim East Jerusalemite as *rebbe* because of his encyclopedic knowledge of Judaism. Khaled Rishek takes pride in being able to argue, in Hebrew, over the finer points of Abraham's biblical land claims. Given the chance, he will talk for hours about the complex meaning of obscure Old Testament stories.

"*Khaled,*" they say, with a friendly pat on his balding head and a squeeze of his clean-shaven face, "*knows Judaism better than most Jews.*"

For 30 years, Khaled has worked at the YMCA in West Jerusalem, an island of Arab-Jewish coexistence whose 152-foot-tall Byzantine bell tower has served as a geographic guidepost and solitary icon for decades.

To his Jewish coworkers at the Y, to his Jewish neighbors on Assael Street, to his Jewish friends in Israel, Khaled is the Good Arab.

"*You're not like those other Arabs,*" they tell him before retreating into their homes. "*You're not like those Arabs down the hill—causing all the trouble.*"

"*People always focus on the negative,*" his Jewish colleagues at the Y say when things get tense, "*but look at us: We are Muslim and Jew, working together.*"

To all of them, Khaled represents the Israel they imagine it to be: a place where Arab and Jew live and work—side by side—in peace. Especially when things get tense, Khaled's colleagues and neighbors turn to him for reassurance that everything is going to be all right.

"They say: 'You are not like the other Arabs.' But this doesn't make me feel good," he said one night in 2014 outside his home on Assael Street, while Israeli soldiers and masked Palestinian kids fought running street battles a few blocks away.

"I am part of them," he said of the stone throwers. "I am not part of you."

To Jewish families on the western side of Assael Street, families like Khaled's on the eastern side serve as a buffer from the disaffected Palestinians living in cramped homes and neglected neighborhoods right below.

"I say to anyone who wants to move into this area: 'You've got to realize that you're living right next to the ghetto,'" said Elon Bezalely, a British-Israeli financial adviser who lives with his wife and two kids across Assael from Khaled.

"That street," he said with a nod toward Assael, "is the border."

Practically and metaphorically, Khaled represents the first line of defense for his neighbors on the other side of the street. The entrance to Khaled's home sits in the middle of a steep, narrow stairway next to the Bazlamit compound. Most likely those stairs sit on the old dirt path that the UN inspectors walked up to the Yaghmour house in 1966 when they came to find out who had returned to No Man's Land. Khaled bought the Yaghmour house in 1990 from Ziad, grandson of Eid, the farmer who'd handed some poppies to Rachel Machsomi over the border fence. Like that of the Bazlamits' across the concrete stairway, Khaled's alley wall features hand-painted images of the Dome of the Rock, the black Ka'aba of Mecca, and celebratory crescent moons.

While Assael has been swept up in sporadic demonstrations over the years and has occasionally been tagged by political vandalism, the street had never been at the epicenter of major confrontations between Israeli soldiers and Palestinian stone throwers.

In the summer of 2014, Khaled could feel the troubles closing in on Assael Street. The kidnapping and killing of the three Israeli teenagers—Naftali Fraenkel, Gilad Shaer and Eyal Yifrach—was followed by the kidnapping and killing of 16-year-old Mohammed Abu Khdeir. When Israeli police arrested the Jewish suspects four days after the Palestinian boy's killing, his father wondered if the government was going to destroy the homes of the suspects the way they'd destroyed the home of the Palestinian killer. Angry mourners at the boy's funeral threw rocks at Israeli soldiers keeping watch. The soldiers responded with tear gas and rubber-coated metal bullets. Demonstrations spread to the West Bank.

Then Netanyahu sent the Israeli army back to crush Hamas in Gaza. As with previous clashes, the Palestinian death toll vastly outnumbered the Israelis'. Sixty-six Israeli soldiers and six civilians were killed during the 50-day operation. In Gaza, more than 2,000 lost their lives, including about 500 children—an average of ten kids a day. Israel was accused of killing scores of civilians by hitting crowded UN schools being used as shelters that offered minimal protection from Israeli artillery, mortars, rockets and bombs. The story from Gaza that Khaled and his family were seeing on the Arabic language cable stations was not the same one their Jewish neighbors on the other side of Assael Street were getting on their Israeli news programs.

The new surge of violence created deep psychological gashes for Palestinians and Israelis. Parents on both sides had reason to worry that their kids might not come home at night. People began to wonder if they were about to be consumed by a new Palestinian uprising. Pundits alternatively dubbed it the Silent Intifada, the Jerusalem Intifada, the Firecracker Intifada, the Children's Intifada and, perhaps most wryly, the Post-Modern Intifada.

Then the troubles washed over Abu Tor. The killing of Mu'atez Hijazi set off nightly clashes that forced people to close their windows to keep the tear gas out of their homes. Mothers on Assael worried about sending their children to take out the trash. Israeli border police installed concrete barriers to temporarily close off the main entrance connecting lower (Arab) Abu Tor to the upper (Jewish) part. That's when Khaled's Jewish neighbors started seeking some reassurance when they saw him on the street.

It was what Khaled did. He was the kind of tall, unassuming guy women would feel comfortable asking for directions if they saw him on the street. He could fade into the background at parties and easily settle into conversations with almost anyone. The sternest thing about Khaled seemed to be the dark, bushy eyebrows that sometimes made it look as if he was scowling.

Khaled was a Jerusalem baby, the oldest of 11 siblings. Before 1967, his father helped make uniforms for the Jordanian army at a factory in Amman. Khaled was born in the Muslim Quarter of the Old City in 1966. The next year, Israel seized control of the Old City, East Jerusalem and the West Bank. The tailor's son grew up playing soccer on the Old City's tourist-clogged streets and walking with his family to Friday prayers at al Aqsa mosque.

LIVING ON THE EDGE OF THE "GHETTO"

For neighbors like Elon Bezalely, Khaled and the families on the other side of Assael Street weren't part of the problem. The Arabs across the street weren't the ones stirring up trouble. It was Arabs coming from the valley, from the heart of Palestinian Abu Tor.

"I think the major issues that happen in Abu Tor—such as the car burnings and Molotov cocktails—are, I feel, I've got no evidence, I feel it's predominately from the other side of the valley," said Elon, who moved from London to Israel in 1997, when he was in his late 20s and the voices of hope in the Middle East seemed to have a slight advantage over the voices of despair.

"I'm not so sure about that," his wife said.

Linda Bezalely had less faith in her neighbors.

"I know you'd like to think it's all from Silwan, but I think there are a lot of people who don't like us in Abu Tor," Linda said after putting their two young kids to sleep.

Elon moved to Assael Street in 2007. For Elon, living on the invisible border meant that the price was right. Elon bought the two-bedroom home for $275,000. Linda moved in two years later when the couple got married.

"Everyone asks: 'What made you choose Abu Tor?' and I say: '*I didn't. I chose the man*,'" Linda said.

"This," she said with a nod toward Assael Street, "came with it."

The couple's home is one of the few on the western side of the street that still has an open door leading out onto Assael. And it's one of the few with a small stoop—a stoop that became an ideal place for the Bazlamit boys to hang out every night and smoke shisha while texting friends and watching who was coming and going on Assael Street. Most days, Linda found the boys on her steps when she came out with her stroller to take her little boy and girl for a walk to the park. Linda was a skinny, athletic, self-assured, curly haired British immigrant who had given up a career as a financial adviser to run dating seminars that offered women advice on how to avoid marrying a "jerk." Like Alisa Maeir-Epstein, Linda decided she wasn't going to steer clear of Assael Street. She said hello and tried to be friendly. She didn't know most of her Palestinian neighbors' names, but at least she could recognize some of them.

"I wouldn't have chosen this area for myself," she said, "but the truth is we love it."

"If you're willing to put up with, again, the best way to describe it is living right next to the ghetto, then it's good," said Elon who, even at home, has the frenetic energy of the hedge fund manager he once was.

Elon bought his house from Carol, the Israeli realtor effectively driven from the neighborhood because of the bad blood with the Bazlamits across the way. Elon did his homework before he bought the place. He looked up stories on Assael. He checked out Carol and came across an article detailing her clash with the Bazlamits. For Elon, the problem seemed easily surmountable.

One of the first things Elon did when he moved in was to reach out to the big Palestinian family across the way to let them know that he was totally cool with them painting on what was now *his* outside wall, not Carol's. The Bazlamits were happy to take Elon up on his offer. The next time the family held a welcome home party for someone returning from their pilgrimage to Mecca, the kids brought out their stencils and spray paint cans.

"Welcome back from Hajj, Abu Zakaria" ran in uneven black Arabic script across the white cement wall that had been the spark for the feud between Carol and the Bazlamits.

For Elon, the offer was strategic. It allowed him to build up some goodwill with a family that knew what it was like to live on a dividing line. And, perhaps, the Arabic graffiti would serve as a modern-day Passover symbol, shielding his family from problems he hoped would pass over his house, much the same way God passed over the homes of Jews held captive in Egypt who painted red Xs in lamb's blood on their doors to protect their firstborn children from His wrath.

"I don't think people come up this street," Elon said one night in the fall of 2014, as Israel tried to put a lid on the stone-throwing protests. "But, just in case, there's a bit of artwork on our side."

Their neighbor, Sara Arnold, wasn't sure letting the family paint graffiti on the wall was such a good idea. Sara had lived above Assael much longer than Elon and Linda. She considered herself a bridge-builder and worked with Arab kids in Jerusalem schools. But she wondered how much goodwill there really was on the street.

"Are you sure it says what it says?" she asked Elon that fall night while they considered the possibility that they might be on the front lines of the third Palestinian intifada.

"Yeah," he told her. "My mom read it."

By happenstance, Elon was the latest Israeli of Iranian descent to live on Assael Street. His mom was born in Iran and emigrated to England in the 1960s, where she met her Israeli-born husband, married and started their family.

"Does she really know?" Sara asked again. "If it says 'Kill the Jews' or something, I don't know that you'd want it on your wall."

Elon took it as a measure of faith, verified by his mother, that their neighbors hadn't written "Kill the Jews" on his wall. But, in some ways, he understood where that kind of hostility came from.

The political stalemate had, to his mind, created an untenable status quo that was eating away at Israel's morality. Many Israelis, he said, wanted the West Bank, but not the Palestinians living there. Realists across the political spectrum understand that annexing the West Bank, absorbing its 2 million Palestinians as citizens with full rights and abandoning the two-state solution could eventually lead to the end of Israel's self-identity as a Jewish state. But the creation of the Palestinian Authority and the reduction of the Israeli military presence across the West Bank created enough separation between Arabs and Jews to effectively obliterate the popular characterization of the West Bank as Occupied Territory.

"There are many people, including people we know, who would be happy to say: 'Well, I want to annex it and not give them passports and give them second-class citizenship,'" Elon said. "We go through school, life, and people say to us, 'Well, calling it the 'Occupied Territories' is anti-Semitic.' It's not. They're occupied territories. It hasn't been annexed."

Most Israelis reject any comparison of their country to racist, 1970s-era South Africa and its discriminatory Apartheid state. Not Elon, who seemed like the kind of British transplant who'd be happy to debate the issue for long hours over pints at a pub almost anywhere in the world.

"People liken us to Apartheid," he said. "It *is* like Apartheid. Fifty years we've been on the fence and we haven't done one thing or another. We haven't annexed or not—and there's a couple of million there who haven't got citizenship."

"THERE ARE MANY ARABS LIKE ME"

Elon and others living on Assael know when Khaled is home because he parks his red-and-white motorbike under a canopy of bougainvillea climbing the stone walls across from his house. Khaled has worked for years as an emergency medical technician with United Hatzalah, the countrywide emergency response group run by ultra-Orthodox Jews.

In more tranquil parts of the world, being an emergency paramedic means responding to car accidents and heart attacks. In Jerusalem, working for United Hatzalah means that Khaled has been one of the first responders to years of Palestinian suicide attacks. It is always risky business.

Emotions run hot in the aftermath of suicide attacks in Jerusalem. It's not uncommon to see groups of young Jewish men, often led by ultra-Orthodox nationalists, chanting "Death to Arabs" as medics carry off the injured and religious crews try to collect every piece of the victims' bodies that they can find.

United Hatzalah started hiring EMTs like Khaled to work in the Arab neighborhoods, where its Jewish paramedics were often afraid to go. Riding their bikes, with red sirens attached to the top of their medical-gear boxes on the back, the paramedics are able to zip through traffic and respond more quickly than conventional ambulances trying to squeeze through Jerusalem's narrow, traffic-clogged roads. And living in Abu Tor meant that Khaled was often one of the closest EMTs when a suicide attack occurred in the center of the city.

Khaled said he feels protected when he wears the full, heavy motorcycle helmet and leather jacket bearing the United Hatzalah logo. It sends a clear message that Khaled is there to help. Especially with his helmet on, people can't tell if Khaled is Arab or Jewish. Khaled's fluent Hebrew means that he understands everything going on around him when he gets to the scene. He can tell when emotions are running high, and it makes sense to stick close to friends for protection. And he's got plenty of allies among the medics and police officers who are part of the city's unique fraternity.

"They hurt the other Arabs," he said of the vitriolic activists who seem to converge on every major Palestinian attack in Jerusalem. "But not me."

Khaled was willing to take the risks—as long as his wife and kids were safe. That wasn't something Khaled was always able to guarantee, especially when his son reached his teens. At the scene of one West Jerusalem attack in 2008, just down the street from the YMCA, Khaled saw his only son Jamal, who was about to turn 12, in the crowd, standing among the TV cameras and angry young bystanders. While police prepared to remove the body of a Palestinian assailant who'd commandeered a tractor and wounded two dozen people before being shot dead, Khaled rushed over to see Jamal.

"What are you doing here?" he asked his son. *"Get out of here. It's not safe."*

Khaled's sinking feeling got worse during the summer of 2014. He could see a little bit of Mohammed Abu Khdeir in his son. Had fortune been against Jamal, he could just as easily have been the one snatched off the street that summer day. Like the 16-year-old Khdeir, Jamal was thin, with adolescent acne and few signs that he'd be able to grow a beard any time soon. As much as Jamal wanted to think he was tough, he probably couldn't put up much of a fight.

"I'm afraid for Jamal all the time," Khaled confessed one evening as he sat in his living room with his son in the fall of 2014. Khaled was always on alert because of his work. It made him hypersensitive to shifts in the atmosphere. That November, Khaled had been one of the first to reach the scene of an attack in which an East Jerusalemite plowed his van into people waiting at a light rail station on the wide highway that was part of the border dividing the city from 1948 to 1967, just down the road from the old Mandelbaum Gate that once connected Jordanian-controlled East and Israeli-controlled West Jerusalem.

The attack, captured on film by various security cameras, showed a white van careening into people as they scrambled for safety at the rail station. The driver jumped from the car and vainly tried to get away. Dozens of drivers watched police officers shoot the man in the middle of one of Jerusalem's busiest intersections. For many, the attack was a clear sign that random attacks were going to be the hallmark of the third intifada.

Khaled's emergency alert went off on his phone while he was working at the Y. He grabbed his leather jacket, put on his helmet and jumped on his scooter for the short ride to the scene. He zipped past the French hospital that once sat on the edge of No Man's Land, where Catholic nuns carried out their unusual search for a patient's missing dentures in 1956.

When Khaled got to the scene, he saw the attacker, shot dead by police in the intersection. Nearby, he saw an older couple trapped in their car, which had been sideswiped by the van. The couple looked terrified as Khaled walked up to them, still wearing his helmet. Khaled saw Muslim prayer beads on their dashboard as he approached.

"A-salaam allekum," he said to them as a wave of relief washed over both their faces, knowing they weren't going to be lynched by an angry mob.

"Ilhamdulilah," they said in thanks to God. "You are Arab."

Three people were killed by the driver: a 17-year-old Jewish religious studies major, a 38-year-old Druze border policeman, and a 60-year-old Palestinian man from the West Bank. Hamas claimed responsibility for the attack, but it seemed more likely that the driver was a lone wolf.

Khaled saw his work as an EMT as perhaps the most important thing he could do to shatter misconceptions most Israelis seemed to have about Palestinians.

"Every time I volunteer somewhere in Israel, when I go inside a house, I say: 'My name is Khaled and I am a volunteer,'" he said. "They are surprised because, to them, they have a stereotype in their head that, as an Arab, you're not supposed to be doing any good in any way."

Khaled takes that view as a personal affront. He's made it a personal mission to change people's minds.

"I try always to challenge that idea and say: 'Don't be surprised. I'm not unique. There are many Arabs like me.'"

In 2014, Khaled appeared in a two-minute advertisement to promote United Hatzalah. The video was meant to showcase the private aid group's diverse volunteers. It begins in a mosque where Khaled, wearing saggy, dad-style blue jeans and a short-sleeved green polo shirt, is praying with dozens of men. It cuts to a young, bearded, ultra-Orthodox Jewish colleague, draped in a white prayer shawl covering his head and the small black box filled with Torah verses strapped to his head, praying in a synagogue. Then it cuts to an attractive sandy blond (apparently secular) woman, in jeans and a black T-shirt, listening to music on headphones in a CD shop. All three of them rush from what they are doing when they get a medical alert on their phones. This time, it's not about a suicide bombing or lone-wolf car attack. The three join forces to save a young red-haired Israeli girl who is choking in her kitchen. Khaled and the other man jump on their scooters while the woman gets behind the wheel of an ambulance. The three, all wearing United Hatzalah's neon orange emergency vests, work together to save the blue-faced girl's life. As the girl's relieved mother hugs her daughter, the screen fades to white with the group's slogan, in Hebrew, Arabic and English, appearing on the screen: "United Hatzalah of Israel: United for Life."

The work bolsters Khaled's reputation among Israelis as "one of the good ones." It gives Khaled unusual credibility when he criticizes Israeli policies. Though he can ramble on in a voice that can lull you to sleep, Khaled's words can be cutting.

One night, Khaled took his wife to a special screening of a documentary about an Israeli high school up north that decided to produce a play with kids from a nearby Arab village. The film captured the tensions between the Muslim and Jewish kids as they tried to overcome their preconceptions and misconceptions to put on a musical about the Israeli-Palestinian conflict.

Khaled knew the film's producer from his work at the Y, so he and Rita walked down to the Cinematheque, Jerusalem's art-house theater set in the lower part of the Hinnom Valley, the Valley of Slaughter, across from the Old City walls. A few dozen people turned out to see the film in a large, mostly empty auditorium. Most decided to stay after the film was over for a discussion with the producer. Khaled and Rita seemed to be the only Palestinians in the small audience.

The screening attracted like-minded people who wanted to see Arabs and Jews living together. Mostly.

One man wondered who Israel belonged to: The Jews? The Arabs? Both? He mentioned the Holocaust and reminded everyone about why Israel had been created in the first place.

"The Arabs have a lot of countries and the Jews have but one," he said during the discussion. *"It has to be protected."*

People in the crowd murmured amongst themselves and Khaled could tell that most people weren't on this guy's side. Khaled raised his hand to speak and stood up so everyone in the movie theater could see him. He wore a worn, espresso-colored tweed blazer over a simple striped polo shirt and khaki brown pants. Dressed in a well-fitting, hip-length scarlet jacket over black tights and pointed, ankle-high, black leather boots, Rita looked on as Khaled spoke his mind.

"With all due respect to the victims of the Holocaust, many of the Arabs in this country feel that they, too, paid a price for the Holocaust," he told the small group that stayed for the postmovie talk. *"Because of the guilt of the world after World War II, the world supported the creation of the State of Israel, which came at a great price: the* Nakba, *the Catastrophe, for Palestinians."*

The audience wasn't sure what to say. The producer thanked Khaled for his thoughts and the moviegoers soon made their way out into the chilly Jerusalem evening. Khaled rarely seems to doubt his place in Israeli society. He sees it as his duty to challenge Israelis, especially those who consider themselves open-minded. One Jewish colleague at the Y told Khaled a story about left-leaning Israelis living along the coast in an old Palestinian home in Jaffa, the funky Brooklyn of Tel Aviv, just up the Mediterranean coastline. One day, Khaled's friend told him, the original Palestinian owners of the home turned up and told the progressive Israelis that they were living in their old house. In a conciliatory gesture, the Israelis invited them in, but things quickly went badly and the Israelis kicked the original owners out of the house. The story struck Khaled for its fundamental hypocrisy.

"If these were leftist Jews, what do you expect of the extreme Jews?" Khaled said. "I guess people talk big about coexistence until the topic comes home. Then they show their true colors."

COEXISTENCE IS A JOKE

What to some people might come across as anti-Israeli seems to Khaled's son to be just the opposite.

"Every time he discusses political issues it seems like he's backing the Jewish narrative," Jamal said. "My father sees only the positive side of the story and not the negative side. He has never been to a checkpoint. That's why he only sees the good side of Jews. Because he works with them."

Jamal's studies at Bir Zeit University outside Ramallah regularly brought him into the West Bank for classes. In an effort to show Jamal the value of coexistence, Khaled sent him to an Arab-Jewish peace camp in Ottawa, Canada, in the summer of 2013.

The kids spent hours talking about their lives, went on field trips, played confidence-building games together and vowed to keep in touch before heading home. A year later, Jamal ran into one of the Israelis from the peace camp. She was serving as a guard at the Qalandiya checkpoint, one of the regular battlegrounds for Israeli soldiers and Palestinian demonstrators. One summer she was celebrating coexistence in Canada. The next, she was wearing an Israeli military uniform, armed with a machine gun, manning one of Israel's biggest West Bank chokepoints. That moment told Jamal all that he needed to know about the value of coexistence.

"Look at her now," Jamal said. "She's checking IDs."

To avoid being scrutinized by the Israeli soldier he'd met at peace camp in Canada, Jamal ducked his motor scooter into a different lane, flashed his Jerusalem ID to another soldier and sped home. Jamal came to regret taking part in the Canada peace camp after a religious teacher told him it was tantamount to "normalization."

"Our religion bans us from having peace with them," Jamal said. "Because they betray you, just like they betrayed the Prophet Muhammad."

Khaled saw his son's views as an uneducated interpretation of Islam. Sure, Muhammad expelled Jewish tribes that had broken their pledge to support him in Medina when Islam was taking root. But he also gave Jews and Christians religious autonomy in Medina, referring to them, like Muslims, as "People of the Book," and reminded his followers that all of them prayed to the same god.

"If Jamal were to read more, he would not base his views on what he hears," Khaled said while his son checked his cell phone messages.

Khaled had the same debate with Jamal all the time.

"There's a school of thought that we should not talk to the other side at all," he said as his son listened from the other side of their living room. "I disagree with that, and I present myself to them, always, as a human being. I am a human being like you. Don't lie to me. Treat me with respect."

Khaled's wife was torn. She was one of the only wives on the eastern side of Assael who didn't cover her hair. She has no problem wearing tight jeans and sleeveless shirts that might elicit catty comments from more conservative women on the street. But she feels just as Palestinian as they do. One of her relatives is a high-ranking member of the Palestinian Authority intelligence service. Her sister is a well-known host on Palestine TV in the West Bank.

"I love the West Bank," she said. "Whichever Arab country we visit, I feel they have more commitment to their Arab and Pan-Arabness than here. Once we have Jerusalem as our capital, we will make lots of mistakes and we will suffer tremendously, but at least it will retain its Arab character."

Khaled sees the fundamental imbalance in the way Arabs and Jews interact in Israel. The question always comes up in the various coexistence workshops Khaled takes part in.

"Whenever I ask: 'Do you know any Arabs?' They say: 'Oh, yes I do. I know this worker in my father's company.' To them an Arab is a worker. An Arab is an assistant. An Arab is a waiter. They only know Arabs in terms of a menial service that they provide. They never look at the Arab on the same level as themselves. They have a superiority complex. Just because of the sheer fact that they're at a meeting, they feel they have given a lot to the relationship. There are so many in Israeli society who believe the stereotype completely about the Palestinians and are completely convinced the country was created only for them," he said. "To them Arabs are Bedouins."

"YOU DIRTY ARAB"

Khaled sees the uncensored animosity in the Facebook posts of his Israeli friends who proudly upload photos of Hebrew "We don't employ Arabs" signs in store windows, placed there to appeal to Israel's basest fears. He sees it in the small humiliations he endures while out doing errands.

"One day I went to the post office," he said. "A woman in front of me in line left and it was my turn. She came back a few minutes later and said: 'Where's my phone?'"

Khaled knew this wasn't going to end well. He shuffled through his paperwork to make sure her phone wasn't hidden. No luck.

"Where's my phone?" she started screaming at Khaled. *"You're a thief. You're a dirty Arab."*

Scores of people in the post office held their tongues, including people working there who knew Khaled. Khaled wasn't going to keep his mouth shut.

"Shame on you," he told her. *"I didn't take your phone."*

The women became unhinged.

"Don't talk to me like that," she said before storming off. *"Shame on you, you dirty Arab. You thief."*

Khaled was shaken by the confrontation. He looked around for some sympathy or support, but he found none. A Jewish-Israeli acquaintance at the post office scolded Khaled for talking back.

"I'm not upset with that woman," she said, *"I'm upset with you. I don't want you to defend yourself. I know your situation is difficult. But it only makes things worse."*

As if to prove her point, the customer came back in and started lecturing the Jewish customers about the silent dangers they all faced from people like Khaled.

"Your naïveté is what encourages these people to commit terrorist acts," she said to everyone who would listen.

Khaled wrapped up his errand and returned to the Y. He was angry and upset. But he found some solace being back at the Y, a small oasis in Jerusalem. The building was designed in the 1920s by Arthur Loomis Harmon, the man who helped create what was at the time the world's tallest building: the Empire State Building in New York.

The Y was built to be a sanctuary for Jerusalem's three major religions: Judaism, Christianity and Islam. The architects and builders injected symbolism into the smallest details. Some call it a "sermon in stone."

The foundation stones came from the same quarries that the Jews of Jerusalem used to build the second temple in 500 BC. The builders planted 12 cypress trees, said to represent the 12 tribes of Israel, the 12 disciples of Jesus Christ and the 12 followers of Muhammad. They courtyard contains 40 pillars to commemorate the 40 years Jews spent in the desert and the 40 days Jesus fasted.

The bell tower features a bas-relief sculpture of a six-winged angel, a seraphim, that flew around the throne of God crying "holy, holy, holy" in the Book of Isaiah. The sprawling lobby, with its vaulted ceilings and stone pillars, is home to a mosaic replica of the Madaba Map, an iconic sixth-century Byzantine map at a church in Jordan that depicts the ancient Middle East, including Jerusalem.

Part of the ceiling features painted panels from Damascus that were dismantled in Syria and brought to Jerusalem. The courtyard walls are engraved with three phrases honoring the city's Muslim, Christian and Jewish faiths.

In Hebrew, one phrase from the Old Testament reads: "The Lord our God the Lord is One." In the middle, in Aramaic, are the words of Jesus Christ: "I am the way." On the left, in Arabic, is the Quranic profession of faith: "There is No God but God."

The entrance also features a quote from Lord Edmund Allenby, the British military officer who captured Jerusalem from the Turks during World War I.

"Here is a place whose atmosphere is peace, where political and religious jealousies can be forgotten, and international unity fostered and developed," Allenby said at the opening ceremony for the YMCA in 1933.[1]

Over the years, it has served as home for the International Red Cross, the UN Consulate General and UN mediator Count Folke Bernadotte, who was assassinated in 1948 by the Jewish Stern Gang while he was trying to broker peace in the region.

The arched courtyard colonnades are pockmarked with blasts of shrapnel from the 1948 war—a visible scar meant to serve as a reminder that preventing war requires actively working for peace.

On that afternoon, Khaled was feeling little of the peace and tranquility that the Y was meant to offer. When he got back to work he ran into Rena Sered, the Y's health and fitness manager, an energetic, Chicago-born American-Israeli who had been working with Khaled for seven years.

"What's wrong?" Rena asked Khaled, who was unusually distraught. Khaled felt comfortable talking to some colleagues at the Y about personal problems, but he was hesitant to tell Rena about the post office. The two of them would talk about the Jewish Torah and they'd both been to each other's houses to offer condolences for the loss of their mothers. But Khaled didn't think he could talk to Rena about what happened.

"Our relationship isn't made for me to talk to you about anything like this," Khaled told her.

But Rena wanted to offer a sympathetic ear. She got him some water and a towel to dry his sweating face. Rena seemed to be genuinely concerned, so Khaled decided to tell her the whole story.

"In my opinion," Khaled said later, "this was one of my life mistakes."

Khaled was wound up. He took a slug of water and told her what happened, in Hebrew. He told her about the missing phone and the woman's accusations. He told her about the conspicuous silence from his so-called friends at the post office. He told her about the scolding he'd gotten for speaking up for himself. It was too much for Khaled.

"Israelis say they are for coexistence, but they're all terrible," he told her.

"Wait a minute," Rena said. *"It's not all Israelis. Don't say all Israelis are bad. The people in the post office might be bad people, but that's not all Israelis."*

"As a nation," Khaled said. *"Israel is terrible."*

Rena was shocked by what Khaled was saying. This wasn't the man she'd worked with for years. This wasn't the man she'd come to call a friend.

"Do you want me to go back to the post office with you?" she asked.

"No," he said. *"What good will that do?"*

"Well," she replied. *"You can't generalize about all Israelis or all Jews. It's like me saying that all Arabs cut people's heads off, that all Arabs are ISIS."*

Khaled couldn't believe what he was hearing. *All Arabs are ISIS? All Arabs are savages?*

"What are you saying?" Khaled told her. *"Shame on you. You're a racist."*

"You're the racist," she replied. *"You're very hostile towards the Jews."*

"I'm wasting time with someone like you," Khaled said as he considered walking out.

They argued for an hour. Rena couldn't believe Khaled seemed to be demonizing all Jews. Khaled couldn't believe Rena seemed to be stereotyping all Arabs. While they were arguing, the Y's executive director heard the bickering and stepped into the membership office to find out what was going on.

Though he was only 36, Forsan Hussein held the distinction of serving as the only Muslim CEO of any YMCA in the world. Born in a small

Arab village in Israel's Lower Galilee, Forsan went from being a construction worker to becoming a respected advocate for Israeli-Palestinian coexistence.

Forsan had all the natural qualities of a leader. He received a full scholarship from Israel's Abraham Fund to study at the predominantly Jewish Brandeis University, a small liberal arts college outside Boston, Massachusetts. When he arrived as the only Arab student on campus, he dove into campus life and teamed up with a Jewish-Israeli student to start a weekly student talk radio show.

Forsan got a master's degree in international relations from Johns Hopkins University's School of Advanced International Studies in Baltimore, Maryland, and an MBA from Harvard Business School. He was fluent in English, Arabic and Hebrew. His voice was soothing, his cadence lyrical. It could sound almost seductive, even in meetings. To top it off, Forsan's lean figure, square jaw and slight five o'clock shadow made him look like he walked off a Tommy Hilfiger fashion shoot. He married the daughter of Israel's first Arab ambassador and dreamed of following in his father-in-law's footsteps. His supporters dubbed him the "Israeli Obama."

As Arab-Israelis, Khaled and Forsan had lots in common. Language. History. And a belief in their identities as Palestinians living in Israel.

Like Khaled, Forsan saw his life as a reflection of his philosophy. And serving as the first Muslim head of any Y in the world, not to mention the first Palestinian Muslim to serve as head of the Y in West Jerusalem, was a testament to his ideology.

"Jerusalem is a place of many divides: social, political, religious, cultural and in education," Forsan wrote in his vision statement for the YMCA. "On every level, Jerusalem is a place of tension."

Forsan wanted "to contribute to the wellbeing of our society through bringing people together, bringing these conflicting narratives and sects together to a place where they can actually realize the humanity in the other," he wrote. "What I have done throughout my life has taught me that hopelessness and helplessness are not options. They simply aren't."[2]

Forsan was firmly rooted in Israel: a Palestinian whose conversations would meander back and forth between Hebrew, Arabic and English, much the way a conversation in Toronto would seamlessly shift from French to English and back. Forsan saw himself as someone who could transcend those ethnic, social, cultural, religious and political divides in Jerusalem.

"The YMCA was created to set an example of what Jerusalem can, and should be," he said in a video promoting coexistence made for his American alma mater, Brandeis University. "I take my life as an example of a successful co-existence story. I'm an Israeli-Arab, and not [just] any type of Arab, I am a Palestinian—with pride."[3]

"I feel that I am that bridge," he continued. "Not just me, but the entire Palestinian-Israelis, or the Israeli-Arabs, a million and a half people, that could completely serve as a bridge between Israel and the rest of the Arab world."[4]

"We aspire to bring a new generation of Palestinians and Israelis who understand the values of shared society and shared citizenship," he said. "We need a new leadership that emerges out of a different narrative, a different psyche. Not the psyche of fear. Not the psyche of occupation. Not the psyche of injustice."[5]

Forsan tried to cultivate those ideals at the YMCA. But on that afternoon, he could see that the psyche of fear and injustice was winning the day.

Forsan tried to defuse the situation. He knew Khaled and Rena were both well-intentioned. They both played important roles at the Y. When Forsan had to lay people off, he'd made sure that both of them were taken off the list. Rena was a great people person who helped keep the Y running. Khaled was a jack-of-all-trades who knew how to do just about anything at the Y. He sympathized with both of them.

"Khaled was hurt because, to them, he's one of the 'good Arabs,'" Forsan said. "He feels like he's an ambassador and, for that to happen to him, it's unfair."

"Rena," he said, "Rena is American-Jewish. She is completely PC. She would never say anything that hurts people. Nothing racist would come out of her mouth. I don't think there's anything wrong with what she said, but Khaled did perceive what she said as racist."

If Khaled had a particular flaw, Forsan thought, it was his emotions. Khaled let them get away from him too often.

"I don't think Khaled has processed things," he said. "There's a lot inside him. There's anger. There's resentment. He's a wonderful representative of Arabs to the Jews. But it's hard for me to see Khaled as a bridge. I know Khaled very well. Khaled is a great guy. He's a good family man. But I think Khaled would explode if you pressure him and, if you push, he might actually do damage when it comes to Israeli-Palestinian relations."

While Forsan valued Khaled's work at the Y, he thought his friend and employee was more effective as a Palestinian goodwill ambassador to Israel in the work he did as a medic.

"I don't see him as a symbol," he said. "I think he's much more effective doing United Hatzalah. The work of United Hatzalah is the most human thing you can do. And that's already a symbol."

Khaled and Rena's argument blew over and the two got back to work.

Rena, who spent most of her life working in fitness, still turns to Khaled as a confidante. Khaled may unfairly lash out at Jewish-Israelis sometimes, she said, but he can be even more critical of Arab Muslims. His emotional disdain for Palestinians can be just as cutting, if not more.

"I don't think he's one-dimensional," Rena said. "I think he's frustrated with his people as well."

Khaled knew his emotions got the better of him that afternoon when he got back from the post office and lashed out at Rena, and the two of them later commiserated over their passionate discussion. Things blew over and they moved on. That's how it went at the Y.

"THEY LIVE THEIR LIES IN THEIR COCOON"

While Forsan didn't see Khaled as a bridge-builder, Micah Hendler did. Forsan hired Micah to set up his Arab-Jewish youth choir at the Y. And Micah hired Khaled to be one of the choir's dialogue supervisors. It was Khaled's job to facilitate, and translate, the difficult discussions the Arab and Jewish kids had every time they met.

"I don't think I know anyone in Jerusalem who understands more of what's going on in the city, from every perspective, than Khaled," Micah said. "I have so much respect for his understanding of what's going on here. And he really lives all of the tensions, even just living on the street and with his identity."

Even though Khaled has to defend his work when he goes home, he doesn't see any other way. Cutting ties, living separate lives, isn't a solution.

"They live in their lie, they live in their cocoon, and if we do not approach them, if we don't start somewhere, we will achieve nothing," he said. "We have to start somewhere."

Forsan saw his work in similar terms. Activists often accused people like Forsan and Khaled of embracing "normalization"—a derogatory term for coexistence programs like those at the Y. They were often accused of undermining Palestinian independence by giving legitimacy to anti-Palestinian policies and working within the Israeli system. Forsan rejected the criticism.

"I am totally pro-normalization," he said. "I am pro–people talking to each other. I don't see coexistence as a political issue at all. I see it as a way of life, and I refuse to brand it, or even to speak of it in tones of politics."

Khaled was constantly questioned about his loyalties—by Israelis, by Palestinians, by his own family. His identity and sympathies were challenged at every turn. Everything Khaled did was subject to scrutiny—even how he identified himself: Arab-Israeli? Palestinian-Israeli? Palestinian? Each label came with its own baggage.

Whatever they called themselves, the 1.5 million Arabs living in Israel were always an awkward reality for the country. Israel was established as a home for the Jewish people. Its founders envisaged a democratic, pluralistic nation. But they always imagined Israel would be a Jewish nation—one way or another.

At best, the Arab-Israelis were meant to be a peaceful, fully assimilated minority with full rights and freedoms. At worst, well . . .

In the worst of times, Arab-Israelis were viewed with suspicion. Where *exactly* did their loyalties lie? If they *had* to choose, which side of the hyphen would they lean toward? That's why people paid so much attention to how people like Khaled identified themselves. Were they Arab-Israeli or Israeli-Arab? Were they Israelis of Palestinian ancestry or Palestinians living in Israel?

Israel's most nationalistic leaders saw the nation's Arab minority as a dangerous fifth column that threatened the country's very existence. The hostility tended to rise and fall depending on the political season. Typically, it got worse when things were bad.

"We will have to take another decision, and that is to sweep the Israeli Arabs from the political system," Effie Eitam, a controversial Israeli war hero and politician, said in 2006 after the country's war with Hezbollah in Lebanon. "We've raised a Fifth Column, a league of traitors of the first rank. Therefore, we cannot continue to enable so large and so hostile a presence within the political system of Israel."[6]

Even in the best of times, Israel's Arab minority was seen as a source of concern. Israeli politicians and demographers carefully monitored the birth and death rates of Arabs and Jews. They watched with increasing alarm as the Arab birth rate rose and encouraged the country's Jewish residents to have as many kids as possible, something Israel's ultra-Orthodox community was more than happy to embrace.

In 2003, Netanyahu, then serving as Israel's finance minister, called the country's Arab minority a "demographic bomb."[7] Netanyahu's critics denounced his characterization as racist. Netanyahu worried that a rising Arab population would transform Israel into a binational state—an idea anathema to the Israeli leader and most of the country's Jewish population.

Fear of the Arab minority in Israel fueled the rise of politicians like Avigdor Lieberman, the ultranationalist who gained enough clout to be named foreign minister in Netanyahu's 2009 government. Lieberman consistently backed inflammatory proposals. He suggested that Arab-Israelis be forced to sign a loyalty oath if they wanted to stay in Israel. In 2006, he denounced Arab-Israeli lawmakers who met with Hamas as collaborators and suggested that they should be tried as traitors before being killed.[8] While campaigning in Israel's 2015 national election, Lieberman suggested that Arab-Israelis who didn't back the country be beheaded, an inflammatory declaration that drew immediate condemnation from Arab lawmakers who compared him to Islamic State militants videotaping their gruesome beheadings in Syria.[9]

"Those who are with us deserve everything, but those who are against us deserve to have their heads chopped off with an axe," Lieberman told one campaign rally.[10]

Israel's Arabs were always made to feel like second-class citizens. And the problem was especially pronounced in Jerusalem, where half of the city is considered by international law to be occupied land. Though Israel effectively annexed East Jerusalem after the 1967 war and declared the entire city to be its "complete and united" capital in 1980, most of the city's Arab residents had fewer rights than their Jewish neighbors.

When Israel took over East Jerusalem in 1967, the government offered citizenship to Arab residents who were willing to pledge their allegiance to the state of Israel and renounce loyalty to any other nation. It was a step few Arab residents of East Jerusalem have ever been willing to take.

The alternative was permanent residency—and a blue ID card—a status that prevented them from voting in Israel's national elections.

Jerusalemites with the blue IDs could vote in city elections, though few Arab residents ever do. There was another problem that made it hard for permanent residents of East Jerusalem: They couldn't automatically pass along the benefits of residency if they married Palestinians from the West Bank or Gaza Strip.

Jerusalem was united geographically, but still divided politically, economically, culturally and socially. The political stratification meant that people on Assael Street had different rights. Some Arab families, like Abu Fadi and his kids, were full Israeli citizens. Others, like Khaled, his wife and their kids, were permanent residents.

Though there was a stark imbalance in the services provided to those living in East and West Jerusalem, the city's permanent residents came to appreciate the benefits the blue ID provided them, things they weren't eager to give up.

Soon after Mohammed Abu Khdeir was killed in the summer of 2014, Jamal Rishek and his friends went into the heart of West Jerusalem to meet up with a Canadian friend who had come to town for a visit. The guys tried their best not to "look Arab," but their Arabic singing at a bus stop caught the attention of plainclothes security who asked to see their IDs, grilled them about what they were doing on that side of town and told them they should go back to East Jerusalem.

To Jamal, it was another reminder that he wasn't welcome, that Israel really wasn't his country. Although he was better off than Palestinians living in the West Bank and Gaza Strip, Jamal knew their fates were all intertwined.

"I hate the government a lot," Jamal said. "You can see what happened in Gaza."

Jamal, a part-time waiter at the Y's restaurant, felt the pull of the street clashes he could hear rolling through the streets below Assael.

"One day I will go," he said one night in the family living room in the fall of 2014. "I have to go."

It sounded unconvincing, more like an idle boast than a vow. Jamal was a shy teen who liked to look at the world from behind a camera lens. He was thinking about being a journalist, but the idea didn't seem certain to stick.

Khaled shot Jamal a glare from across the room. His son returned the look with silence.

"If I had a West Bank ID I would go throw rocks," Jamal eventually said. "But because I have an Israeli ID, I can't. They will catch me."

For Jamal, the benefits of being an Arab-Israeli outweighed the potential costs of joining the stone throwers. By that fall, Netanyahu and his cabinet had backed tougher penalties for stone throwers, who faced the possibility of spending 20 years in prison. Israel also started making moves to strip troublemakers of their blue IDs. Prison and exile weren't things Jamal was willing to face.

"I have to go to university," he said. "I have my life."

It was exactly the kind of view many Israelis hoped would prevent Jerusalem from being consumed by another intifada. For Israel, the more kids who saw that they had something to lose by taking to the streets, the better.

"JERUSALEM IS A CAGE"

Khaled was well known on Assael for his work. He tried to bridge the divide whenever he could. Khaled served as a vital link for David Maeir-Epstein's coexistence work. Khaled took part in the community meetings and backed the group's effort to provide common ground for people living in Abu Tor.

The group succeeded in getting new garbage bins—with lids—for the street. They backed a plan to install two benches and a chain-link fence on the edge of a neglected open lot at the beginning of Assael Street.

To some people in the neighborhood, including Khaled's younger brother, the benches are a joke. And the meetings were meaningless. Amjad Rishek refused to take part.

"David can do nothing," Amjad said. "There is something bigger than David."

Amjad, a beefy man with bookish, wire-rimmed glasses and a shaved, shiny head, was a relative newcomer to Assael. In 1993, he and his wife moved into the newly built, two-bedroom second-story home, right on top of Khaled's place. The couple had four girls, bestowing Amjad with the honorific title *Abu Banat*—Father of the Daughters.

Like many men in the neighborhood, Amjad married a young woman from Hebron and brought her to Jerusalem. Three years earlier, Khaled had married Rita, his stylish wife from a successful West Bank family.

Khaled had been able to secure a Jerusalem ID for Rita under Israel's "family reunification" program. But when Amjad went through the same process for his wife, Wafa, he found that the rules had changed. The process was frozen, leaving Wafa in limbo.

Every year, Amjad had to return to Israel's Interior Ministry to secure permission for his wife to stay with him in Jerusalem. The different IDs sometimes made it difficult for the family to travel together outside the city. Some checkpoints are only for those with West Bank IDs. Others bar West Bank residents. That meant the couple had to return to Jerusalem through different checkpoints. That sometimes made short trips outside the city more trouble than they were worth.

"Here in Jerusalem, you live in a cage," said Wafa, one of the many wives on Assael to wear a hijab and conservative Palestinian dress. "In Hebron, you're able to live."

As a young man, Amjad was an ambitious contractor who snatched work away from big Israeli firms. He worked as a subcontractor building apartments, offices and stores in high-rises. But contracting feuds consumed Amjad, so he moved on to work for an Israeli nonprofit that helps hundreds of elderly Jerusalemites each day with food, medical care and workshops to make a little money in their golden years.

The Rishek family pooled its money to buy the rectangular stone home in 1990 from the Yaghmours—with the clear understanding that they would be able to get a license to build another story. They even had a paper from the city telling them they would be able to build, Amjad said. But when the time came to apply for permits, they got a different story.

"They started giving us excuses by saying the percentage of the building versus the size of the land blah blah blah, which did not make sense to me at all," Amjad said.

The city came up with reason after reason to say no to the Risheks. Then, one morning, Amjad began to see construction crews coming down the street, passing his house and going to work on the western side of Assael. Developers were transforming the old Machsomi property into a new, modern apartment building. As it rose, Amjad couldn't believe what he was seeing. Amjad took photos of the construction site. He took pictures of his own property. And he brought them all to the city for comparison.

"*Why are you giving them a permit, but not us?*" he asked.

They came up with more reasons why it was OK for those property owners to build a big apartment building on one side of the street while denying modest building permits to those living on the other.

"We were surprised to see that a Jewish neighbor managed to build a high-rise," Amjad said dryly. "Bottom line: They do not want to grant any licenses to us."

So the Risheks decided to do what most Palestinian families on Assael had done: Build without permits. City inspectors came out to check the work, but they couldn't stop it. Amjad and his family moved in, knowing that the wrecking ball was going to shadow their lives until they got an OK from Israel for their house.

The families on Assael grumbled about the building inequities, but they only got worse.

"I'm not concerned on a personal level," Amjad said. "I am only concerned so that I can get a license."

LIVING WITH A LOOMING WRECKING BALL

The disparities drove Amjad toward a meticulous obsession with life on Assael. He tracked down rare satellite maps of the street taken right after the 1967 war. He collected city maps and legal documents that he stuffed in white plastic bags that became his makeshift filing cabinets. He filled his shelves and drawers with demolition orders for their home, paperwork from attorneys, and fines from the city.

The Risheks got their first home demolition order in 1993, soon after they built the second-story addition. The threats to demolish their house come every year, sparking an annual battle to prevent wrecking crews from turning up on their front door. They hire attorneys and seek court intervention to block the demolition orders. Every year they pay thousands of dollars in fines.

Dressed in jeans and a black T-shirt, Amjad rummaged through bags and bags of paperwork while his wife looked on with a mix of admiration and disbelief. One of his teenaged daughters came home from school and changed into a zip-up sweatshirt, black tights and a T-shirt with a simple statement on the front, in Arabic: "We are all Gazans." She slumped on the living room couch while her dad dug through his paperwork, searching for one thing or another. When it became clear that her dad was going to keep talking about boring stuff, she retreated to the small room she shared with her sisters.

Amjad's wife laughed at the stacks of maps, architectural drawings, reports, letters and legal papers and wondered what good would come of it all.

"All you have gotten for us is no space to live in a house threatened with demolition," Wafa told her husband.

It was a joke. But the problems constantly weighed on Amjad.

"We are living in the context of a racist Israeli policy against the residents of East Jerusalem in every sense of the word," Amjad said as he held up the latest demolition order imposed on his home.

The Risheks know that the orders aren't hollow. The Bazlamits had to destroy part of their compound after losing a battle with the city. To prevent the city from sending bulldozers into his yard, Moussa Salhab personally dismantled a veranda the city said he'd illegally built. The families lived under a constant psychological siege while defending their homes. They were never sure where the next attempt might be made to drive them off. Amjad didn't know where the next threat might come from. In 2009, he found out.

That year, Amjad got an official letter from the Israeli Interior Ministry. Israel had concluded that Amjad was living outside the country— a precursor to stripping an East Jerusalemite of their residency permit. Amjad gathered up his water bills, his electricity bills and his tax bills and brought them all down to the ministry to prove that he was living in Jerusalem.

"*Is Assael Street in Israel or Romania?*" he sarcastically asked the city worker.

The official didn't like Amjad's tone and had him thrown out. Amjad had to beg for another meeting to clear things up. Amjad saw it as part of a calculated effort by Israel to force Palestinians out of Jerusalem.

"They send letters hoping people will panic," Amjad said. "It's one way of decreasing the Palestinian population. They exploit our ignorance of the law and our fear of confronting them."

The following year, Amjad went to the city to get a copy of their land registry document—the coveted *Tabu*. He paid for the copy, but when the clerk returned to the desk he told Amjad he couldn't find anything with his name on it.

"Check again," Amjad said. *"Look, here's my ID."*

"No," the clerk told him. *"Your name's not here."*

"Forget my name," Amjad told the clerk. *"Check the previous owner: Ziad Yaghmour."*

The clerk checked the records again.

"There is no Yaghmour," he said.

"Who owns the land then?" Amjad asked.

"This land," the clerk told him, *"is owned by the Moriah Company of Jerusalem."*

The clerk gave Amjad paperwork showing that their property was owned by Moriah, the city's development arm.

"This is my land," he told the clerk before leaving, *"not Moriah's."*

Amjad was in a panic. He called his wife at home to confirm he had the right number for his land. He went back to the clerk, who told Amjad that if he had a problem he should make an appointment with the head of the land registry office.

"I want to see her now," Amjad said. *"You can call the police and kick me out, but I'm not leaving until I find out what's going on."*

After some arguing, Amjad talked his way into a meeting. The director dispatched someone to research the history of the land and bring it back to her.

"Sorry," she told him after reading the paperwork, *"your name was never put on it. There's no such thing as an Amjad Rishek."*

"I called my brother," Amjad said. "I told him: 'We're in big, big trouble.'"

Khaled was in his manager's office at the Y when Amjad called.

"I have the original land documents," Khaled told him, *"but I don't know where they are."*

Amjad drove back home, found the *Tabu*, returned to the office and marched back to the manager where they tried and failed to keep him from going in to see her. Amjad laid the documents down on her desk.

"One says I don't belong and one says I do," he told her. *"Which is the correct one?"*

The director looked over the paperwork, checked her computer and turned back to Amjad.

"Have you ever used this paper for anything?" she asked, referring to the city documents claiming the land as city property.

"No," Amjad told her.

"There has been a mistake," she said before tearing up the paperwork showing Moriah as the owner of his land. *"Don't pay anything,"* she told him. *"We will give you all the documents that you want."*

The endless uncertainty hangs over Amjad and his family. And it reinforces his feeling that coexistence programs in Abu Tor that promote yoga and street fairs are pointless.

"Why would I go to David's meeting?" Amjad asked. "Look at my life. David doesn't know anything. These are systemic policies from the highest levels of government. It is bigger than me and bigger than David. It's not that I rejected David's invitation for personal reasons. I rejected it because it doesn't make sense."

THE "MONSTROSITY" ON ASSAEL STREET

Nothing stands as a larger testament to the inequities on Assael Street than the massive apartment building that Jewish and Arab neighbors both call a "monstrosity." It is distinctly out of place on the eastern side of the street. None of the neighbors can figure out how the Jewish-Israeli developers got permission to build it.

The apartment building was built on land once owned by a distant relative of the Salhabs. From what Amjad knew, the Salhabs had sold the land to Canadians who then sold it to Israeli developers. It was the kind of land sale that could get an Arab property owner killed. The new owners came as a shock to longtime residents on Assael Street. For the first time, the Risheks and Bazlamits had Jewish homeowners on their part of the street. It didn't go unnoticed that the property sat next to the home of the collaborator, Abu Fadi.

When the developers started work at the site, Amjad and everyone else on the street could see that something wasn't right. The footprint was huge. It ran from the edge of Assael Street down to the edge of Ein Rogel one block below. There was no open space left. It seemed to be taking up more land than builders were allowed. Amjad took photos of the construction site and brought them to the city.

"How are they able to build this, but I can't get a permit for my home?" he asked.

The planning office cited various rules and regulations about green space percentages and construction square footage that didn't seem to make much sense. But there was nothing Amjad could do. From the street above Assael, Judith and Jeffrey Green were aghast to see the building going up.

"It was such an eyesore," she said. "It was just so obviously out of place."

By law, a building in this part of East Jerusalem was typically not supposed to be more than two stories high. This building looked like it was going to be three, four, maybe five or more. Judith sent a letter to the planning commission that was slightly tongue-in-cheek: *"If you're looking for illegal construction in East Jerusalem to demolish,"* she wrote, *"I know just the place."* When it became clear that the building was going to tower over its neighbors and block the Old City views of many homes, the Greens and other Jewish residents asked the city to shut the construction site down.

"It was so obvious that what they were doing there was illegal," Judith said. "We took them to the planning committee and they gave them a command to stop building. They had 200 building violations."

The developers were furious.

"They were so mad that they threatened to kill our dog," Judith said.

Construction came to a halt for a few years and the unfinished building sat like countless others across Jerusalem. One day, the workers returned. They had new orders, new money, new permits. How the property owners got them, no one seemed to know. Everyone suspected that they had used some political connections with the city.

"It's definitely a scandal," Judith said.

The building was like no other in the neighborhood. The red-tile roof was reminiscent of the ones in Israeli settlements spread across the West Bank. From the street below, the floor-to-ceiling wraparound windows of the penthouse looked like they could be the bridge for a *Star Trek* starship. On either side, the building was surrounded by Arab neighbors—the Bazlamits, the Risheks, the Salhabs, the Mujaheds—all of whom were entangled in costly legal battles over their homes. The message to them seemed clear: If you were Arab, you couldn't do anything. If you were Jewish, the sky seemed to be the limit. Perhaps worst of all for the Bazlamits, the new building entirely blocked their view of the Dome of the Rock and al Aqsa mosque—a view they had cherished for generations.

"It always seems like they want to kick us out," said Nawal Bazlamit.

Rumors began to spread that the developers planned to rent the place to nationalistic Israeli settlers who would likely raise a massive Israeli flag from the roof and use the property as a wedge to splinter the neighborhood.

When asked about his building for this book, property developer Yakov Almakayes tried to deflect questions. At first, he claimed that his building was on the western side of the street and wasn't subject to East Jerusalem building restrictions. Then, though he lived in the building for years, he said he couldn't remember exactly where it was. Then he got defensive. He dismissed the neighborhood whisper campaign as hollow talk and salacious rumors.

"Maybe they have different laws and we have different laws," he said of his Arab neighbors on the eastern side of Assael Street.

Yakov dismissed his neighborhood critics as crazy and embittered.

"People that don't have any future are jealous about people that have a future and success," he said. "That's it."

Yakov laughed at any suggestion that he'd threatened to kill the Greens' dog.

"They can say what they want to say, I don't care," he said. "How can it be true? I have two dogs and a cat in my house. If you can have someone who has two dogs and a cat that wants to kill dogs, I don't know."

Yakov told neighbors in Abu Tor that he hoped to sell the apartments to rich Jews from overseas who wanted, and could afford, a place in Jerusalem with romantic views of the Old City. But the arrival of the second intifada put a damper on every Jerusalem property owner's aspirations. Hopes of making millions by selling the luxurious, modern apartment building with wraparound windows dried up. Instead, Yakov and his family started renting out the expensive apartments on Assael to Western journalists, US workers and a series of other foreigners.

The building looms over the Arab families as an example of the inequities they face in Jerusalem. It literally casts a shadow on the illegally built homes around it. For Amjad, the building stands as a constant reminder that David's small street improvement projects mean nothing if his home is demolished.

"I still greet my Israeli neighbors and I feel they have the same interest in peace as us," Amjad said. "I encourage my daughters to go play with David's daughter. But his meeting was meaningless to me."

David understood the criticism. He knew dumpsters and potlucks weren't going to be a catalyst for Middle East peace any time soon. But, on a street with physical, psychological, political, cultural and linguistic walls, you had to start somewhere.

"It's true that talking about coexistence fairs and graffiti things and changing garbage pails pale in comparison to the fact that somebody can't get a building permit to build something that they can get on the other side of the street, and that when they go ahead and build it anyway 'the law' is enforced because they have violated the law," David said. "It's a catch-22 kind of a thing. Down the line, if we work well, we should get to some of those things that are more meaningful. But both sides have to build up a track record of doing some things before we reach those kinds of more difficult things."

David said he isn't afraid to tackle political issues like building permits—when the time is right. The question then becomes: Will the city be as helpful on building permits as it was on dumpsters?

"I've been meeting so far with a great deal of willingness to cooperate on the part of the establishment. In other words: Are they smart enough to say we should be giving Abu Tor at least what we are giving other neighborhoods, if not more? Whether that will continue when we start talking about the sensitive issue of building permits, which is part of an ideological, nationalistic and, some would say, Machiavellian policy to prevent and try to reduce the Arab presence in Jerusalem, and whether or not the city will be equally open to the influence of the grassroots, Arab and Jewish, is a big question," he said in 2014. "Just as the city official said we can't have a coexistence festival tomorrow, we also can't deal with this issue. We have to find the right timing and process."

While David waited for the "right time" to bring up the most difficult issues on the street, Amjad kept being drained, spiritually, financially and psychologically.

"They have exploited me, they have drained me of all my resources, just because they know I'm holding onto my rights and they know I have no alternative," he said.

If the Palestinian Authority really wanted to foment change in Jerusalem, Amjad said, it should stop giving people a little bread here and a little cash there.

"Tell them the following: 'Build without licenses,'" Amjad said. "And do not respond to house demolition orders. Let Israel come and demolish in the hundreds. How many houses can it demolish? It will be the scandal of scandals."

When trouble boils up in East Jerusalem, Amjad understands the pent-up frustration. But the encroaching clashes worried Wafa, whose four girls all attended school down in the valley.

"The other day, my children were on their way to school," she said in the fall of 2014. "They didn't know there were problems down below. On the way to school they ran into Israeli soldiers who chased them, shot tear gas at them and fired sound bombs. They came home panic-stricken. We've been living a peaceful life. Up until now they've only seen problems and clashes on television. They haven't seen it in real life. Now they are being confronted with it in real life."

The spike in violence presented a test for East Jerusalemites like Amjad and Khaled, whose lives had become rooted in Israel. One day at the nonprofit, a co-worker asked Amjad what he thought of Mu'atez Hijazi, the convict from Abu Tor who had been killed by police days earlier.

"When the issue of Mu'atez Hijazi came up, one person at work asked me: 'Is Mu'atez a martyr?'"

It's the kind of charged question Israelis often ask their Palestinian friends, co-workers and neighbors as a litmus test after terrorist attacks. It's a way to see where they stand. And it's a question people like Amjad have learned to deflect when needed.

"I'm not God to decide," Amjad told his co-worker.

As tensions rose in Jerusalem that fall, Amjad's boss asked about the clashes in his neighborhood.

"*You're living in Abu Tor?*" she asked. "*How are things?*"

"*These things are not born overnight,*" Amjad told his boss. "*Whether the escalation is from the Israeli side or the Palestinian side, it has a reason, it has a feeling that has been building on both sides.*"

At the end of the day, Amjad told her, the root of the problem was Israel's control over the fate of the Palestinian people.

"*Do you feel that you are living under occupation?*" she asked Amjad.

"*Yes, I do,*" he told her. "*And this is what I tell my daughters.*"

Amjad's boss was startled by his candor.

"*I'm not going to tell you what you want to hear,*" he told her. "*I'm going to tell you the truth.*"

No matter which country controls Assael Street, Amjad said, he isn't moving.

"We are Jerusalemites and Muslims," he said. "My family is from Jerusalem. My father was born in Jerusalem. My grandfather was born in Jerusalem. Our family house is in the Muslim Quarter. They say that this is the land of steadfastness and protection of the holy sites. I consider my project one of steadfastness. I could easily buy somewhere else, but I am staying."

EIGHT

THE ARCHITECTS
OF DIVISION

Presidents, generals, dictators and kings have all taken their shot
at solving the Israeli-Palestinian conflict. Now the architects want
their chance. They have a vision: Divide Jerusalem, once again—
right down the center of Assael Street.

For better and for worse, Assael Street is still Jerusalem's dividing line.
Like the grease pencils that created the thick, poorly defined lines through
Abu Tor in 1948, the borders here are blurry. Things bleed over. But, if
there is to be an Israeli state living alongside a Palestinian one, the line has
to be drawn somewhere.

For Karen Lee Bar-Sinai and Yehuda Greenfield-Gilat, that somewhere may be down the middle of Assael Street, where the barbed wire
once split the neighborhood. It's not a fanciful idea. There are plenty of
good reasons for Assael to become the eastern edge of Israel and the western edge of Palestine. And these architects have influential backing for
their evolving designs. The pair developed the meticulously mapped plan
for the Geneva Initiative, an independent coalition of well-known Israeli
and Palestinian politicians who have spent more than a decade fine-tuning
their peace plan. The group was created by Yasser Abed Rabbo, a veteran
Palestinian peace negotiator, and Yossi Beilin, one of Israel's most dedi-
cated diplomats.

In the late 1990s, Beilin served as a minister for Prime Ministers Yitzak Rabin and Ehud Barak. He was part of Barak's 2001 negotiating team during peace talks in Taba, Egypt, where the Israeli leaders had opened the doors to dividing Jerusalem and accepting East Jerusalem as the Palestinian capital. Though those talks fell apart and Barak was soon defeated, Beilin embarked on two years of secret talks with a small group of Israeli and Palestinian negotiators who set out to come up with their own plan. In 2003, the group unveiled the Geneva Accords, a 50-page framework that called for making East Jerusalem the capital of a new Palestinian state, officially absorbing Ma'ale Adumim and most other major West Bank settlements into Israel, and sending international forces into the West Bank to keep a check on security.

They then spent another six years doing the detailed work that Dayan and Tell had been expecting someone to do soon after they divided Jerusalem in 1948. The group wrestled with every curve in the road. They examined the demographics of mixed neighborhoods like Abu Tor as they hunted for border lines to separate Israel and Palestine. They knew there would be no perfect compromise.

"How can you really divide a street?" said Beilin, a soft-spoken politician with wire-rimmed glasses that sealed his image as a bookish intellectual. It was a conundrum they had to face. There were plenty of places where borders seamlessly blended from one place into the next. But Jerusalem wasn't likely to be one of them. The group eventually released an exhaustive 400-page plan that detailed what the dividing line between Israel and Palestine in Jerusalem would look like (wall, fence and border crossings), how Palestinians could get between the West Bank and Jerusalem (a four-lane sunken highway), and where the border would run. The plan to divvy up Jerusalem was largely the work of Karen Lee and Yehuda, idealistic young architecture students who thought the world's architects didn't have enough of a voice in deciding where and how to draw borders in the Middle East.

"Architecture is a problem-solving profession," said Yehuda, a quiet thinker with shaggy brown hair and glasses that make him look a bit like an adult version of Waldo from the popular children's books *Where's Waldo?* "It's not philosophers."

The two teamed up while studying at the Technion, Israel's premier technology institute on the country's northern coast in Haifa. They shared a common belief that their work could change the way people saw the stagnant peace process.

"There's nobody who is an expert on space in the negotiation rooms," said Karen Lee, a fast talker with thick, curly black hair, who always seemed like the more optimistic of the pair. "It's amazing. Not even a single one. We think this, inherently, should change. We design in order to show and expand the possibilities in somebody's mind."

The Geneva Initiative unveiled its plan while Karen Lee and Yehuda were studying at the Technion. The two were inspired by the ideas and disturbed by the impact of Israel's separation barrier as the country continued to carve an unrecognized new border through the Middle East. To the pair, it was a major political and moral question that needed to be confronted.

"It was one of the biggest spatial facts in the Middle East—and nobody was talking about it," Yehuda said.

Karen Lee and Yehuda planned to work on a project to protest the new dividing line. But when Beilin and the Geneva Initiative came out with their plan for splitting Jerusalem, the pair decided to present the Israeli diplomat with their ideas for dividing the city. Beilin was so impressed that he hired them to create the entire blueprint for Jerusalem. Yehuda and Karen Lee joined the team intent on finding a compassionate way to separate Israelis and Palestinians.

This, Karen Lee said, is "a family that desperately needs a divorce."

Yehuda agreed. "There's no 'Kumbaya' here," he said.

For starters, they threw out the pre-1948 plan, pushed by many countries, that would make Jerusalem an international island with special status short of being its own country (like Vatican City). The idea, known as *corpus separatum,* was a nonstarter for many reasons. One of the biggest was Israel's 1980 Jerusalem Law, which declared the city the country's "complete and united" capital.

"There is no way on earth that Israelis will give up their sovereignty of their capital," Yehuda said. "It's not gonna happen."

Even if it was possible politically, the pair found the idea of creating a secure border around Jerusalem to be much more problematic than drawing one straight line through the city.

"While this idea is a beautiful one—let's share Jerusalem—de facto what it will mean in terms of securing that Jerusalem and separating it from

Israel and Palestine, it would mean that you encircle the whole of Jerusalem with some kind of wall or fence or border of some sort—and you capture people in that entity," Yehuda said.

It didn't make sense. Instead, the pair looked for obvious breaking points.

"It makes a lot more sense to separate the city where it's so naturally separated, even today, where the scars of earlier separations still are, and do that in a sensitive manner, in a manner that allows connections together, with separation," said Yehuda.

Karen Lee and Yehuda looked at the border as a living being, a creature with muscle that stretches.

"We talked about division, but division in a sense of a living tissue that still needs to work together on many, many levels," Yehuda said one afternoon in 2014 at a downtown Jerusalem café where he and Karen Lee detailed their ideas.

"Normally cities are divided by war and united in peace," Karen Lee said. "Here we are talking about the opposite need. We need to separate for peace."

The models for things like this—the partition of India among them—weren't great success stories. The architects were well aware of the thick, broken lines drawn by Dayan and Tell in 1948 when they started trying to craft their own.

"There's a huge gap between policy making and the broad sketches on the map, like Moshe Dayan [made]," Karen Lee said. "There's a huge gap between that and the reality on the ground. How do we come and say: 'What does the city need? Can we create new connections that don't exist today?'"

For years, the team argued over the route they were creating. Their first idea was to divide the city along the eastern edge of the old No Man's Land, a route that would have naturally cut along the ridgeline above the Valley of Slaughter. When the group unveiled the plan in 2009, the team proposed a route that would have put the top part of Abu Tor—and *all* of Assael—inside Israel. The natural drop-off below Abu Tor's Ein Rogel Street, they argued, created a natural barrier that would reduce, if not eliminate, the need for concrete walls or barbed-wire fences.

"The spine of Abu Tor is really there," Karen Lee said.

A NEW NO MAN'S LAND FOR ABU TOR

They also proposed creating a new buffer zone in Abu Tor by transforming part of the valley into a park that would be open to citizens of Israel and Palestine. The team dreamed up a shared space that belonged to everyone and no one, a kind of international community park connecting the two nations.

"The idea here was to create a border garden that can be used as almost a No Man's Land that everybody can use together," said Chen Farkas, one of the Israeli architects who worked on the plan. "It's not owned by either side, but it could be, depending on different circumstances. It could be Israeli, Palestinian, divided half-and-half, or shared completely."

While the idea of resurrecting the neighborhood No Man's Land—the setting for decades of disputes—might make some neighbors shudder, Yehuda said creating a new one might be cathartic.

"It's kind of a healing process, in a sense," he said, "saying that there really are going to be shared areas."

Abu Tor, Yehuda said, "is the most intense part of the division, because it's really in the urban fabric."

"The real division in Jerusalem is in Abu Tor, and it's only about 500 meters," he said. "It's a unique challenge."

The team tried to "avoid the city line and its scars, both physical and mental, that it left on the population," Yehuda said.

Avoiding the city's physical and mental scars proved to be impossible. There was simply no way to carve up Jerusalem without offending a lot of people. As criticism for the proposed split piled up, Karen Lee and Yehuda fine-tuned their plan. The group commissioned a detailed survey of Abu Tor that pinpointed which homes in Abu Tor were Arab-owned and which ones were Jewish-owned. When they looked at the results, they could see that their plan would place all of Abu Tor's old No Man's Land inside Israel. That would place all the Palestinian families on Assael Street, along with dozens of other Arab homes, inside Israel. Palestinian architects working on the maps weren't willing to accept that kind of division.

"While our stance was: 'Let's create what's best for the border infrastructure, let's use the best possible landscape,' they said: 'Look at how many Palestinians live on that side. Are you mad?'" Karen Lee said. "That was a discussion."

"Each house you annex to Israel is a huge loss for Palestinians, so they couldn't accept any change of ownership," Chen said.

Although they were hesitant, Karen Lee and Yehuda agreed to move the proposed border line so it ran down the center of Assael Street—a decision they made without even knowing that the dead-end road separated East and West Jerusalem from 1948 to 1967.

"It just made sense," Yehuda said.

The architects' initial plan envisioned a concrete wall running down the center of Assael Street, where the barbed wire once separated the neighbors, creating a physical barrier to replace the invisible one many say has risen there over the years.

But the proposed border went even further than Dayan and Tell's marks by actually cutting Assael in half. Palestinians would access the street from the south. Israelis would get to their homes from the north. If the walls went up as planned, Arab families at the beginning of the street, like the Risheks and Bazlamits, would be Palestinian citizens, able to get to their homes via Assael Street. For those living at the top end, like Imm Fadi and Maha Salhab, Palestine would end right outside their front doors. Assael Street on their doorstep would be part of Israel. The wall would cut Assael in the middle, right where Yakov Almakayes's widely reviled building towers over its neighbors. That building could play a special role in the Geneva Initiative plan: One proposal suggests turning the multistory apartment complex into a place that would be shared by Israel and Palestine. Like the No Man's Land promenade, the building's ownership could shift as circumstances demanded: it could be shared; it could be split in half; one side or the other could assume complete control.

The architects saw a shared building as one way to consciously create careful connections between Israelis and Palestinians. Karen Lee found precedent for the idea on the border of France and Switzerland, where half of Basel's international airport—known as EuroAirport Basel-Mulhouse-Freiberg—is run by the Swiss, and the other half is run by the French.

"It's not only a hope that the building, the structure, the landscape will do it alone," Karen Lee said. "You have to remember that the resentment people have of the past is also a result of that contradiction they lived in. It was not something they chose. It was the result of the war. It was the result of Jerusalem being annexed."

The simmering resentment, she said, would evaporate once residents in Abu Tor were living on a dividing line Israelis and Palestinians agreed upon.

"When Israelis and Palestinians sign something and say, 'This is how we see our future coexistence, side-by-side,' it's a whole different ball game," Karen Lee said. "Abu Tor could be a case study that everybody looks up to, not the thing that illustrates the worst that has happened. In that case, yes, the landscape has to facilitate and build and nurture the future coexistence in a way that they don't know it yet."

The idea of creating buildings and parks run by both sides sounds like a fantasy to plenty of people who look on the decades of mistrust and conflict as a bad precedent. The families who lived here are scarred by their personal histories. They're wary of the people who want to divide them once again. Yehuda and Karen Lee say they aren't unmoored from reality. Like many Israelis, the pair pride themselves on their ability to stand firm in the face of what often seems like impossible odds.

"We are not naïve," Yehuda said. "It seems, in the beginning, that we are kind of rainbow people."

The two are used to being ridiculed for their ideas. When they first presented their plans in college, they were humiliated in front of their peers. They were told they would never make it as architects. But they persisted.

Yehuda and Karen Lee came to their work from two very different places.

Karen Lee was an adopted daughter raised in an apolitical home by a stay-at-home mom and air-traffic-controller dad. She was always searching for different ways to look at the conflict that framed their lives. But it may have been her move to the Gaza Strip border in 2008 that galvanized her belief in dividing Jerusalem. Karen Lee and her husband decided to move to a southern Israeli kibbutz founded by his grandparents. The couple and their two kids moved into their home a few weeks before Israel launched a major ground invasion into Gaza to stop Palestinian militants from firing rockets that seemed to be getting bigger, faster and more dangerous.

Karen Lee woke in the middle of the night to rattling windows that made her wonder if the explosions were from Hamas rockets hitting their kibbutz or from Israeli missiles slamming into Palestinian homes on the other side of the border. She worried incessantly about the possibility that she might have to use her body to protect one of her two children—a modern-day Sophie's choice she wasn't willing to entertain. She never had to make that kind of decision, and living through the short war didn't transform her into a hard-line "Bomb Them Into the Stone Age" kind of Israeli hawk. It actually cemented Karen Lee's commitment to trying to come up with realistic alternatives.

"We all fear for our kids, and it makes no sense," she said of her life on the kibbutz during the war. "It strengthened our belief that this all needs changing."

Yehuda came to the work as the son of a left-leaning Israeli lawmaker. He was raised to take a stand and defend his point of view. Along with his work with the Geneva Initiative, Yehuda signed up to help moderate Israeli leaders like Tzipi Livni and President Reuven Rivlin as they tried to beat back the conservative political tide that seemed to be saturating Israel. Yehuda is part of a new generation of disillusioned Israelis trying to decide how much of their lives to invest in attempting to soften their country's edges. Yehuda believed in Israel. He was willing to fight for his country. But if Israelis were going to keep backing hard-line politicians who refused to seriously pursue peace with the Palestinians, Yehuda said he'd be among many that would think seriously about leaving.

"If the majority of Israelis decided that they are going to live on our sword for the next generation, I suspect that some people will say, 'This is not for me,'" he said. "We want to be here. We think it's a fantastic project. We think it's a miraculous project. But we won't sustain this deterioration."

The architects face a path cluttered with obstacles. Their attempts to present their plan for dividing Jerusalem as a unified Israeli-Palestinian proposal were undercut because their Palestinian colleagues wouldn't let their names appear on the report and refused to do media interviews. It made clear what Karen Lee and Yehuda already knew: The idea of dividing Jerusalem is still one of the most contentious issues in the conflict. And being linked to a plan that cedes Palestinian land could be seen as traitorous to some.

"PEOPLE ARE NOT LEGO"

Among the critics is Senan Abdelqader, one of the most celebrated modern-day Palestinian architects in the world.

"This is a joke," Senan said of the Geneva Initiative plans for splitting Jerusalem.

Senan is one of a growing number of Palestinians in Israel who has full citizenship. He carries an Israeli passport that prevents him from traveling to most countries in the Middle East. Senan teaches architecture at Tel Aviv University and works on a variety of projects in Israel. But he eschews the label "Arab-Israeli" and instead refers to himself as "Arab-Palestinian." Senan sees the modern mapmakers as extensions of a misguided colonial mindset that has for centuries repeatedly tried—and failed—to draw stable borders in the Middle East.

"People are not Lego," he said.

Senan doesn't want to see his city divided. He is among those who would rather see Jerusalem united under some international authority that allows the city to retain its unique character.

"When you think to separate it, you would interrupt its urban net and it would lose its historic character," said Senan, who doesn't see architecture as the kind of political tool Karen Lee and Yehuda imagine it to be.

"Architecture is not a solution," he said, "it's a concept."

Senan's office sits in Beit Safafa, a neighborhood between Jerusalem and Bethlehem that, like Abu Tor, was split between Israel and Jordan in 1948. Beit Safafa is filled with block upon block of conventional Jerusalem stone homes and apartment buildings that give the neighborhood little to distinguish it from other parts of the city. Senan's unusual four-story building is one of the architect's subtle protests against Israel's inequitable development policies. The outer frame is made to look like a traditional Arabic latticed room separator known as a *mashrabiya*. The gray stone walls are cut with small holes that create a feeling of openness and intimacy that still provides some privacy for the people living and working inside. The stone mashrabiya acts to keep the inside cool while serving as a shell protecting those living inside.

Senan's mashrabiya is not only infused with modern and traditional Middle Eastern ideas, it was designed in quiet opposition to discriminatory Israeli construction policies that constrain Palestinian development. The outer stone façade conforms to restrictive Israeli construction rules and envelops the actual living area like a box. Three of four yards separate the external shell from the contemporary glass-walled house on the inside, which serves as Senan's home and office.

Senan's criticism of his Israeli counterparts' plans touched a nerve for Yehuda, who chafed at being compared to the British colonialists who carved up the Middle East.

"Everybody tries to divide us, it's true," Yehuda said. "Some people won't like it. But in the greater picture, this is probably the only way to get some kind of agreement, some kind of peace. It's not pretty. I would prefer not to have to divide the city. We're not in love with this concept of division, but it's a necessity."

Popular support for the idea rises and falls, depending on the political climate. Stalemates often give rise to talk of a "one-state" solution where Israel would officially annex all of the West Bank and give the Palestinians living there full rights and citizenship.

Palestinians sometimes float the idea as a threat, knowing full well that most Jewish-Israelis would reject the idea of absorbing more than 2 million Palestinians, a move that would more than double the size of the country's minority population and stoke Israeli fears that its 6 million Jewish citizens could one day become a minority in a country established as a modern-day homeland for the Jewish people.

"The spirit of an agreement between Israelis and Palestinians—its DNA—is separation and, in Jerusalem, it's more obvious than anywhere else," Yehuda said. "There are two cities here. There's a clear line between them. Now, sometimes the line is within an urban fabric—like Abu Tor—but also, there, the line is very clear. You know immediately when you pass from a Jewish street to an Arab street. You feel it immediately. Not only in the language, but in the space, in the air. It's a different environment, and this is the most complicated place."

Yehuda sees himself as a political realist and views critics like Senan as naysayers still holding onto some unattainable, idealistic peace plan.

"I think some Palestinians, for some reason, I don't know why, they have this romantic view of what Jerusalem needs to be," Yehuda said. "They haven't decided what they want. Do they want hard Palestinian nationality? Are you connected to reality? Because you have to choose. If you want Palestinian nationality, that means making hard choices about cutting Jerusalem in half. It means having to swallow living side-by-side with Israelis, but taking responsibility for your own people."

It is up to Palestinians to bite the bullet, accept their decades of losses and agree to a less-than-ideal compromise, he said.

"Do you want this, or do you want to sit in a colonized place and whine that Israelis are colonizers?" he asked. "I find a lot of Palestinians really haven't made that decision."

Yehuda finds the skepticism of people like Senan, whose career and success are intertwined with Israel, to be especially ironic. Senan teaches architecture at Tel Aviv University and at Jerusalem's more funky, alternative Bezalel Academy of Arts and Design. He works on projects with the Israeli government, often in the country's Arab communities.

"Senan lives on the Israeli fabric," said Yehuda, who wondered what the alternative—the realistic alternative—is to dividing the city.

"What? What do you offer?" Yehuda asked of the critics. "What's your proposal? This place is going for division. It's not going anywhere else."

There's no realistic scenario Yehuda can see in the short term that would lead to the dream of an undivided Jerusalem that is the capital of both Israel and Palestine.

"I don't understand that, not on the architectural-planning level and not on the cultural-societal level," he said. "There's no level on which Jerusalem exists as one, no level besides the Jerusalem of the heavens. I understand it's frustrating. I understand it's frightening. I understand it will change realities in ways people can't understand. It's emotional, but laying on this false sentiment of a united Jerusalem, it sounds like Netanyahu saying that Jerusalem is united and will never be divided, so the extreme right and the extreme left meet on their backs."

"DIVIDE WHAT? IT'S NOT A CAKE"

The prospect of being part of a new Palestinian state puts the families on the eastern side of Assael in a quandary. No one would dispute that becoming part of any new nation is going to be fraught with risk and uncertainty. And a new Palestinian nation, if it ever becomes a reality, will face more challenges than most new states. For now, the opportunities for Palestinians living in Jerusalem are much better than those living in the West Bank or the Gaza Strip.

The route of the proposed dividing line matters less to the families on the western side of Assael Street than those on the eastern side. The big concern for the Joudans, the Maeir-Epsteins and the Bezalelys is whether they might someday find themselves living on the edge of Israel, as the families here did when the nation was first created. The families on the other side of the street—the Bazlamits, the Risheks, the Salhabs—would have to decide whether they wanted to give up their Israeli passports and ID cards to live their lives on the outer edge of Palestine.

While most of the people on the eastern side of the street want to see a Palestinian state, not everyone wants to live in it. Many people simply avoid answering the question when asked which country they would want to live in, given the choice.

When asked in various polls, Arab East Jerusalemites have been split on the issue. In one 2011 survey, 35 percent said they would choose Israeli citizenship if given the choice between living in Israel and a new Palestinian state. Another 35 percent wouldn't answer the question. Thirty percent said they wanted to be citizens of Palestine.[1]

The possibility that leaders like Palestinian Authority president Mahmoud Abbas could ever oversee security, electricity, garbage collection and water on the lower half of Assael Street seems improbable to many who live here.

"It's a dream," said Moussa Salhab, the Assael father embittered by years of fighting losing battles with Israeli bureaucrats over who owned the gardens outside his front door. "Who will come here? Abbas? It will never happen."

Maha Salhab, Moussa's daughter, doesn't want to see Jerusalem split again. Maha is among the young, hijab-wearing Palestinians in Jerusalem who benefit from life under Israeli rule, even if she sometimes has to deal with terrifying threats from young Jewish punks trying to intimidate her when she goes out in West Jerusalem.

"Divide what?" she said of her hometown. "It's not a cake."

There's little reason to carve up a city that is already fragmented by Israel's concrete separation walls and security fences, said Maha.

"It's only a little city," she said. "It's nothing on the map. We're not talking about Chicago. It's Jerusalem. It's like dividing your own house. You're already surrounded. You already have a wall, so what are you going to divide? Another wall? It's like having a door—and another door."

Right next door, Imm Fadi has no intention of giving up her Israeli passport. If her home were to become the edge of Palestine, she would almost certainly move into Israel, even though it would leave family members on the other side. Imm Fadi may not support the same right-wing Israeli leaders as her late husband anymore, but she still sees the benefits of being an Israeli citizen. Palestinians and Arab-Israelis may be second-class citizens in Israel, but corruption in the new Palestinian government would be intolerable.

"I will not have a chance to be a first-class citizen in Palestine because I don't have connections," Imm Fadi said. "In Palestine I wouldn't even be a tenth-class citizen. Here, I am second class. Second-class citizenship is better than tenth-class citizenship."

Her son Fadi disagrees. After being raised by a father who vehemently opposed the idea, Fadi said he now supports a two-state solution.

"I want a Palestinian state," Fadi said one afternoon in his mother's living room.

Imm Fadi scoffed at her son's views and reminded him of the inefficiency and corruption of the Palestinian Authority in Ramallah, which relies on international aid to keep it from collapsing.

"They went to Ramallah," she asked Fadi. "Did they do anything?"

"The economy in Ramallah is good," he replied.

Imm Fadi wanted no part of it.

"Only those that work in the Palestinian Authority become rich," she said. "All others are poor."

She reminded her oldest son that his family is intimately intertwined with Israel.

"We studied in Israel," she said. "We complement them and they complement us. The people from the West Bank, if they were to be given a chance to come back under Israeli occupation, they would love it."

When Fadi left the room, Imm Fadi said her son was delusional.

"Fadi is a liar," she said. "He cannot live in a Palestinian state. Fadi's heart gets ahead of him. My other kids wouldn't live in the Palestinian Authority. They studied in Israel. We work here."

Everyone's lives on Assael now seem inextricably connected to Israel. It's hard for many residents here to imagine anything else. Like many idealists, Khaled Rishek doesn't want to see Jerusalem divided again. He envisions a united, open, international city for Israelis and Palestinians.

"My plan is to keep it as an open city, where everybody lives in dignity, as a capital for both countries and, at the end of the day, no one is able to choose his neighbor."

His brother Amjad disagrees. He's one of the few people on Assael Street who says plainly that he wants his home to be part of a new Palestinian state.

"If a Palestinian state is established and where I am living is still part of Israel, I will always feel like I am living under occupation," he said. "If a Palestinian state is formed and where I am living becomes part of a Palestinian state, I will feel that I am independent."

Members of the Bazlamit family firmly support a Palestinian state. But they're suspicious of the plan to divide Assael and see it as another malicious attempt by mapmakers to sow the neighborhood with dissent, distrust and division.

"Splitting the street is a way for them to keep control of the city," said Abdel Halim Bazlamit, whose son Jawad was killed in 1996 at al Aqsa mosque.

Abdel Halim's wife thinks Israelis pushing the idea aren't altruistic supporters of Palestine. They're doing it to push their own agenda.

"They think about dividing for their own security," said Dawlat, Abdullah Bazlamit's wife, who thought a book about the street should be titled *The Rapists* because "everything is against our will."

"Whether they divide or not, whether they separate or not, we will never feel secure," she said. "We always feel unsafe."

Jewish residents across the way are just as skeptical of putting another dividing line down the middle of the street. Some Israelis on the western side worry about living on the edge of a fragile new nation, a border that could be tested by radicals looking to challenge Palestinian security forces by launching attacks on Israel.

The concerns were amplified in 2014 by the spread of instability across the Middle East, where the euphoria of the Arab Spring revolts had given way to a sobering new landscape dominated by civil wars and extremism. The most alarming development was the disintegration of Syria, where three years of civil war had created a chaotic battlefront filled with competing militant groups fighting President Bashar al-Assad's military and each other.

That summer in Syria's Golan Heights, Jabhat al-Nusra, al Qaeda's front line force in the civil war, had taken control of the country's western border crossing with Israel. The militants temporarily detained dozens of UN peacekeepers and raised their black flag in the Syrian border town of

Quneitra as Israeli forces and the United Nations shuttered the tiny crossing point with Israel.

The Golan Heights crossing has been used primarily to export apples from Druze farmers in Israel to Syria. It also served for decades as the backdrop for scores of emotional farewells of Druze brides crossing from Syria into Israel, or vice versa, to marry men on the other side—a union that was almost always a one-way trip for the bride. Those crossings came to a halt in the summer of 2014 when a border that had once been one of Israel's more stable suddenly became one of its biggest concerns. Israel started bombing Syria more frequently to stop what it said was an increasing flow of advanced rockets bound for Hezbollah militants in neighboring Lebanon. And thousands of extremists, backed by a concerning flow of true believers from England, France and America, had seized enough land in Iraq and Syria to declare themselves the Islamic State.

In a part of the world in constant conflict, 2014 seemed to Alisa Maeir-Epstein to be an especially perilous time in the Middle East.

In concept, Alisa wants to see a Palestinian state. But she's not sure if she wants to see it right across the street.

"If it would work, that would be wonderful," she said. "But will it work?"

Alisa watched Iraq and Syria struggling to defeat zealous Islamic State fighters and wondered if Palestinian soldiers would really be up to the task.

"Will the Islamic State come to the West Bank?" she asked. "It's a hard one. That's a hard one for me to think about. Look at all these countries. As soon as there's turmoil the Islamic radicals take over—and they're very uncompromising. It's not like they'll say: 'OK, we'll take over the West Bank and then we'll have a peace treaty with Israel.' That's not what it's about."

Alisa saw the Islamic State as the resurrection of a thousand-year-old religious war—a New Crusade—only this time Muslim soldiers are leading the charge, not Christian warriors.

"We always used to think maybe Jerusalem will be an international city, maybe it will be the capital of two states," she said. "I don't have a problem with that, but I know that there are people who won't agree and would go to war over that."

Elon Bezalely, the guy who'd bought Carol's home and then urged his Palestinian neighbors to use his wall as their canvas, understands the rationale for making Assael the borderline again.

"Jerusalem is split," he said one night in his living room in the fall of 2014. "This side of the street is Jewish and that side of the street is Arab. It's a clear line. The question is where do you put the wall? Do you put the wall over here? *Can* you put the wall over here?"

His wife, Linda, worried less about where the line is drawn and more about making sure that a new state doesn't become a launching pad for attacks aimed at Israel.

Linda sees Gaza as a cautionary tale. Israel pulled all of its settlers and soldiers out of the Gaza Strip in 2005 as part of a unilateral move, ending 38 years of Israeli occupation and effectively ceding responsibility for the area to the Palestinian Authority. The move gave Gaza's 1.5 million residents a level of freedom most had never known. But Israel and Egypt, which shares a short border with Gaza's southern edge, kept tight control of who and what went in and out. Gaza militants accused Israel of creating an open-air prison and continued to use the Mediterranean strip to launch attacks. A year after Israel pulled out of Gaza, Palestinian militants used a tunnel they'd dug under the border to kidnap a young Israeli soldier, Gilad Shalit, who remained a lonely captive until he was freed in 2011 as part of a prisoner exchange.

In 2007, longstanding divisions between Hamas and Fatah boiled over into a civil war between the rival political factions that ended with a humiliating defeat for the Palestinian Authority and Hamas seizing full control of Gaza. The Palestinians finally had their two-state solution. It just wasn't the two-state solution they had been working for. While Israel and Hamas agreed to a series of truces that brought temporary halts to rocket fire from Gaza, Palestinian militants persisted in firing rockets into Israel.

Between 2008 and 2014, Gaza militants engaged in three short, intense wars with Israel, fueling perceptions in Israel that the 2005 withdrawal had been a failure.

"There are lines, but they're bombing us," Linda said. "So, it was easy to show where the lines would be, but look at what happened. Now they could say: 'Let's draw the lines here and here,' but the point is what may happen afterwards. I want peace."

"But first you want security," Elon said.

"Well, it's the same thing. Peace as in: 'No one's going to hurt anyone.'"

"You're never going to be able to get several million people to sign on a contract that says we're not going to shoot back at you," Elon said. "You separate into two countries. If they fire rockets at you, it gives you a right to fire rockets back and defend yourself."

Yaacov Davidian, the guy known as Yanki and one of the few people born on the western side of Assael who still lives there, doesn't think dividing Assael will bring any measure of peace or quiet.

"Even if there will be some agreement, it's not going to be like this," he said. "Next door to you? What will they do? A 50-meter wall? It will not help."

Karen Lee and Yehuda aren't dead-set on dividing Assael Street once again. But they both say the line has to be drawn somewhere. And Assael makes a lot of sense.

"This is what's on the table," Yehuda said. "People are dreaming of a lot of nice dreams, but it's not on the table. The real people who are talking, or not talking anymore, who used to be talking, this is the only valid scenario. Now the question is: 'How do you create the least damage with this scenario?' Symbolically and nationally, people want to be divided."

But division doesn't have to come in the form of Berlin Wall–style concrete barriers.

"The symbol of division today is the barrier," Yehuda continued, "because people don't think there is another choice, because it wasn't planned, because architects weren't involved, and planners, and maybe even artists. But if you understand that they want to be freed of occupation, the price within territory doesn't have to be that harsh, it could be much more thoughtful."

History makes it clear that the fortunes of Jerusalem will almost certainly shift. The borders here are likely to keep changing. And who lives in which houses on Assael Street could determine where the lines are drawn. That is why the families here, on both sides of the street, hold firm to their often divergent beliefs. They know that their decisions matter. It matters if they stay or move. It matters if they fight or surrender. They all see their lives as part of the fabric that has made Jerusalem what it is today. And they all plan to leave their mark on the city's future.

"We did not write the Bible," Beilin said of the plan to divide Assael Street. "One should take into account the wishes of the people at the end of the day. If they want something else, then the decision makers of the day will have to take some other decision. Our main idea was not to say that this is the only solution. Our goal was to show that a solution is possible."

EPILOGUE

"THE SIEGE OF ABU TOR"

I n the spring of 2015, as this book was getting ready to head to the publisher, I got a phone call from Jerusalem. It was Sarah Sallon, an Israeli doctor who made a name for herself by germinating a 2,000-year-old date palm seed from the Judean Desert.

I'd met Sarah in 2009, when she was looking for a place to buy in Abu Tor. Sarah came to check out the place I was renting and fell in love with the rooftop view. It took awhile, but she eventually convinced the owners to sell. The apartment offered an enviable view of Jerusalem that Sarah wanted to look out on every day. Sarah always hated Yakov Almakayes's big monstrosity of a building on Assael Street. The towering eyesore was an ugly gash in her panoramic rooftop view. She looked at the place every day. She couldn't avoid it. She knew there was a scandal there waiting to be uncovered. But now, she said, a new outrage was brewing: Developers had their greedy eyes on the Hill of Evil Counsel.

To Sarah, this was an incomparable outrage, a disgrace that had to be exposed.

"It's the Siege of Abu Tor," Sarah said. "Only now it's a different kind of siege."

In this case, mysterious developers had secured a long-term lease for the most coveted, undeveloped spot in Abu Tor: the two-acre hilltop compound owned by the Greek Orthodox Church that was home to the Goelis; a small Sephardic synagogue with a dwindling attendance; the locked, rarely used monastery; and a few people who paid the church rent to live in a small block of boxy, one-story homes. After dark, cars and trucks would sometimes rumble into the compound and park under the pine trees, for some seclusion, to do one thing or another. People would throw beer cans into makeshift campfires while neighbors took their dogs out for late-night walks nearby.

The Greek Orthodox Church was more than a major Christian fixture in Jerusalem. It was one of the city's largest landowners. Second only, perhaps, to Israel itself. The Israeli prime minister's house and the country's parliament were built on church land. That put the Greek patriarch in Jerusalem at the center of feud after feud. In 2005, the church was accused of secretly selling prized East Jerusalem land to Israeli settlers as part of a campaign to drive Palestinians out of the city. The patriarch accused of orchestrating the deal was ousted, but he locked himself in the church's Old City compound, not far from the Church of the Holy Sepulcher, and refused to leave.

When Sarah called me that night in early 2015, the ousted patriarch was still hunkered down in a modest apartment inside the tranquil stone Christian Quarter compound, where he used a shopping bag and rope lowered from his room to get food and supplies from his supporters. Now, Sarah said, the church had ignited a new furor by selling part of the Abu Tor compound to greedy developers. The Hill of Evil Counsel might become Jerusalem's next big apartment complex or, even worse, some new high-tech business hub. This would not stand.

Some Abu Tor residents were quite happy to see development coming to Abu Tor, especially in the church property.

"It's neglected, it's abandoned, good things at night do not happen there," said one neighborhood resident who lives near the compound. "It's not good to have open space with no one in charge. It's kind of abandoned property. If a developer comes in and at least takes care of it, it's at least good for the neighborhood."

But Sarah and a group of neighbors were preparing to fight. Abu Tor residents had lost their battle to block a big shopping and entertainment complex from being built on the edge of Abu Tor, right next to the Peace Forest. But they weren't going to let that defeat deter them.

"It's a tragedy," said Sarah, a London-born founder of the Natural Medicine Research Center at Israel's Hadassah University Hospital. "It's a scandal. This compound has enormous significance in early Christianity. This is absolutely unheard of."

If there was to be a coda to this story of Assael Street, David Maeir-Epstein didn't think it should be about the so-called Siege of Abu Tor and the fight over developing the church property. That had little to do with the trajectory of relations on the dividing line. No, he said, the thing people should be left with was the story of the newly refurbished soccer field at the Abu Tor community center, which was one of the last places where Arab and Jewish kids could still find some common ground in the neighborhood. The field, spruced up at city expense, was poised to become the site of a new soccer program for middle school kids—Jewish *and* Arab—where they would be able to kick the ball around and get help with their homework. Then there were the plans to offer Hebrew lessons to as many as 30 Palestinian women and Arabic classes to the same number of Jewish women, or however many signed up. It was something. Especially since the community center had been thinking about banning Palestinian kids altogether when things got tense in Abu Tor the previous year. It was progress. It was a victory, however small.

While David worked away on his bridge-building projects, city officials turned up across the street to carry out a surprise inspection of the Bazlamit compound. They came to see if Mohammed had done as he'd promised and torn down the rooms he'd built without city permission. Mohammed, son of Nawal and Zakaria, grandson of Hijazi, did destroy the rooms in 2012. But, before too long, he quietly started rebuilding. His family needed somewhere to live. So he decided to take the risk. Now the city inspectors were back.

The Bazlamits didn't know who, but they figured somebody had snitched on them. Maybe it was the son of the collaborator, the one living a few doors down who'd clashed with Ahmad over and over again until the young Bazlamit was thrown in an Israeli prison for who knew how long. Maybe it was Yaacov, the owner of the yappy dog and son of their old friend Imm Ismael, the Iranian immigrant who'd scolded Israeli soldiers for beating Palestinians after the 1967 war.

It didn't really matter who made the call. It ended the same way. The city hit the family with another costly fine for illegally building on their property. The Bazlamits watched the inspectors leave and added the order to an ever-growing stack of crippling penalties they had to pay to avoid being kicked off the family land where Hijazi Bazlamit had been brought down by an Israeli bullet in 1951.

NOTES

Note: Italicized quotes in the book are based on memories of one or more people who were part of the conversation.

INTRODUCTION

1. Dr. Seuss, *The Sneetches and Other Stories* (New York: Random House, 1961), 33.

CHAPTER ONE: NO MAN'S LAND

1. Meron Benvenisti, *City of Stone: The Hidden History of Jerusalem* (Berkeley: University of California Press, 1996), 63.
2. Ibid., 57.
3. "Report of the Special Mixed Armistice Commission Meeting Called by the Chief of Staff on 23 April, 1953," May 13, 1953, Jerusalem, Reports, United Nations Archives and Records Center, New York City, New York (hereafter UN Archives).
4. Ibid.
5. Ibid.
6. Ibid.
7. Ibid.
8. Ibid.
9. Ibid.
10. Ibid.
11. Ibid.
12. Maj. Gen. Vagn Bennike, Letter to UN Security Council, UN Truce Supervision Organization, December 12, 1953, Jerusalem, UN Archives.
13. New York Times News Service, "Nuns Recover Dentures from No Man's Land," *Milwaukee Journal*, May 23, 1956.
14. Ibid.
15. E. H. Hutchison, *Violent Truce: A Military Observer Looks at the Arab-Israeli Conflict, 1951–1955* (New York: The Devin-Adir Company, 1956), 11.
16. "Jordan Yields Wrong Sheep," *Jerusalem Post*, February 11, 1958.
17. Ibid.
18. "Betrothal in No-Man's-Land," *Jerusalem Post*, November 15, 1956.
19. "Couple Married in No-Man's-Land," *Jerusalem Post*, September 14, 1956.
20. "Husband Cools Off in No Man's Land," *Jerusalem Post*, August 16, 1959.

21. "Jerusalem Area—Abu Tor—Construction Between the Lines," unsigned memo, Israel-Jordan Mixed Armistice Commission, February 11, 1966, Jerusalem, UN Archives.

22. "One-Sided Investigation of Jordan Complaint No. M-91," memo from Maj. J. C. Jenkins and Capt. C. Bernard to Chairman, HJK-I-MAC, February 28, 1966, Israel-Jordan Mixed Armistice Commission, Jerusalem, UN Archives.

23. "Second Session of Emergency Meeting No. 420," March 8, 1966, Israel-Jordan Mixed Armistice Commission, Jerusalem, UN Archives.

24. Ibid.

25. Ibid.

26. "Fourth Session of Emergency Meeting No. 420," March 14, 1966, Israel-Jordan Mixed Armistice Commission, Jerusalem, UN Archives.

27. Uzi Narkiss, *The Liberation of Jerusalem* (London: Valentine Mitchell, 1983), 35.

28. Ibid.

29. "100,000 Trees for Jerusalem Border," *Jerusalem Post,* August 15, 1957.

30. "Report by the Acting Chief of Staff to the United Nations Truce Supervision Organization in Palestine," September 24, 1957, Jordan-Israel Mixed Armistice Commission, Jerusalem, UN Archives.

31. Ibid.

32. "Text of Complaint by the Jordanian Delegation," July 24, 1957, Jordan-Israel Mixed Armistice Commission, Jerusalem, UN Archives.

33. Yossi Katz, "Israeli Tree Planting in the Armon Hanatziv (the former British Government House) Area in the Summer of 1957," (unpublished manuscript, March 2015), provided to author by Jewish National Fund.

34. Ibid.

35. Ibid.

36. Ibid.

37. Ibid.

38. Ibid.

39. Ibid.

40. Ibid.

41. Ibid.

42. "Verbatim Record of the 787th Meeting," September 6, 1957, UN Security Council, New York, Library of Congress, Washington, DC.

43. Ibid.

44. Ibid.

45. "Verbatim Record of the 788th Meeting," September 6, 1957, UN Security Council, New York, Library of Congress, Washington, DC.

46. Ibid.

47. Ibid.

48. Ibid.

49. Ibid.

50. Shalom Israel Tours website, http://shalomisraeltours.com/peace-forest/.

CHAPTER TWO: FATHER OF THE BULL

1. W. Besant and E. H. Palmer, *Jerusalem, the City of Herod and Saladin* (London: Committee of the Palestine Exploration Fund), 433.

2. Doron Oren, personal research.

3. Ibid.

4. Ibid.

5. Ibid.
6. Ibid.
7. Ibid.
8. Ibid.
9. Atria Winchester, "Creativity on the Cusp," *Jerusalem Post,* March 25, 2005.
10. Ibid.
11. "Two More Held for Flat-Jumping," *Jerusalem Post,* July 20, 1967.
12. "High Court Throws Out Flat-Jumpers Claims," *Jerusalem Post,* July 21, 1967.

CHAPTER THREE: THE MARTYRS

1. Memo from UN Operations Officer to Chairman of Jordan-Israel Mixed Armistice Commission, November 7, 1957, UN Archives and Records Center, New York City, New York.
2. Ibid.
3. Oded Shalom and Gideon Maron, "And in Its Center, a Transparent Wall," *Yedioth Ahronoth,* April 23, 2007.
4. Ibid.
5. Ibid.
6. Ibid.
7. Ibid.
8. Ibid.
9. Ibid.
10. "48th MAC Meeting," February 12, 1951, Jordan-Israel Mixed Armistice Commission, Transcript, Jerusalem, UN Archives.
11. Ibid.
12. Ibid.
13. Ibid.
14. Ibid.
15. Ibid.
16. Raphael Israeli, *Jerusalem Divided: The Armistice Regime, 1947–1967* (London: Frank Cass & Co., 2002), 56.
17. "High Court Throws Out Flat-Jumpers Claims," *Jerusalem Post,* July 21, 1967.
18. "Israel Declines to Study Rabin Tie to Beatings," *New York Times,* July 12, 1990.
19. Herb Keinon, "Baum Appointment Draws Protests, Praise Tough New Commander in Abu Tor," *Jerusalem Post,* December 8, 1989.
20. Ibid.
21. Ibid.
22. Stephen Franklin, "Uprising Shattering Jerusalem's Dream of Coexistence," *Chicago Tribune,* January 14, 1990.
23. Keinon, "Baum Appointment Draws Protests."
24. Ibid.
25. Ibid.
26. Franklin, "Uprising Shattering Jerusalem's Dream of Coexistence."
27. Ibid.
28. Ibid.
29. Ibid.
30. "Flurry of Meetings Seek to End Israeli-Palestinian Fighting," CNN.com, September 26, 1996.
31. Eitan Felner, "Playing with Fire on the Temple Mount," B'Tselem, December 1996, http://www.btselem.org/publications/summaries/199612_playing_with_fire.

32. Ibid.
33. Ibid.
34. Ibid.
35. Ibid.
36. Ibid.
37. Bill Delaney, "Proximity, History Bind Jerusalem Israelis, Arabs," CNN.com, September 29, 1996.
38. Ibid.
39. Ibid.
40. Said Ghazali, "Palestinians and Israelis Live Under Fragile Coexistence," Associated Press, September 28, 1996.
41. Ibid.
42. Suzanne Goldberg, "Rioting as Sharon Visits Islam Holy Site," *Guardian* (UK), September 28, 2000.
43. Ibid.
44. Ibid.
45. Ibid.
46. David Rohde, "Mideast Turmoil: Jerusalem; Israelis Seek to Build Physical Barrier in West Bank," *New York Times,* May 7, 2002.
47. Ibid.
48. Deal Hudson, "A City Divided: How Israel's Wall Is Splitting the Holy Land," *Crisis Magazine,* January 10, 2005, http://www.crisismagazine.com/2005/a-city-divided-how-israels-wall-is-splitting-the-holy-land.
49. Ibid.
50. Ibid.
51. Ibid.

CHAPTER FOUR: THE SETTLERS

1. "Immigration to Israel: Operation Magic Carpet—Airlift of Yemenite Jews," http://www.jewishvirtuallibrary.org/jsource/Immigration/carpet.html.
2. Naomi E. Pasachoff and Robert J. Littman, *A Concise History of the Jewish People* (New York: Rowman & Littlefield, 2005), 301.
3. Martin Gilbert, *In Ishmael's House: A History of Jews in Muslim Lands* (Toronto: McClelland & Stewart, 2010).
4. Colin Shindler, *A History of Modern Israel* (Cambridge, UK: Cambridge University Press 2008), 63.
5. Rhona D. Seidelman, "Encounters in an Israeli Line: Sha'ar Ha-'aliyah, March 1950," *AJS Perspectives* (Fall 2014).
6. Rhona D. Seidelman, "Conflicts of Quarantine: The Case of Jewish Immigrants to the Jewish State," *American Journal of Public Health* (February 2012).
7. Seidelman, "Encounters in an Israeli Line."
8. Abraham Rabinovich, "No Politics Are Talked in Abu Tor," *Jerusalem Post,* May 16, 1969.
9. Ibid.
10. Ibid.
11. "One-sided Investigation of Israel Complaint No. M-425 dated 24 September 1966," September 30, 1966, Jordan-Israel Mixed Armistice Commission, Jerusalem, UN Archives and Records Center, New York City, New York.
12. Ibid.
13. Ibid.

14. Ibid.
15. Ibid.
16. Rabinovich, "No Politics Are Talked in Abu Tor."
17. Ibid.
18. Ibid.
19. Abraham Rabinovich, *The Battle for Jerusalem: June 5–7, 1967* (Philadelphia: Jewish Publication Society of America, 1972), 91.
20. Rabinovich, "No Politics Are Talked in Abu Tor."
21. Ibid.
22. Ibid.
23. Ibid.
24. Ibid.
25. Ma'ale Adumim City Stats, http://machat.co.il/news/maale-adumim-stats/.
26. Uzi Narkiss, *The Liberation of Jerusalem* (London: Valentine Mitchell, 1983), 35.
27. Eyal Weizman, *Hollow Land: Israel's Architecture of Occupation* (London: Verso, 2007), 114.
28. The Old Testament, Joshua 6:21.

CHAPTER FIVE: THE COLLABORATOR

1. "Fatwa from Religious Scholars of Palestine, 1935," http://www.muslim-lawyers.net/research/index.php3?aktion=show&number=58.
2. Ibid.
3. Associated Press, "Firing Squads Killed Alleged Collaborators," *USA Today,* January 13, 2001.
4. Saleh Abdel Jawad, "The Classification and Recruitment of Collaborators," The Issue of Collaborators in Palestine, *PASSIA,* March 2001.
5. Ibid.

CHAPTER SIX: THE PEACENIKS

1. "What is Reiki?" International Center for Reiki Training, www.reiki.org.
2. Timothy Egan, "A Conscience Haunted by a Radical's Crime," *New York Times,* September 17, 1993.
3. Alexander Marquardt and Bruno Nota, "Israeli PM Calls Killers of Three Israeli Teens 'Human Animals,'" ABCNews.com, June 30, 2014.
4. Itamar Sharon, "Abu Khdeir Murder Suspect Gives Chilling Account of Killing," *Times of Israel,* August 12, 2014.
5. "Bereaved Mother Offers Condolences to Slain Arab Teen's Family," *Times of Israel,* July 7, 2014.
6. Ibid.
7. Ibid.
8. Daniel K. Eisenbud, "Jewish Abu Tor Residents See Spike in Arab Violence," *Jerusalem Post,* July, 28, 2014.
9. Ibid.
10. "Assassin Was a Serial Arsonist, Assaulted 3 Wardens in Prison," Ynetnews.com, October 30, 2014.

CHAPTER SEVEN: THE GOOD ARAB

1. Jerusalem International YMCA website, YMCA.org.il.

244 | A STREET DIVIDED

2. "A New Narrative," YMCA mission statement, http://ymca.org.il/about-us/ceos-view/.
3. "Making Connections Across Cultures," YouTube video, 4:04, posted by Brandeis University, August 9, 2011, https://www.youtube.com/watch?v=Hp8F WNCYANo.
4. Ibid.
5. Ibid.
6. "Leftist MKs Blast Eitam's Statements on Arabs, Urge AG to Investigate," *Haaretz*, September 11, 2006.
7. "If Israel's Arab Citizens Indeed Are a 'Demographic Bomb,' Can It Be Diffused?" JTA.org, December 22, 2003.
8. "Lieberman Calls Arab MKs Who Meet with Hamas 'Collaborators,'" *Jerusalem Post*, May 4, 2006.
9. Jack Moore, "Lieberman Is 'Jewish ISIS' Says Israeli Politician after Beheading Comments," *Newsweek*, March 10, 2015.
10. Moshe Cohen, "Lieberman: Disloyal Arab-Israelis 'Should Be Beheaded,'" *Arutz Sheva*, March 8, 2015.

CHAPTER EIGHT: THE ARCHITECTS OF DIVISION

1. Natasha Mozgovaya, "Would East Jerusalem Arabs Rather Be Citizens of Israel or Palestine?" *Haaretz*, January 13, 2011.

BIBLIOGRAPHY

"100,000 Trees for Jerusalem Border." *Jerusalem Post*. August 15, 1957.

Amichai, Yehuda. *Poems of Jerusalem and Love Poems*. New York: Sheep Meadow Press, 1988.

Bennike, Maj. Gen. Vagn. Letter to UN Security Council. UN Truce Supervision Organization, December 12, 1953, Jerusalem. UN Archives and Records Center, New York City, New York.

Benvenisti, Meron. *City of Stone: The Hidden History of Jerusalem*. Berkeley: University of California Press, 1996.

"Betrothal in No-Man's-Land." *Jerusalem Post*. November 15, 1956.

"Couple Married in No-Man's-Land." *Jerusalem Post*. September 14, 1956.

Felner, Eitan. "Playing with Fire on the Temple Mount." *B'Tselem*, December 1996, http://www.btselem.org/publications/summaries/199612_playing_with_fire.

Franklin, Stephen. "Uprising Shattering Jerusalem's Dream of Coexistence." *Chicago Tribune*, January 14, 1990.

"High Court Throws Out Flat-Jumpers Claims." *Jerusalem Post*. July 21, 1967.

Hudson, Deal. "A City Divided: How Israel's Wall Is Splitting the Holy Land." *Crisis Magazine*, January 10, 2005, http://www.crisismagazine.com/2005/a-city-divided-how-israels-wall-is-splitting-the-holy-land.

"Husband Cools Off in No Man's Land." *Jerusalem Post*. August 16, 1959.

Hutchison, E. H. *Violent Truce: A Military Observer Looks at the Arab-Israeli Conflict, 1951–1955*. New York: The Devin-Adir Company, 1956.

Israeli, Raphael. *Jerusalem Divided: The Armistice Regime, 1947–1967*. London: Frank Cass & Co., 2002.

"Jordan Yields Wrong Sheep." *Jerusalem Post*. February 11, 1958.

Katz, Yossi. "Israeli Tree Planting in the Armon Hanatziv (the former British Government House) Area in the Summer of 1957." Unpublished manuscript, March 2015. Provided to author by Jewish National Fund.

Keinon, Herb. "Baum Appointment Draws Protests, Praise Tough New Commander in Abu Tor." *Jerusalem Post*, December 8, 1989.

Narkiss, Uzi. *The Liberation of Jerusalem*. London: Valentine Mitchell, 1983.

New York Times News Service. "Nuns Recover Dentures from No Man's Land." *Milwaukee Journal*, May 23, 1956.

Reports, Jordan-Israel Mixed Armistice Commission, UN Archives and Records Center, New York City, New York.

Rabinovich, Abraham. *The Battle for Jerusalem: June 5–7, 1967.* The Jewish Publication Society of America, 1972.

Transcripts, UN Security Council Meetings, September 6, 1957, Library of Congress, Washington, D.C.

"Two More Held for Flat-Jumping." *Jerusalem Post.* July 20, 1967.

Weizman, Eyal. *Hollow Land: Israel's Architecture of Occupation.* London: Verso, 2007.